RETHINKING OUTDOOR, EXPERIENTIAL AND INFORMAL EDUCATION

This book seeks to bring together the two disciplines of informal and outdoor education, and challenges readers to think differently about outdoor and adventure education. It develops core ideas and thinking about informal education within outdoor settings, and explores how its principles and practice can enhance outdoor education.

A wide range of contributors look in detail at the concept of change in the outdoors, whilst also considering the ways in which this expanding field might exploit opportunities offered to young people and adults to engage in reflective informal education. It encourages outdoor educators to experience their immediate surroundings in new and innovative ways and grasp the challenge of promoting a sustainable lifestyle.

Offering a fresh perspective on shifting the outdoor education agenda from that of narrow knowledge and skills acquisition and 'shallow learning' to the social and political, as well as aesthetic and philosophical opportunities embodied within the outdoor experience, this book will be valuable reading for those studying or working in the field of outdoor education.

Tony Jeffs recently retired from Department of Applied Social Sciences, Durham University, UK, where he still teaches in a part-time capacity. He was founding editor of the journal *Youth and Policy* and is currently a member of the journal's Editorial Board.

Jon Ord is Associate Professor at Plymouth Marjon University, UK.

RETHINKING OUTDOOR, EXPERIENTIAL AND INFORMAL EDUCATION

Beyond the Confines

Edited by Tony Jeffs and Jon Ord

Routledge
Taylor & Francis Group

LONDON AND NEW YORK

First published 2018
by Routledge
2 Park Square, Milton Park, Abingdon, Oxon OX14 4RN

and by Routledge
711 Third Avenue, New York, NY 10017

Routledge is an imprint of the Taylor & Francis Group, an informa business

British Library Cataloguing in Publication Data
A catalogue record for this book is available from the British Library

Library of Congress Cataloguing in Publication Data
A catalog record has been requested for this book

ISBN: 978-0-415-70310-9 (hbk)
ISBN: 978-0-415-70311-6 (pbk)
ISBN: 978-1-315-10176-7 (ebk)

Typeset in Bembo
by diacriTech, Chennai

CONTENTS

ACKNOWLEDGEMENTS

The editors wish to thank the authors of the chapters for their contributions, as well as the staff at Routledge who have handled our enquiries efficiently and managed the transition of the manuscript from submission through to publication very well.

Acknowledgement is also made for the permission to use the following Figure 3.2 from Kolb, David A., *Experiential Learning: Experience as the Source of Learning and Development*, 2nd ed., Englewood Cliffs, NJ: Prentice Hall. © 2015 Reprinted by permission of Pearson Education, Inc., New York.

CONTRIBUTORS

Dr Susan Cooper is a senior lecturer at the Plymouth Marjon University and leads the BA and MA Youth and Community Work courses. She joined the university in 2005 following 20 years as a youth work practitioner in a variety of settings. Her specialisms include group work, evaluation and participatory research methods.

Dr Annette Coburn is a lecturer in Community Education at the University West of Scotland. She has taught on programmes in Higher Education since 2003 and prior to that she was a youth and community worker for over 20 years. Annette's research interests include questions about how equality work is developed in youth work and how a critical pedagogy can enhance human flourishing.

Tony Jeffs now teaches part-time at Durham University. He is a member of the editorial board of the journal *Youth and Policy*.

Dr Mark Leather is a senior lecturer in adventure education and outdoor learning at the Plymouth Marjon University where he teaches on undergraduate and post-graduate programmes that utilise the outdoors and an experiential pedagogy. He enjoys researching and connecting with people, places and the planet, on or near water, especially the sea.

Chris Loynes worked as an outdoor educator in schools and youth work before becoming an educational advisor and lecturer. He is now a reader in Outdoor Studies at the University of Cumbria. He is currently chair of the European Outdoor Education Network.

Dr Liz Mallabon is a senior lecturer in Outdoor Studies at the University of Cumbria. Liz has a particular interest in applying theories of ecological psychology to our understanding of coaching and learning in different outdoor contexts, ranging from performance-driven skill acquisition coaching to wilderness journeys focused on sense of place.

Dr Jon Ord worked as a youth worker for nearly 20 years, some of which was in the outdoors, and has taught youth and community work at Plymouth Marjon University since 2003. He is the author of a number of articles on youth work and experiential learning, and has written the books *Youth Work Process, Product and Practice* and *Critical Issues in Youth Work Management*.

Jean Spence has been a youth worker and a lecturer in community and youth work. Having taken early retirement from her lectureship in Durham University, she now continues to teach and research on a part-time basis, whilst pursuing more fully her interest in photography and representation of the natural world.

David Wallace is senior lecturer in community, participation and education at the University of West of Scotland. He has 25 years' experience in community work as an activist, youth worker and manager. He has engaged in a number of research evaluation exercises on youth work programmes, projects and initiatives. He is co-author of the book *Youth Work in Communities and Schools* (2011) with Annette Coburn.

Dr Sue Wayman is a senior lecturer at the Plymouth Marjon University. Her research interests lie in the areas of education for sustainability, global education and practitioner/action research.

1

ORIGINS OF OUTDOOR AND ADVENTURE EDUCATION

Tony Jeffs

Outdoor and adventure education is a long rope comprising many strands. That rope remains unfinished. Thanks to the creativity of practitioners it is still being extended as long-standing modes of practice are remodelled and renewed. Simultaneously it is broadened as new pursuits, such as freerunning, coasteering, urban exploring and skyrunning are woven into the fabric to meld with traditional formats. In part the rope's strength derives from the accumulated experiences and theories of practitioners seamlessly transferred via conversation, observation and instruction from one worker to another, one generation to another. Just as conversation and dialogue with colleagues helps us to accumulate knowledge of experiences and dangers we have never encountered or techniques as yet untried, so by the same means we acquire theories and ideas from articles and books we may never read or hear of. This is why even snatched 'professional' conversations can be so productive. Just as the sensible practitioner values the chance to learn from their contemporaries so the wise outdoor educator relishes the prospect of learning from the expertise of those who went before.

The strength and resilience of outdoor and adventure education emanates from a blending of fieldwork and research which broadens our understanding and deepens our awareness. Consequently, holding onto the analogy of the rope, we can picture an entity that takes ideas and activities, history and vision, analysis and action, and by drawing them together like the strands of a rope gives strength from one to another. This creative interplay of theory and practice, ideas and action, with each nurturing the other and each modifying the other, is not unique to outdoor and adventure education; indeed it is the hallmark of any vibrant profession or area of study. This process, whereby theory changes practice and practice changes theory is what philosophers and educationists often refer to as *praxis*. It is not a new concept. Aristotle, over 2,300 years ago, maintained there were essentially three fundamental human activities – *theoria* (thinking), *poisis* (making) and *praxis* (doing). He believed 'life is *praxis*, not doing. Mere doing is the function of the slave' (1999, 7.2: 1325). Praxis ultimately entails making wise and prudent practical judgements 'about how to act' in given situations (Carr and Kemmis, 1986: 190). Hannah Arendt (1958), one of the last century's most influential political philosophers, argued it was this application of *theoria* via *praxis* that uniquely makes us human, dissimilar from animals and plants. Paulo Freire, who acquired a similar status to Arendt in relation to adult and informal education, likewise spoke of humans 'as beings of *praxis*' who as such had the ability to 'transform' the world and 'humanise it' (1970: 455).

Exploiting the past

Nothing stands still. Outdoor and adventure education has been unrelentingly reshaped by 'praxis' – the interplay of theory and practice, ideas and activity, policy and procedure – much as it has been buffeted by changes occurring in the wider social, economic and physical environment. This perpetual state of flux is at best exciting, at worse unsettling, but either way it is possible to secure a better grasp of what is happening today and construct a notion of the current trajectory of travel by acquiring an awareness of the dynamics of how the building blocks of practice abrade one against another. However this can only be achieved by first interrogating our knowledge of where we have come from. But Galbraith warns us one cannot simplistically require history to 'pay a dividend' (1964: 59), for it never obligingly tells us with unerring accuracy what will unfold in the near or distant future. A knowledge of history will, however, help us acquire a superior comprehension of the world around us and contemporary forms of practice, thereby ensuring we are equipped to more adroitly handle the inescapable changes we inevitably encounter during our working lives. Isaac Newton, in a letter written in 1676 to Robert Hooke, a fellow scientist and long-term rival, reminded his colleague that one can always see 'a little further' by 'standing on the shoulders of Giants' (Iliffe, 2007). It is a maxim that applies with equal force to outdoor and adventure education. To better second-guess where outdoor and adventure education is heading, we, like Newton, must be prepared to stand 'upon the shoulders' of the giants who preceded us. Indeed to comprehend contemporary outdoor and adventure educational practices it is wise to secure an appreciation of the ideas and *modus operandi* that have shaped it, much as 'one cannot understand the English landscape, town or country, or savour it to the full, apprehend all it's wonderful variety without going back to the history that lies behind it' (Hoskins, 1963: 219). Thankfully to help us do so we have Ogilivie's (2013) magnificent history of outdoor education as well as articles proffering adroit summations of the sector's development, such as Nicol (2002a,b, 2003), Cook (1999) and Brookes (2016). In addition, fine biographies are available on the lives and work of many pioneers including Kurt Hahn (Rohrs, 1970; Miner, 1990), John Muir (Worster, 2008) and Robert Baden-Powell (Jeal, 1989). Consequently, diligent students and inquisitive practitioners can autonomously carve a route through the thicket to piece together a comprehensive insight into the key events, thinkers and pioneers who created the field of practice they now occupy.

Burrowing down

Given the availability of the literature underscored at the close of the last paragraph, this chapter opts to concentrate on ideas that shaped current provision. But how far back should one delve? That question generates some palpable obstacles not least because the terms 'outdoor education' and 'adventure education' surfaced relatively recently. According to Knapp (2000), the former emerged in a 1943 article by Lloyd Sharp, a noted American pioneer within the field (Carlson, 2011: 123). This was two years after Hahn, described somewhat quaintly by Priest and Gass as the 'grandparent of adventure programming', opened Aberdovey, the first Outward Bound centre (2005:28). Much has been written regarding Hahn's singular contribution to the advancement of outdoor and adventure education and it is to that launch, according to Hattie and colleagues, 'most researchers trace the origins of modern adventure education' (1997: 44). Irrespective of the validity of that assessment, 'Outward Bound' programmes certainly incorporated, like the earlier Moray Badge scheme Hahn launched in 1937, an activity package that included orienteering, search-and-rescue training, athletics and gymnastics, small-boat sailing, ocean and mountain expeditions, obstacle courses and community service – which encompass the core ingredients of what soon became known as outdoor education. Baden-Powell similarly formulated a syllabus for Scouting, which he launched in 1908, that comprised most of the activities that the Moray Badge scheme and outdoor education amalgamated within their remit. Therefore in essence the format pre-dated the title. 'Adventure education' was similarly absent from our lexicon prior to 1971 and the inauguration of the Massachusetts-based Project Adventure Program (Prouty, 1990). Again the designated activities and educational layout can be encountered long before the categorisation entered everyday language. Therefore a compromise is required if we are to avoid burrowing ceaselessly back in time fruitlessly searching for when, say, the first individuals took a boat out for pleasure rather than to fish or trade, or walked a hillside for enjoyment rather than to scavenge or hunt. To escape this entrapment the author is going to begin with the decades either side of 1712.

Why 1712? First because it was in that year Thomas Newcomen, a village blacksmith in Dartmouth, assembled the first practical steam engine, thereby signalling the onset of the Industrial Revolution. Second, during the same year Jean-Jacques Rousseau was born in Geneva and England's last trial of a woman for witchcraft took place; the last executions occurred four years later. What links these disparate events was that they are signifiers of the passing of one historical era and the onset of another. Another was the publication in 1690 of John Locke's *Essay on Human Understanding*, widely seen as the precursor of a century of 'rationalism and reason'. Dubbed the 'Age of Enlightenment' or the 'Age of Reason', this was an 'age' shaped by a philosophical and social movement that swept across Europe. The Enlightenment was a philosophical idea and an historical phenomenon. Rousseau was by no means the preeminent Enlightenment thinker, but he more than any other paid sustained attention to the content and format of education, and linked it to a consideration of the dynamic relationship between mankind and nature. Thus Rousseau, despite his shortcomings as a philosopher and human being (he was a neglectful parent and fickle friend), has a special place in relation to the development of outdoor education. Finally, in 1720 Gilbert White was born in Selborne (Hampshire). White authored *The Natural History of Selborne*, commonly viewed as the first 'ecological book'. Comprising White's letters to colleagues, it laid the foundation for the modern study of nature and rural life. One measure of its importance is that it has been re-published every year since its launch in 1788 (Scruton, 2012: 332). A German edition, the first of numerous translations of White's book, appeared four years after it was initially published in Britain (Mabey, 1986). Now we will look at what links Newcomen's and White's work and an emerging philosophical movement to the advancement of outdoor and adventure education.

Satanic mills

By stages the machines that tumbled forth following Newcomen's breakthrough eliminated many time-honoured restraints upon mankind's productive capacity, thereby manufacturing the conditions for a seemingly limitless multiplication of goods, wealth and people. Usually referred to in its initial stages as the Industrial Revolution, it is a revolution whose momentum up to the present has never totally subsided, although it has always progressed in fits and starts. Currently it seems to be once again gathering impetus with the advance of robotics, AI (Artificial Intelligence) and computerisation. This upsurge is transforming the world in ways Newcomen and his contemporaries surely never predicted. But it is never solely the means of production that alters. As Virginia Woolf, whose father Leslie Stephen between 1858 and 1871 conquered nine previously unclimbed Alpine peaks and was for a time president of the Alpine Club, recalled during the period stretching from her youth to the late eighteenth century, the process of industrialisation meant:

> *All human relationships have shifted: those between masters and servants, husbands and wives, parents and children. And when human relations change there is at the same time a change in religion, conduct, politics and literature. (1924: 5)*

Britain's population in 1712 was six million, eighty per cent of whom lived in small towns, villages and hamlets. Mostly tied to the land, they produced food-employing techniques familiar to generations of their ancestors. By the time Woolf was born in 1882, scientific methods, new machinery and the application of industrial techniques meant British agriculture, supplemented by imports made feasible by the arrival of railways, canals and steamships, was able with an ever-diminishing workforce to feed a population six times larger than that of 1712. Year-on-year a steady flow of farm workers departed (or were evicted from) the countryside and relocated in the new industrial centres or emigrated, until around 1810 Britain became the first urbanised nation, one where a majority lived in towns or cities of over 20,000. It was a contagious trend, as gradually across the world in terms of population and wealth the urban began to eclipse the rural. The shrinkage of the agricultural workforce meant the countryside's appearance altered, as working communities decayed or were transformed into dormitory units for urban areas within 'easy' reach, retirement havens or tourist destinations. It has been this restructuring that made available so much of the 'open space' outdoor and adventure education, and other 'leisure' pursuits have been able to colonise.

As the nation urbanised, so the population grew. Between 1800 and 1850 it doubled, then doubled again by 1900, despite millions emigrating to the USA and colonies. Cities such as Liverpool, Middlesbrough and Leeds seemingly emerged from thin air and wealth accumulated, albeit somewhat haphazardly, on an unprecedented scale. There were tangible benefits, but industrialisation and urbanisation generated what social scientists term 'diswelfares'. Diswelfares are the price some, often a majority, pay for the progress enjoyed by others. Reisman explains this process as follows:

> *A opens a railway and B makes a trip – but C loses his forest as a consequence of the sparks. D opens a factory and E buys his goods – but, the river polluted, F as a result can neither fish nor swim. (2001: 159)*

Reisman's examples show how diswelfares are inescapable by-products of unregulated industrialisation, for new technological developments and workplace innovations propagate losers as well as winners. In relation to the environment it warns us we face a perpetual struggle to manage the diswelfares resulting from the extraction of minerals, the use of agri-business techniques, the enlargement of the tourist industry and a demand for greater mobility.

Initially during the first century of industrialisation the diswelfares included overcrowded slums; poor or non-existent sanitation; excessive working hours; grinding poverty; an absence of health care; minimal educational provision; adulterated food; hazardous working conditions; and despoliation of the natural environment in pursuit of raw materials and cheap food. Cumulatively these resulted in urban dwellers having a life expectancy half that of their rural compatriots. In Manchester during the 1830s sixty per cent of children died before their fifth birthday and those who survived enjoyed a life expectancy of just nineteen years (Jones, 1991). Little by little consciences were pricked, righteous anger harnessed and self-interest redirected until the worst excesses were set aside. Since 1840 life expectancy across Britain has improved along with living standards, educational provision, housing and access to free time. Post-1840 it has on average increased by three months per annum (Gratton and Scott, 2016).

Industrialisation and urbanisation redefined our relationship with the countryside and nature. In 1712 three-quarters of the British population worked the land;

today it is barely one per cent of the labour force. Yet current output eclipses that of earlier periods; these new farming methods have altered the social structure, appearance and ecological balance of rural Britain. Variations in life expectancy and living standards between urban and rural localities in advanced industrialised nations are now a distant memory. But the overcrowding, pollution, crime rates and sheer ugliness of so much of urban Britain ensure the countryside is still viewed as a healthier alternative, the 'other' promising respite, relaxation, rest and recuperation. Hence the countryside and coast are where outdoor and adventure education predominately occurs, the destination to which parties are transported to improve their physical and mental well-being, the setting which promises a chance to step back, relax and form fresh perspectives on life.

Working weeks of seventy-plus hours meant the overwhelming majority of urban dwellers were effectively imprisoned in the towns and cities where they laboured during those first decades of industrialisation. Only the better-off were able to escape to the countryside or coast for holidays or exercise. Nevertheless by 1800 the outflow of 'visitors' was sufficient to warrant the publication of the earliest guide books. Amongst the first was William Hutchinson's 'account' of his 'Excursion' to the Lake District complete with accounts of his ascent of selected peaks including Skiddaw. By the 1790s 'tourist' had entered into the vernacular, sufficiently so for William Wordsworth to utilise it in his *Guide Through the District of the Lakes in the North of England* published in 1810 which sought to teach 'persons of taste' how to appreciate the natural world. With some justification the *Guide* is 'said to have initiated the modern environmental movement' (Yoshikawa, 2016: 4). For in it Wordsworth presciently designated the Lake District,

> *A sort of national property, in which every man has a right and interest who has an eye to perceive and a heart to enjoy (Wordsworth, 1810/2004: 93).*

This portrayal by the most popular poet of his age of a segment of the countryside as a 'national property' had a far-reaching impact on public opinion. Not least it helped inspire a network of social movements devoted to protecting, and also extending public access to, the countryside. Campaigning bodies such as The Rights of Way Society (1845), the Commons, Open Spaces and Footpath Preservation Society (1865) and the National Trust (1895) emerged in the wake of a plethora of local initiatives such as The Association for the Protection of Ancient Footpaths in the Vicinity of York founded in 1824 and the Manchester Footpath Preservation Society launched two years later (Taylor, 1997). Large and small, national and local, these strove to protect access by keeping ancient footpaths and rights of way open and secure legislation to safeguard fauna, flora and places of natural beauty.

Aided by the construction of a national rail network and postal service, the second half of the nineteenth century witnessed the formation of numerous clubs and societies designed to enable individuals to share and collectivise outdoor 'hobbies' and 'activities' such as climbing, hiking, angling, shooting, sailing and cycling (Oglivie, 2013). This trend helped stimulate the construction of resorts and hotels catering to this new clientele, who initially comprised mainly upper and middle-class males; however this gradually altered as women began to take up mountaineering as the nineteenth century progressed (Smith, 2004: Coley, 2010), as well as pursuits such as hiking, cycling and rowing (Schweinbenz, 2011). Working-class involvement also grew notably following the 1850 Factory Act, which enshrined the principle of the sixty-hour week with compulsory closing at 2 p.m. on a Saturday. Designated holiday entitlements, over and above statutory Bank Holidays, followed in 1871. Large swathes of the working population, notably women in domestic service and retail trades, barely benefitted from the 1850 Act, however the fortress wall was breached. Henceforth in Britain and other industrialised nations, thanks largely to trade union pressure, a gradual shrinking of the working week and an increase in allotted holidays took place (Barton, 2005). Yet it was only towards the end of the 1860s that 'weekend' emerged to describe two days free from toil. Year-on-year greater access to leisure meant ever more individuals and groups were able to enjoy the countryside and coast. Clubs and societies typically self-managed and commonly linked to religious bodies arose to facilitate outings and holidays. As legislation increasingly excluded young people from employment and drove them, often unwillingly, into full-time schooling and curtailed the length of the working week of those in work, so organisations emerged to offer them 'inspiring', 'healthy' and 'improving' alternatives to 'hanging about the streets'. After 1850 a myriad of local and national youth organisations, now mostly forgotten, were founded, the most successful and long-lasting being the Young Men's Christian Association (founded 1845), Young Women's Christian Association (1855), Girls' Friendly Society (1873), Settlement Movement (1883) and Boys' Brigade (1883). These and others opened thousands of boys' and girls' clubs, and branches which cultivated youthful engagement with morally improving and physically beneficial outdoor activities. Leaders believed, on the basis of evidence placed before them by writers such as G. Stanley Hall and Geddes, that urban living interfered with the proper and wholesome development of young people (see Hall, 1904; Savage, 2007). Boys' and girls' club leaders in droves embraced the concept of trips, camps and residentials (see Pilkington, 1896), not only because of the damage the urban environment wrought upon the health and well-being of young people but also because these 'events' generated opportunities for sustained coherent learning experiences, interludes when leaders might supplement the informal educational contact they had with members in the club, unit or association setting with a more substantive and focussed educational input. They also sensibly ran trips because they were exceedingly popular with members, so the summer camp, weekend away and outing became a fixture of club life. Club leaders' enthusiasm for and belief in the benefits of outdoor activities ensured many took leading roles in the bodies formed to extend and encourage public enjoyment and usage of the countryside. Probably the best remembered amongst these is Octavia Hill, a pioneer of community, play and social work, girls' clubs and adult education – she managed the first adult education college and designed the earliest children's playground opened in 1857 (Cranwell, 2001). Hill also played a central role in establishing the original social work training programme; the construction of Britain's first social housing units; and the founding of the Commons, Open Spaces and Footpath Preservation Society in 1865, the Army Cadets in 1889 and the National Trust in 1895 (Darley, 1990). This impressive portfolio reflects Hill's commitment to ensuring working people enjoyed access to the outdoors and that the countryside was protected for the benefit of all. In an influential article entitled "Space for the People" Hill spoke for thousands of fellow campaigners when she summarised her ambition as being to provide for young and old, rich and poor, 'places to sit in, places to play in, places to stroll in and places to spend a day' (1883: 90).

Now barely recalled, the Boer War (1899–1902) dispensed a dreadful shock to the self-confidence of Britain and especially its military elite. The poor physical condition of approximately a third of those who volunteered raised serious doubts concerning the nation's capacity to police the Empire and simultaneously fight a European war. Industrialisation and urbanisation had exacted a dreadful toll. The well-grounded fears of imperialist politicians and military leaders now coalesced with the demands for social reform articulated by trade unionists, radicals and philanthropists. Together this unholy alliance forced the state to play a more interventionist role with regards to boosting the health and well-being of young people and families. The resultant legislative package incorporated measures to give greater legal protection to open spaces, and fostered the creation of parks and policies designed to encourage young people to engage in sports and physical activities. These humble statutory beginnings, although significant, were at least until the late 1930s eclipsed by the contribution of the voluntary sector, which was now reinforced by new bodies created to combat the crisis highlighted by the Boer War – notably the Boy Scouts (1908), Girl Guides (1908), Federation of Ramblers' Clubs (1905), School Journey Association (1911), School Nature Study Union (1902) and National Camping Club (1901) founded by Thomas Hiram Holding (Abaitua, 2011), all focussed on cultivating healthy bodies and minds, and a love of the outdoors. By 1914 the combined membership of uniformed youth organisations, boys' and girls' clubs and youth associations alone was approaching a million. Apart from social and sporting activities, they organised visits to the country and some taught what might be termed survival skills. Members usually enjoyed an annual week or weekend away either camping or at a rural residential centre. An indication of the popularity of outdoor activities during the Edwardian period can be gauged from the sales of Baden-Powell's *Scouting for Boys: A Handbook for Instruction in Good Citizenship*. Published in 1908, by 1913 it had gone through six editions and over twenty reprints to eventually become the fourth best-selling book of all time (Boehmer, 2004). One eventual legacy of these pre-1914 developments was the emergence in the 1920s of a movement spearheaded post-1930 by the YHA dedicated to providing 'cheap holiday accommodation' for young and old in the form of campsites, huts, residential centres and hostels (Coburn, 1950). The contribution of religious-orientated providers fell away in line with a steady decline in church attendance post-1919 as did that of youth work organisations in the wake of the gradual falling-away in youth club membership post-1945. A consequence of these changes was the staged emergence of new organisations to cater to a seemingly relentless demand for outdoor and adventure activities. Amongst these were a network of local authority outdoor centres, Outward Bound, the Duke of Edinburgh Award and for-profit providers. Their focus, apart from that of the for-profit providers, remained consistent with that of their predecessors. However the diswelfares they sought to address altered: some disappeared, while others to varying degrees remained to be supplemented by new scourges such as obesity, stress and depression, which in some cases have in terms of impact overshadowed those illnesses and maladies that troubled earlier generations. These afflictions pose fresh challenges whilst presenting new opportunities for outdoor and adventure education to respond to societal needs. Modes of production and the composition of our urban landscape remain in a ceaseless state of flux, and as both are reconfigured, so new problems and predicaments will arise that individuals and societies must address. As before, some can be alleviated, even overcome, by the intervention of outdoor and adventure educators; the challenge now, as in the past, is how to identify where and when that may be the case.

Thinking anew

The pace of social and economic change is never fixed. Within the context of outdoor and adventure education, as with other spheres, the popularity of given activities wax and wane. For instance, during the last two decades, after years of relative decline, cycling has enjoyed a revival. No solitary reason will suffice to account for such fluctuations. Partly in relation to this example it is fuelled by technological advances which made 'off-road', 'trail' and 'mountain' biking more practicable and cheaper, and cycling on roads 'less demanding'. But it is also driven by heightened demand. Therefore we must look beyond the technology for additional social causes. One such is that the resurgence may be correlated to a structural adjustment within society, in particular a widespread tendency within the English-speaking world for people to become less collectivist and more individualistic with respect to their choice of leisure activities (Putman, 2000; Bauman, 2001; Elliott and Lemert, 2006), a cultural shift that has cultivated a decline in participation in team games and group activities and fostered a turn towards pursuits which individuals can partake in isolation such as cycling, running and visiting a gym. Likewise changes within the world of ideas surface at variable rates of velocity and for similarly disparate reasons; just as the popularity of activities will rise and fall so also do philosophical concepts or ideas. Philosophy, like most human activities, has heightened periods of vibrancy and times when it languishes in the doldrums. Gottlieb (2016) identifies two junctures when the greatest leaps forward were accomplished. The first occurred during the time of Socrates, Plato and Aristotle; the second was the *le Siecle de Lumieres* (the Century of Lights) or Enlightenment which flourished between the final quarter of the seventeenth century and the first of the nineteenth century. What helped make the latter exhilarating was that, as Cassirer noted, it attributed 'to thought not merely an imitative function but the power and the task of shaping life itself' (1951: viii). Here then was an epoch when philosophy focussed as much on changing the world for the better as helping us to understand it with greater clarity. As this implies, it was always more than purely a philosophical movement, for from the outset it impacted upon other arenas such as religion, politics, science and as we shall see education.

Kant, in a short essay written in 1784, sought to answer the question *Was ist Aufklarung* [What is Enlightenment?]. His response, which follows, still serves as a useful guide to our understanding of this phenomenon:

> *Enlightenment is the emergence of man from his self-imposed infancy. Infancy is the inability to use one's reason without the guidance of another. It is self-imposed, when it depends on a deficiency, not of reason, but of the resolve and courage to use it without external guidance. Thus the watchword of enlightenment is* Sapere aude! *Have the courage to use one's own reason. (Kant, 1996: 11)*

Sapere aude, borrowed from the Roman poet Horace, translates as 'Dare to Know' or more loosely 'Dare to Be Wise'. It is an axiom that encapsulates much of the spirit of the Enlightenment which held that:

1. Reason is an individual's central capacity which enables them to think and most importantly act correctly.
2. People are by nature rational and good therefore 'evil' can be overcome.
3. Individuals and society have the potential to progress to perfection.
4. Beliefs should be adopted only on the basis of reason, not taken on the authority of others, including religious leaders and texts.

Enlightenment thinkers broke through barriers of prejudice by urging tolerance towards the views and lifestyles of others, and the removal of injustice. Condorcet, a leading Enlightenment figure whose political activism eventually cost him his life, was not atypical in advocating an end to discrimination against homosexuals, the granting of full political and social equality to women, provision of free education for all and the abolition of slavery (Schapiro, 1963). By adopting these and other liberal positions, he and others radically reorientated the way many perceived their own place in the world, and importantly for many reading this chapter, our appreciation of nature and the natural environment. The very existence of outdoor and adventure education to a substantive degree is a by-product of this re-conceptualisation of the relationship between human beings and nature as well as a philosophical realignment that encourages 'aesthetic taste and natural piety' to stand 'vigil over our surroundings' (Scruton, 2012: 253). For Enlightenment thinkers, irrespective of whether we classify them as conservatives, such as Edmund Burke and the William Wordsworth of his later years, or as radicals, say Condorcet or Friedrich Schiller, shared a belief that 'the beautiful and the sacred were connected' and must therefore 'be rescued together from the human urge to exploit and destroy' (op. cit). In line with Locke's belief that 'no man's knowledge can go beyond his experience' (Locke, 1689/2000: 71), those who sought wisdom and understanding were encouraged to turn, at least in part, towards nature and the physical world for guidance and inspiration. A widespread acceptance of this sensory basis for ideas promoted not only a greater respect for the natural world but both a desire to explore it scientifically and engage with it aesthetically. Here we can perceive the beginning of an expedition of discovery and scholarship of which outdoor and adventure education has belatedly become a constituent part.

Given the educational focus of this book, it is helpful to note for informal and outdoor education alike the Enlightenment was also of crucial importance for two discrete reasons. First it initiated a profound realignment in social attitudes towards education's role. Enlightenment thinkers were aware their ambitions to set aside prejudice and ignorance and create a new world order founded upon reason and justice required an educated populace. At the outset John Locke, a key figure in the early stages, set this process in motion with *Some Thoughts Concerning Education*, published in 1693. Its first principle was that:

> *A sound mind in a sound body, is a short but full description of a happy state of mind in this world: he that has these two has little more to wish for. (1693: 33)*

Although few might disagree in the abstract with this premise, in reality the balance advocated by Locke has within the context of the school rarely been prioritised. The need for a 'sound body' has been consistently sidelined, demoted in comparison to the teaching of 'employment skills' and 'examinable subjects', an oversight which, in no small measure, led to the emergence of a discrete form of pedagogic practice – outdoor and adventure education. Supporters of the Enlightenment certainly prioritised the need to equip young people to think for themselves, live by reason and fulfil their destiny as autonomous citizens. Those early advocates of democracy rightly held that if an electorate were not to be presided over by self-perpetuating educated elites or manipulated by charlatans, thereby making a mockery of this system, high-quality universal education was essential. Herein emerged a difficulty, one never fully resolved by latter generations, namely if young people were to acquire the arts and knowledge required to be free sovereign citizens how can this be accomplished if the educational institutions are controlled by the very religious bodies, governments and employers who initially denied them liberty and equality and whose self-interest is best served by producing a supine, easily manipulated populace? Various writers and theoreticians outlined solutions to this dilemma. Thomas Jefferson, principle author of the American Declaration of Independence, believed the answer resided in ensuring education was controlled by locally elected and accountable officials; Condorcet argued 'all authority' of both church and state 'is a natural enemy of enlightenment', so opted for education to be provided by an independent Guild of Teachers (quoted Schapiro, 1963: 211); and Rousseau held the solution lay in allowing children to develop 'naturally', which meant sheltering them from unwarranted and excessive interference. Indeed it is in the writings of Rousseau we encounter the modern origins of 'experiential education' and the rudiments of an analysis that morphed into a substantive strand within the theoretical underpinnings of contemporary outdoor and adventure education. Rousseau's rule of thumb when it came to giving children and young people guidance with respect to their learning was:

> *Let it be very little, and avoid the appearance of it. If he goes wrong, do not correct his errors. Say nothing till he sees them and corrects them himself; or at most arrange some practical situation which will make him realize things personally. If he never made mistakes he would never learn properly. (1979: 13)*

Here we find an educational model resting upon a belief that young people have a natural proclivity towards activity, inquisitiveness, inventiveness and self-discovery. One embellished in the two decades following Rousseau's death by a second Swiss educationalist Johann Pestalozzi who, like Rousseau and Locke before him, advocated an approach focussing on the whole person. Unlike those predecessors Pestalozzi implemented his version at his school in Neuhof where he formulated a curriculum designed to engage the student's hands (via creative activity), heart (via the experience of feeling and emotion) and head (by the process of thinking) (Pestalozzi, 1885: Silber, 1994). Here was a model founded upon a belief that:

> *Nature forms the child as an indivisible whole, as a vital organic unity with many sided moral, mental and physical capacities. … Each of these capacities is developed through and by means the others.* (cited in Heafford, 1967: 47)

Once more we happen upon a conceptual configuration encapsulating the essential elements of not only outdoor and adventure education but also the foci of informal education.

Second, many Enlightenment intellectuals, notably those most concerned with educational practice, embraced a desire to devote matched attention to promoting healthy bodies and healthy minds. This may account for why so many were prodigious walkers and in some cases pioneering climbers. Irrespective of whether they embraced physical activity, they collectively viewed the natural world afresh believing it had much to teach us and was deserving of detailed study. Froebel, an admirer of Rousseau and Pestalozzi, born in 1782, four years after Rousseau's death, explained this stance in *The Education of Man*:

> *Young animals and plants are given rest, and arbitrary interference with their growth is avoided, because it is known that the opposite practice would disturb their pure unfolding and sound development; but, the young human being is looked upon as a piece of wax or a lump of clay which man can mold into what he pleases. (1907: 8)*

Such reappraisals of the importance of the outdoors and nature prompted educators to take young people into the countryside so they might learn first-hand about nature and about themselves. The value pioneers such as Pestalozzi, Froebel and Robert Owen, who at New Lanark in 1814 established Britain's first primary school and community centre surround by a network of laid-out paths and woodland walks, placed upon moving young people away from the classroom and into the outdoors was predictably dismissed by the Gradgrinds who controlled the nineteenth-century school system. However, the idea of teaching the 'whole child' and placing due emphasis on the study of the natural world and the acquisition of a healthy body was never entirely lost. Elements of the nature worship linked to Rousseau may be irreconcilable to a modern age, indeed even when it first emerged it attracted criticism from other leading Enlightenment figures. Voltaire, no friend or admirer of Rousseau, dismissed the latter's admiration for the uncivilised 'savage' state as a foolish 'nostalgia for the Neolithic' (quoted Pagden, 2013: 204). Neither is the tutoring model advocated by Rousseau in *Emile* feasible within a system of mass education; however, the influence of his ideas concerning child development and the importance of play retain purchase. Two centuries on elements of his thinking can be encountered in modern primary education, just as they afford a theoretical basis for a great deal of outdoor and adventure education. Those who followed in Rousseau's footsteps learnt the fundamental lessons but, like Pestalozzi and Froebel, proved to be far more pragmatic in tone and, like Lloyd Sharp, were happy to accept:

> That which can best be learned inside the classroom should be learned there. That which can best be learned in the out-of-doors through direct experience, dealing with native materials and life situations, should there be learned. (1943: 363–364)

The influence of Enlightenment thinkers remains alive in the sphere of 'experiential education' and in the importance placed upon fostering a mutually productive relationship between teacher and taught, which is a feature of outdoor education, youth work and adult education. Those thinkers also generated another quantifiable legacy, namely an abiding acknowledgment that nature and the natural environment are of themselves valuable educators, providers of crucial experiences from which men and women secure vital knowledge. This stance promotes a belief that the natural environment as a resource for learning and individual rejuvenation must be protected. Beautiful buildings, the countryside, oceans and rivers, fauna and flora all need to be safeguarded from despoilation; they play such a crucial role we have an individual and societal duty to teach each new generation to appreciate and revere the world we and subsequently they inherit. As Schiller argued in the fourth letter of *On the Aesthetic Education of Man* (1794), the educated man must make nature his friend. Although Schiller profoundly disagreed with Kant on many issues, they shared a deep mutual reverence for nature. It was the latter who in 1788, the same year Gilbert White's text was published in England, remarked, 'There are two things that fill my heart with wonder. One is the moral sense within me, and the other is the order in the heavens above me' (1788: 203). Outdoor and adventure education at their best have taken up these batons acknowledging with equal fervour that nature is a great teacher for those willing and equipped to learn from it. Good outdoor educators seek to 'fill' the hearts of those they work with 'wonder', to encourage them to make friends with nature and cultivate a sense of 'wonder' at the beauty and power of the natural world. Truly outdoor education at its best is a descendent of the Enlightenment.

Studying nature

Gilbert White was not the first person to study the natural world. Others preceded him, including Aristotle, author of *History of Animals*; however, White is possibly the 'first ecologist', the writer who did most to shape 'our modern respect of nature' (Hazell et al., 2005: 99). White's work was founded upon a meticulous study of the pre-industrial natural world he encountered in the environs of Selborne, the village where he was a curate for forty years. White's curiosity and affection for the local countryside and village life is captured in his letters, diaries and poems, writings that can be adjudged to stand as a precursor of a literary genre celebrating the 'minute particulars' of the natural world and country life, a tradition which since his passing has prospered, up to and including present day. Virginia Woolf described *The Natural History of Selborne* as an extraordinarily 'ambitious book' which left a door open 'through which we hear distant sounds' (1950: 15). Besides drawing us back to a natural world that has been largely lost, White opened a door through which others have and will pass. Notably his work also marked the inauguration of a tradition of pastoral prose and reportage that has been blessed by the contributions of outstanding wordsmiths such as Richard Jefferies, Henry Thoreau, Edward Thomas and Flora Thompson, as well as living exponents such as Robert Macfarland and White's biographer Richard Mabey. These and others furnish a literary backdrop before which outdoor and adventure education stands. Sadly too few practitioners choose to immerse themselves in the writings of that genre and tradition; their failure to do so is an individual and collective misfortune for this oversight diminishes the intellectual depth and resonance of their practice and the standing of the profession. It denies them full access to a verdant vocabulary which they can employ to better communicate with their 'students' and clientele plus a wealth of anecdotes which will help practitioners make what they have to offer and teach live in the memory of others. Ignorance of the literary heritage means that ultimately those practitioners who do not seek it out short-change their clientele because they are unable to induct them into a rich seam of literature that will enrich their experiences and aid their understanding of the natural world, the setting that plays host to outdoor and adventure education.

According to James Lovelock, White's work inspired 'what was to become the Green movement of the nineteenth and early twentieth century' (2014: 8). That work was based upon White's studies, for each day he, unprompted, measured the rainfall and monitored the variations in temperature using homemade instruments; studied changes in the behaviour, well-being and distribution of local fauna and flora; and constantly sought answers to questions others had hitherto shown scant interest in. These questions included ones such as where did the swallows and martins go when summer ended? Or what might be the natural length of a pig's life if they were not all prematurely slaughtered for their meat? White proved that 'watching the natural world at close quarters could generate not just understanding but respect, and an insight into the kindredness of living things' (Mabey, 1986: 6).

His desire to better comprehend what, in a poem, he called 'Nature's rude magnificence' (2014: 8), led White to conscript a volunteer band of observers and researchers, a stratagem that may justify flattering him not merely with the title of the 'first ecologist' but that of founder of the 'Nature Study Movement'. Besides being a social and educational movement which came to prominence during the late nineteenth century, this was a pressure group, active through assemblages such as the School Nature Study Union, founded in 1902 by Claude Hinscliff, a curate at the East End church where Samuel Barnett, who opened Toynbee Hall, the first settlement, was vicar (Jenkins and Swinnerton, 1996; Palmer, 2002). The wider movement was entwined with what would now be depicted as youth organisations. One prominent pioneer, Libert Hyde Bailey, was instrumental in founding the 4-H Youth Movement in the USA and Europe. 4-H and its English offshoot, the Young Farmers' Clubs, were also the earliest wholly mixed youth organisations and the first to cater exclusively to young people living in rural areas (Jack, 2008). The Nature Study Movement campaigned for the inclusion of environment education within the school curriculum and the development of what supporters termed 'nature literacy' amongst the wider population (Borland, 2013: 206). It was committed to instilling a respect and love of nature in children and young people in the hope that this would lead to the creation of generations of increasingly conservation-minded adults (Armitage, 2009). The originators of the Nature Study Movement, besides Hinscliffe, included Anna Botsford Comstock (Corcoran, 2001; Woodhouse and Wells, 2011), Liberty Hyde Bailey (Jack, 2008) and Catherine Dodd. They and others merged the ideas of pioneers such as White, Muir and Thoreau with the educational theories of Rousseau and Froebel as well as those of progressive educationalists such as George Counts and John Dewey in the USA (see chapter by Ord and Leather) and Cecil Reddie and Patrick Geddes in the UK (Higgins and Nicol, 2011). Supporters endeavoured to 'put the child in sympathy with nature' (Bailey, 1903). To achieve that end they sought to bring the countryside into the classroom and transport young people into the countryside to initiate 'observation and discussion on geographical, historical, biological and aesthetic topics' (Cook, 2001: 44). As Comstock explained in an influential essay, here was an approach that embodied ideas that resonate within the work of Gilbert White, for the overarching aim of nature study was to activate

> *a love of the beautiful; it brings to ... [the young person] ... a perception of colour, form and music ... whatever there is in his environment whether it be the thunder-head piled up in the western sky, or the flash of the oriole in the elm. (1911: 10)*

Although now barely recalled, the Nature Study Movement had multiple links with figures such as Sharp and Dewey, who played influential roles in relation to the development of outdoor and adventure education (Armitage, 2009). It also laid the foundations in Britain for the creation of local authority study centres established post–1944 in order to enrich the lives of urban young people by enabling them to spend time in the countryside in the company of educators equipped to teach them about the natural world, agriculture and rural crafts. This movement fed into what is now usually called Outdoor Learning, a genre devoted to 'education *in, about* and *for* the outdoors' (Donaldson and Donaldson, 1958: 17, *italics in original*). However with each passing year the odds against the Nature Study Movement are stacked ever higher. We live in an increasingly urbanised world; in 2008, for the first time in excess of half the global population lived in towns and cities (Haut, 2009). In Britain it is 83 per cent. That actuality has serious ramifications for schools, for they come under constant pressure to proffer a curriculum that relates more closely to the lived experiences of their overwhelmingly urban-dwelling students. This requirement, coupled with expectations that they cultivate 'employability', for what is an overwhelmingly urban labour market, means less and less attention is paid to those topics and spheres of knowledge that Gilbert White and the Nature Study Movement held dear and which underpin outdoor and adventure education. Yet paradoxically the need for such programmes may now be greater than ever. Within a generation a quantifiable decline has taken place in the percentage of children and young people who have experienced direct encounters with nature (RSPB, 2010). Since the 1970s the proportion regularly playing in 'wild places' has fallen by a half to fewer than one in ten (Monbiot, 2012). A similar waning in the United States led Louv to identify what he characterised as 'an urban disconnect' from nature resulting in a Nature-Deficit Disorder amongst young people. This results, according to Louv, in 'alienation from nature and a diminished use of the senses, attention difficulties and higher rates of physical and emotional illnesses' (2008: 36). However all is not lost. The legacy of the Nature Study Movement retains an animated presence not solely within the ranks of outdoor and adventure educators. New social movements such as the Campaign for Adventure have appeared that seek to counter the trends indentified by Louv and others, such as Moss (2012) in the UK. The presence of these social movements can be identified in the development of Forest Schools, initiatives such as the John Muir Awards and mounting pressure for educational providers to take cognizance of sustainability issues (see chapter by Wayman).

Conclusion

So far this chapter has concentrated on three drivers that did much to foster the development of outdoor and adventure education. The conclusion that follows briefly mentions one other component that has influenced practice prior to discussing some current 'adjustments' that may also sculpt the future structure and direction of outdoor and adventure education.

Nicol (2002a) highlighted how practice has long been manipulated by governmental policies calculated to modify the behaviour of actual and potential offenders. Given over nine out of ten serious offenders are male and the peak age for offending has for over a century hovered between the mid to late teens, any use of outdoor and adventure education as a mechanism for diverting individuals from criminal and anti-social behaviour has inevitably utilised methods perceived to be attractive to this clientele (Nichols, 2007). Investment in outdoor and adventure education to achieve those ends, which can be traced back to the nineteenth century, has waned in recent years. In part this is a by-product of a fall in overall rates of offending amongst juveniles, but it also emanates from a reorientation towards a harsher regime within the justice sector (Pitts, 2015), a reorientation that has resulted in disinvestment in prevention programmes and in those interventions that are perceived by many voters to be 'soft' options. Diversionary programmes delivered by outdoor and adventure educators tend to be so characterised, which has contributed to cutbacks in their funding (Lotti, 2016). Some slack has been taken up by growth with respect to outdoor programmes funded by schools and colleges, the purpose of which is to improve educational achievement levels by changing students' attitudes towards school and study via the raising of self-esteem and self-confidence (Armour et al., 2008; Sandford et al., 2006). Outdoor and adventure activities have also been employed to heighten commitment amongst school avoiders and truants, and sometimes as a 'reward' for good behaviour and full-attendance (Hodgson and Jeffs, 2013). As with earlier interventions linked to promoting physical and mental 'fitness' for military service, these modern variants tend to reinforce an embedded tendency for provision to be constructed around the assumed needs of certain types of young men. So despite the emergence of the second-wave feminism of the 1960s, which led to heightened participation by young women and girls, it still remains the case that far too often they are simply 'absorbed into courses designed for boys' (Cook, 2001: 50). However, an emergent body of evidence indicates the 'long march' that was started in the nineteenth century by a tiny cohort of women pioneers may be drawing to a close. For by the late 1980s and early 1990s, 'In virtually all aspects of outdoor recreation, the percentage of women participating is increasing faster than [that of] men' (Henderson, 1992:50).

Consequently it is now realistic to envisage a time when within many, if not a majority, of the activity segments of outdoor and adventure education female participation rates overtake those of men. American data for 2014 shows that 46 per cent of participants in outdoor activities were women and still the trajectory is upwards (Outdoor Foundation, 2014). In step with this, a parallel tilting of the axis has transpired in the composition of the professional workforce. Lugg as early as 2003 identified a pattern of 'long term change' which had led to women comprising 'almost half those enrolling on tertiary Outdoor Education courses' (2003: 44), so that within a generation the majority of practitioners may be women, a repositioning that mirrors the feminisation of the workforce in neighbouring sectors such as school teaching, social work, probation and youth work. Collectively these indicators suggest we may be witnessing the beginning of the end of the long 'masculine tradition' that has hitherto dominated outdoor and adventure education (Carter, 2000: 79). When this happens it may prefigure a substantive realignment in the content and culture of the sector. Plentiful evidence exists that men and women tend to exhibit countervailing preferences in relation to both activities and the overall culture. For instance amongst outdoor and adventure participants who were classified as 'risk-takers', men outnumbered women five-to-one (Gordon et al., 2015). Men and women also tend to display different reasons for engaging in outdoor activities, with the former more likely to do so for the physical 'challenge' element, while the latter seek an emotional 'challenge' and a chance to foster relationships with others. Women it seems tend to be 'more concerned with process than outcomes' (Morse, 1997: 131). Alongside this gender rebalancing, a marked adjustment as to the age profile of participants in outdoor activities is taking place. Currently the fastest numerical increase in terms of participation in outdoor and adventure activities is amongst the over 55s (Gordon et al., 2015). If these trends in relation to the profile of participants persist, we can expect to witness a far-reaching reconfiguration in relation to the content, focus and format of programmes in the coming years. Certainly those now commencing a career in outdoor and adventure education will in all likelihood, before they retire, be obliged to operate in ways radically at odds with what is now the norm.

Some signifiers of what might happen can already be discerned. Indivualisation, which was discussed earlier, and the realignment of the clientele in relation to age and gender may now be combining to modify the foci of outdoor and adventure education. One example is what might be designated the 'therapeutic turn', a 'turn wherein the outdoors and wilderness increasingly acquire the mantle of a "healing place"' (Miles, 1987: 5). Of course, as Priest reminds us, within outdoor education 'the emphasis for the subject of learning' has always prioritised 'relationships concerning people and natural resources' (1986: 13). However, whereas traditional practice was underpinned, even at times driven, by a focus on the group and group relationships that were interconnected to an ambition to foster attributes such as a respect for shared democratic decision-making processes, ethically sound interpersonal skills and communitarian social competencies, the therapeutic turn relocates the centre of attention from the development of the group to the needs of the individual. This change of direction can be seen in the emergence of new dynamic and expansionist practice formats such as Wilderness Therapy (Hill, 2007: Russell and Phillips-Miller, 2002: Russell, 2001), Couples Therapy (Fletcher and Hinkle, 2002), Adventure-Based Counseling (Fletcher and Hinkle, 2002), Eco-Therapy (Clinebell, 1996) and Adventure Therapy (Gass et al., 2012). In addition a growing number of outdoor programmes focus on the treatment of mental illness (Hill, 2007). For these and an increasing array of purely recreational programmes, the core role is not the acquisition of outdoor and adventure skills, educating others about the natural world and environmental issues or inculcating a respect for and love of nature, but individual therapy or enjoyment. These exploit nature, and wilderness, as a means to an end, not as an end in itself. Henderson describes this as a process whereby nature and

> outdoor education and recreation is all-too-easily lost in the mania for skill-development, personal growth and technological convenience perhaps a sparring partner to test one's skills and resources. (2007:4)

The machines Newcomen made possible 'set in motion an entirely new and unexpected epoch' of the Earth's history, 'one that we now call the Anthropocene' (Lovelock, 2014: 8). Anthropocene is a concept used to convey the reality that we live in a different world from our ancestors, occupying an era in which, for the first time, the global environment is shaped by the actions of mankind rather than the reverse (Lewis and Maslin, 2015). Set this alongside the arrival of nuclear weapons and power as well as widespread pollution and we are obligated to acknowledge that 'science and technology must be controlled' and that 'we can, in fact, destroy the earth and ourselves' (Singer, 1975: 95, 120). In coming years outdoor and adventure education will, like so many other human activities, need to adjust, willingly or unwillingly, to this new reality as well as the conceptual challenges it will present, much as in the recent past it has been obliged to begin to interact with the notions of 'deep ecology' and 'sustainability' (Heath, 2015; Higgins, 2008), the former being a concept that initially emerged from the work of Norwegian philosopher Arne Naess, who argues the environmental movement encompasses two strands. These he identified as the 'shallow' and the 'deep'. Naess argues the centre of attention for the former lies with 'the health and welfare and affluence of people in the developed world' (1973: 95). The second which Naess promotes concerns itself with deep-seated philosophical questions relating to how humans relate to the environment in its entirety. It views humans not as isolated, discrete objects but as interconnected with each other and in an unbroken relationship with everything around them, part of the web of life in its totality; therefore, according to this perspective, the first priority when analysing environmental issues has to be the transformation of the individual's fundamental way of looking at the world. The need is to foster what Naess calls a 'holistic' outlook that focuses on 'ecological harmony or equilibrium' (1973: 98). Deep ecology seeks a profound change in our worldview and corresponding changes in our environmental ethic. It poses for outdoor and adventure education taxing questions that few have a ready answer to. For just as tourism, according to Urry (1995), selfishly consumes the environment, selfishly exploiting it for human pleasure and gratification, so 'deep ecologists' will require outdoor and adventure educators to defend themselves against similar accusations. These accusations, if they are not effectively countered, may result in the tide of public opinion turning against outdoor and adventure education, resulting in it no longer being viewed as an unquestioned 'educative good', thereby placing it at risk of being categorised as an intervention that, like tourism, exploits the environment and wild places for human pleasure and enjoyment. A pursuit that cumulatively exhausts, depletes and harms the very environment in which it functions.

The future is unknowable. Although outdoor and adventure education's past has largely been an unfolding tale of achievement and positive outcomes of which today's practitioners can be justly proud, we cannot make any assumptions that this state of affairs will continue indefinitely. Like other educators, those within the outdoor and adventure sectors must be prepared to confront new unforeseeable social, economic and technological challenges and a questioning of our values and modes of practice that will demand a partial or even total reappraisal of what we do and how we explain our aims and ambitions to others. A good way of preparing oneself to confront such tribulations is to scrutinise the history of outdoor and adventure education and ascertain how others faced and overcame similar challenges in the past.

References

Abaitua, M. de. (2011) *The Art of Camping: The History and Practice of Sleeping Under the Stars*, London: Hamish Hamilton.

Arendt, H. (1958) *The Human Condition*, Chicago: University of Chicago Press.

Aristotle (1999) *Politics* [translated by B. Jowett], Kitchener, Ontario: Batoche Books.

Armitage, K. C. (2009) *The Nature Study Movement: The Forgotten Popularizer of America's Conservation Ethic*, Lawrence, KS: University Press of Kansas.

Armour, K. M., Duncombe, R. and Stewart, K. (2008) *Final Report: Living for Sport Programme*, Loughborough: Institute of Youth Sport.

Bailey, L. H. (1903) *The Nature Study Idea: Being an Interpretation of the New-School Movement to Put the Child in Sympathy with Nature*, New York: Doubleday, Page and Vo.

Barton, S. (2005) *Working-Class Organisations and Popular Tourism, 1840–1970*, Manchester: Manchester University Press.

Bauman, Z. (2001) *The Community: Seeking Safety in an Insecure World*, Cambridge: Polity Press.

Boehmer, E. (2004) 'Introduction' in R. Baden-Powell, *Scouting for Boys*, Oxford: Oxford University Press.

Borland, J. (2013) 'Outdoor education centres: a sustainable educational model for the 21st century' in A. Kulnieks, D. Roronhiakewen Longboat and K. Young (eds.) *Contemporary Studies in Environmental and Indigenous Pedagogies: A Curricula of Stories and Place*, Rotterdam: Sense Publications.

Brookes, A. (2016) 'Foundation myths and the roots of adventure education in the Anglosphere' in B. Humberstone, H. Prince and K. A. Henderson (eds.) *Routledge International Handbook of Outdoor Studies*, Abingdon: Routledge.

Carlson, J. (2011) 'Lloyd B. Sharp: trailblazer in outdoor education' in T. E. Smith and C. E. Knapp (eds.) *Sourcebook of Experiential Education: Key Thinkers and Their Contributions*, New York: Routledge.

Carr, W. and Kemmis, S. (1986) *Becoming Critical: Education, Knowledge and Critical Research*, Geelong: Deakin University Press.

Carter, M. (2000) 'Developing confidence in women working outdoors: an exploration of self-confidence and competence in women employed in adventure recreation' in B. Humberstone (ed.) *Her Outdoors: Risk, Challenge and Adventure in Gendered Open Spaces*, Eastbourne: Leisure Studies Association.

Cassirer, E. (1951) *The Philosophy of the Enlightenment* [translated by F. C. A. Koelln and J. P. Pettegrove], Princeton: Princeton University Press.

Clinebell, H. (1996) *Ecotherapy: Healing Ourselves, Healing the World*, Minneapolis, MN: Fortess Press.

Coburn, O. (1950) *Youth Hostel Story*, London: National Council of Social Service.

Coley, A. C. (2010) *Victorians in the Mountains: Sinking the Sublime*, Farnham: Ashgate Press.

Comstock, A. B. (1911) *Handbook of Nature Study*, Ithaca, NY: Comstock Publishing Associates/Cornell University Press.

Cook, L. (1999) 'The 1944 Education Act and outdoor education: from policy to practice', *History of Education* 28(2), pp. 157–172.

Cook, L. (2001) 'Differential social and political influences on girls and boys through education out of doors in the United Kingdom', *Journal of Adventure Education and Outdoor Learning* 1(2), pp. 43–52.

Corcoran, P. B. (2001) 'Anna Botsford Comstock 1854–1930' in J. A. Palmer (ed.) *Fifty Key Thinkers on the Environment*, London: Routledge.

Cranwell, K. (2001) 'Street play and organised space for children and young people in London 1860–1920' in R. Gilchrist, T. Jeffs and J. Spence (eds.) *Essays in the History of Community and Youth Work*, Leicester: Youth Work Press.

Darley, G. (1990) *Octavia Hill: Social Reformer and Founder of the National Trust*, London: Faber.

Donaldson, G. W. and Donaldson, L. E. (1958) 'Outdoor education: a definition', *Journal of Health, Physical Education and Recreation* 29, pp. 17–63.

Elliott, A. and Lemert, C. C. (2006) *The New Individualism: The Emotional Costs of Globalisation*, London: Routledge.

Fletcher, T. B. and Hinkle, J. S. (2002) 'Adventure Based Counselling: an innovation in counselling', *Journal of Counseling and Development* 80(3), pp. 277–285.

Freire, P. (1970) 'Cultural action and conscientization', *Harvard Educational Review* 40(3), pp. 452–477.

Froebel, F. (1907) *The Education of Man* [translated by W. N. Hailmann], New York: Appleton and Co.

Galbraith, V. H. (1964) *An Introduction to the Study of History*, London: Watts.

Gass, M. A., Gillis, H. L. and Russell, K. C. (2012) *Adventure Therapy: Theory, Research and Practice*, New York: Routledge.

Gordon, K., Chester, M. and Denton, A. (2015) *Getting Active Outdoors: A study of demography, motivation, participation and provision in outdoor sport and recreation in England*, London: Sport England.

Gottlieb, A. (2016) *The Dream of Enlightenment: The Rise of Modern Philosophy*, Harmondsworth: Allen Lane.

Gratton, L. and Scott, A. (2016) *The 100 Year Life: Living and Working in the Age of Longevity*, London: Bloomsbury.

Hall, G. S. (1904) *Adolescence: Its Psychology and Its Relation to Physiology, Anthropology, Sociology, Sex, Crime, Religion and Education*, New York: Appleton and Co.

Hattie, J. A., Marsh, H. W., Neill, J. T. and Richards, G. E. (1997) 'Adventure education and Outward Bound: out-of-class experiences that make a lasting difference', *Review of Educational Research* 67, pp. 43–87.

Haut, C. (2009) *What Is a City? What Is Urbanization?* Washington, DC: Population Reference Bureau.

Hazell, D., Heinsohn, R. and Lindenmeyer, D. (2005) 'Ecology' in R. Q. Grafton, L. Robin and R. J. Watson (eds.) *Understanding the Environment: Bridging the disciplinary divides*, University of New South Wales Press: Sydney.

Heafford, M. R. (1967) *Pestalozzi*, London: Meuthen.

Heath, G. (2015) 'Re-imagining the outdoor experience' in M. Robertson, R. Lawrence and G. Heath (eds.) *Experiencing the Outdoors: Enhancing Strategies for Well-Being*, Rotterdam: Sense Publications.

Henderson, B. (2007) 'A Canadian meets friluftsliv' in B. Henderson and N. Vikander (eds.) *Nature First: Outdoor Life the Friluftsliv Way*, Toronto: Natural Heritage Books.

Henderson, K. A. (1992) 'Breaking with tradition: women and outdoor pursuits', *Journal of Physical Education, Recreation and Dance* 63(2), pp. 49–51.

Higgins, P. (2008) 'Learning outdoors: encounters with complexity' in P. Becker and J. Schirp (eds.) *Other Ways of Learning*, Marburg: European Institute for Outdoor Adventure Education and Experiential Learning.

Higgins, P. and Nicol, R. (2011) 'Sir Patrick Geddes: Viveno Discimus – by living we learn' in T. E. Smith and C. E. Knapp (eds.) *Sourcebook of Experiential Education: Key Thinkers and their Contributions*, New York: Routledge.

Hill, N. (2007) 'Wilderness therapy as a treatment modality for at-risk youth: a primer for mental health counselors', *Journal of Mental Health Counseling* 29(4), pp. 338–349.

Hill, O. (1883) 'Space for the people' in O. Hill (ed.) *Homes of the London Poor*, London: Macmillan.

Hodgson, T. and Jeffs, T. (2013) *Evaluation of MOBEX Network School Inclusion Project*, London: Paul Hamlyn Foundation.

Hoskins, W. G. (1963) *Provincial England: Essays in Social and Economic History*, London: Macmillan.

Iliffe, R. (2007) *Isaac Newton: A Short Introduction*, Oxford: OUP.

Jack, Z. M. (2008) 'Editor's preface: sower and seer' in Z. M. Jack (ed.) *Liberty Hyde Bailey: Essential Writings*, Ithaca, NY: Cornell University Press.

Jeal, T. (1989) *Baden-Powell*, London: Hutchinson.

Jenkins, E. W. and Swinnerton, B. J. (1996) 'The School Nature Study Union 1903–1994', *History of Education* 25(2), pp. 181–198.

Jones, K. (1991) *The Making of Social Policy in Britain 1830–1990*, London: Athlone.

Kant, I. (1788) *Critique of Practical Reason* [translated by W. S. Pluhar], Indianapolis, IN: Hackett Publishing.

Kant, I. (1996) *Practical Philosophy* [Cambridge Editions of the Works of Immanuel Kant], Cambridge: Cambridge University Press.

Knapp, C. (2000) 'Learning from an outdoor education hero: personal reflections about L. B. Sharp', *Taproot* 12(2), pp. 7–11.

Lewis, S. and Maslin, M. (2015) 'Defining the Anthropocene', *Nature* 219, pp. 171–180.

Locke, J. (1689/2000) *An Essay Concerning Human Understanding,* [edited by G. Fuller, R. Stecker and J. P. Wright and published 2000], London: Routledge.

Locke, J. (1693) *Some Thoughts Concerning Education* [reprinted 1830], Boston, MA: Gray and Bowen.

Lotti, G. (2016) *Tough on Young Offenders: Harmful or Helpful?* Warwick: Warwick Economic Research Papers, University of Warwick.

Louv, R. (2008) *Last Child in the Woods: Saving Our Children from Nature-Deficit Disorder*, Chapel Hill, NC: Algonquin Books.

Lovelock, J. (2014) 'Introduction' in G. White, *The Natural History of Selborne* [first published 1788], Toller Fratrum: Little Toller Books.

Lugg, A. (2003) 'Women's experience of outdoor education: still trying to be "one of the boys?"' in B. Humberstone, H. Brown and K. Richards (eds.) *Whose Journey? The Outdoors and Adventure as Social and Cultural Phenomena: Critical Explorations of Relationships between Individuals, 'Others' and the Environment*, Cumbria: Institute for Outdoor Learning.

Mabey, R. (1986) *Gilbert White: A Biography of the Author of the Natural History of Selborne*, London: Century.

Miles, J. C. (1987) 'Wilderness as a healing place', *Journal of Experiential Education* 10, pp. 4–10.

Miner, J. (1990) 'The creation of outdoor education' in J. C. Miles and S. Priest (eds.) *Adventure Education*, State College, PA: Venture Press.

Monbiot, G. (2012) 'If children lose contact with nature they won't fight for it', *The Guardian*, 19 November.

Morse, A. (1997) 'Gender conflict in adventure education: three feminist perspectives', *Journal of Experiential Education* 20(3), pp. 124–133.

Moss, S. (2012) *Natural Childhood*, Swindon: National Trust.

Naess, A. (1973) 'The shallow and the deep, long-range ecology movement: a summary', *Inquiry* 16, pp. 95–100.

Nichols, G. (2007) *Sport and Crime Reduction: The Role of Sports in Tackling Youth Crime*, London: Routledge.

Nicol, R. (2002a) 'Research topic or universal value? Part one', *Journal of Adventure Education and Outdoor Learning* 2(1), pp. 29–41.

Nicol, R. (2002b) Research topic or universal value? Part two', *Journal of Adventure Education and Outdoor Learning* 2(2), pp. 85–99.

Nicol, R. (2003) Research topic or universal value? Part three', *Journal of Adventure Education and Outdoor Learning* 3(1), pp. 11–27.

Ogilvie, K. C. (2013) *Roots and Wings: A History of Outdoor Education and Outdoor Learning in the UK*, Lyme Regis: Russell House Books.

Outdoor Foundation (2014) *Outdoor Participation Report 2014*, Washington, DC. Outdoor Foundation.

Pagden, A. (2013) *The Enlightenment and Why It Still Matters*, Oxford: OUP.

Palmer, J. A. (2002) *Environmental Education in the 21st Century: Theory, Practice, Progress and Promise*, London: Routledge.

Pestalozzi, J. H. (1885) *Leonard and Gertrude*, Memphis, TN.: General Books.

Pilkington, E. M. S. (1896) *An Eton Playing Field: A Reminiscence of Happy Days Spent at the Eton Mission*, London: Edward Arnold.

Pitts, J. (2015) 'Youth crime and youth justice, 2015–2020', *Youth and Policy* 114, pp. 31–42.

Priest, S. (1986) 'Redefining outdoor education: a matter of many relationships', *Journal of Environmental Education* 17(3), pp. 13–15.

Priest, S. and Gass, M. (2005) *Effective Leadership in Adventure Education*, Champaign, IL: Human Kinetics.

Prouty, D. (1990) 'Project Adventure: A brief history' in J. C. Miles and S. Priest (eds.) *Adventure Education*, State College, PA: Venture Press.

Putman, R. (2000) *Bowling Alone: The Collapse and Revival of American Community*, New York: Simon and Schuster.

Reisman, D. (2001) *Richard Titmuss: Welfare and Society* [2nd edition], London: Palgrave.

Rohrs, H. (1970) *Kurt Hahn*, London: RKP.

Rousseau, J-J. (1979) *Emile: Or on Education* [translated A. Bloom], New York: Basic Books.

RSPB (Royal Society for the Protection of Birds) (2010) *Every Child Outdoors*, Newcastle-upon-Tyne: RSPB.

Russell, K. C. (2001) 'What is Wilderness Therapy?', *Journal of Experiential Education* 24(2), pp. 70–79.

Russell, K. C. and Phillips-Miller, D. (2002) 'Perspectives on the Wilderness Therapy process and its relation to outcome', *Child and Youth Care Forum* 31(6), pp. 415–437.

Sandford, R. A., Armour, K. M. and Warmington, P. C. (2006) 'Re-engaging disaffected youth through physical activity *programmes*', *British Educational Research Journal* 32(2), pp. 251–271.

Savage, J. (2007) *Teenage: The Creation of Youth Culture 1875–1945*, London: Chatto and Windus.

Schapiro, J. W. (1963) *Condorcet and the Rise of Liberalism*, New York: Octagon Books.

Schiller, F. (1794) *On the Aesthetic Education of Man* [translated R. Snell], Mineola, NY: Dover Publications.

Schweinbenz, A. N. (2011) 'Against hegemonic currents: women's rowing into the first half of the twentieth century' in C. A. Osborne and F. Skillen (eds.) *Women in Sport History*, London: Routledge.

Scruton, R. (2012) *Green Philosophy: How to Think Seriously about the Planet*, London: Atlantic Books.

Sharp, L. B. (1943) 'Outside the classroom', *The Educational Forum* 7(4), pp. 361–368.

Silber, K. (1994) *Pestalozzi: The Man and His Work*, London: RKP.

Singer, P. (1975) *Animal Liberation*, New York: Harper Collins.

Smith, J. A. (2004) 'Walker, Lucy (1836–1916)', *Oxford Dictionary of National Biography*, Oxford: Oxford University Press.

Taylor, H. (1997) *A Claim on the Countryside: A History of the British Outdoor Movement*, Edinburgh: Keele University Press.

Urry, J. (1995) *Consuming Places*, London: Routledge.

White, G. (2014) *The Natural History of Selborne* [first published 1788], Toller Fratrum: Little Toller Books.

Woodhouse, J. L. and Wells, C. D. (2011) 'Anna Botsford Comstock: beyond science – learning about self and nature through field experience' in T. E. Smith and C. E. Knapp (eds.) *Sourcebook of Experiential Education: Key Thinkers and Their Contributions*, New York: Routledge.

Woolf, V. (1924) *Mr Bennett and Mrs Brown*, London: Hogarth Press.

Woolf, V. (1950) 'White's Selborne' in V. Woolf (ed.) *The Captain's Death Bed*, London: Hogarth Press.

Wordsworth, W. (1810/2004) *Guide Through the District of the Lakes in the North of England*, [edited by H. de Selincourt reprinted 2004], London: Frances Lincoln.

Worster, D. (2008) *A Passion for Nature: The Life of John Muir*, New York: Oxford University Press.

Yoshikawa, S. (2016) *William Wordsworth and the Invention of Tourism 1820–1900*, London: Routledge.

2

THEORISING OF OUTDOOR EDUCATION

Purpose and Practice

Chris Loynes

Many individuals freely opt to take part in outdoor adventure activities. A high proportion of these first encountered such activities as a consequence of a school or youth group initially offering them an introductory 'taster'. This chapter concentrates on facilitated interventions that offer outdoor adventure experiences explicitly for developmental purposes. Like Roberts (2012), the author makes a distinction between 'learning by doing', that is developing skills and knowledge in order to learn a subject or craft, and 'experiential education', which Roberts notes is concerned with the emerging identities of young people, their relations with others and the world around them, and their trajectory as they negotiate a place in the adult world. Whilst learning the skills and knowledge of an outdoor adventure (OA) activity is a necessary and beneficial aspect of outdoor adventure education (OAE), it is the broader purpose these new skills are used for and what this means to young people that lies at the core of OAE.

OAE has long drawn heavily on theories of experiential education. Dewey's *Experience and Education* (1997) in particular is an oft-cited text notably with regards to his belief that activity does not become experience unless it is purposeful and reflected on. This pragmatic stance has been highly influential within UK outdoor education. A typical example of this usage can be found in the writings of Wojcikiewicz and Mural who apply a Deweyian perspective to the analysis of outdoor experiential education, specifically in their case with regards to sail training. Those writers argue that in order

To foster educative experiences, activities must have the following features:

1. *Activities must have the liveliness and purpose associated with informal learning.*
2. *The learning environment must be knowingly and intentionally shaped.*
3. *The activity must be undertaken with pedagogical purposes.*

4. *The activity must be 'educative,' meaning it must have (a) purpose, in the dual sense of engagement and meaning; (b) intelligent direction with student selection of means to meet ends; (c) discipline, intellectual and social, that is derived from the activity itself; and (d) an open-ended nature, leaving the student willing and able to go on. (2010:110)*

The above list raises at least one prime concern for this author. Dewey understood the 'real' world as one of home, community and work where individuals encountered many experiences that had, as noted earlier under the right circumstances, the potential to be educative. However as Wojcikiewicz and Mural demonstrate, whilst sail training and other adventurous activities are purposeful and social, they are also separated from Dewey's 'real' world. Consequently they can be thought of as separated temporally and spatially from everyday life, which raises issues for some authors relating to reintegration with this 'real' world (e.g. Allison, 2000; Bell, 2003; Loynes, 2007). Irrespective of this, claims are made for the transfer of learning from the outdoor adventure world to what Dewey thought of as the 'real' world of young people and others. However these assertions have in turn been questioned by, for example, Brookes (2003) and Seaman (2008), the crux of this critique being that the threshold is too high and the two worlds so divergent that what is learnt inevitably becomes compartmentalised.

Outdoor adventure context

We live in restless times. Capitalism appears to be struggling, increasing urbanisation is creating new challenges, and the knowledge industries, consumerism, the virtual world and individualism are proceeding apace. We may even have reached or gone beyond environmental limits. The availability and nature of work, the distribution of wealth and access to welfare and education are increasingly problematic. These changes are especially challenging for young people (Bynner et al., 2002; Arnett, 2004). Whilst OAE is worthwhile as a means to develop young people for its own sake (Quay, 2013), this chapter goes further, arguing that if it is possible to address within the context of OAE any of the issues cited then we should do so. Similarly if new educational foci such as 'education for sustainability' (Nicol, 2000; Rawles, 2013) and 'education for resilience' (Ewert and Yoshino, 2011) can be incorporated within OAE, then again these should be placed on the agenda. Likewise attention should be paid to the possibility of adapting traditional elements of OAE such as the development of self-reliance and adventure, and the art of co-operation so that they are made more relevant to the new policy agendas. After all it may be the case that the uncertainty of adventure and ways in which that imprecision stimulates a capacity to cope and even flourish may prove to be a valuable asset whereby OAE can help the citizens of tomorrow deal with a rapidly changing world. Similarly the spirit of collaboration engendered by a group working together to realise their adventurous goals could be an excellent counterpoint to an over-emphasis within society on the need for competition.

This chapter draws upon Kurt Lewin's (1951) notion that there is nothing more practical than a good theory when it comes to helping practitioners reflect on their practice so that they may better develop more future-orientated provision. With this in mind, what follows explores both the social and environmental contexts in which OAE is situated. Whilst acknowledging OAE is a valued form of non-formal education for adults, the focus will be on the benefits to young people. In addition it will review the theories that help secure a better understanding of the design, facilitation and impact of OAE.

Three contexts

This section explores three contexts for OAE that are attracting increasing attention. First from a social perspective is the shift of responsibility from society to the individual in relation to young people steering a course through adolescence. This shift forms a backdrop to much OAE, and yet the approaches so far adopted have failed to be inclusive. Second from an environmental point of view, the construction of the outdoors, and so nature, as remote and hostile or as local and homely underlies a growing debate about the use of unfamiliar settings. Finally, we study the adoption of place-based approaches in a time of environmental crisis.

Social issues

The balance of responsibility for navigating the journey from youth to adulthood and employment has since the 1980s increasingly shifted from wider society to the individual young person (Furlong and Cartmel, 1997; Allen and Ainley, 2010). Despite this realignment the UK has retained an education system overwhelmingly designed to produce conforming workers rather than participating citizens (Bernstein, 1996), even though many observers would claim that, as a nation, we have no idea what the future structure of the labour market is likely to be (see for example White, 1997).

Despite sustained efforts over many years to encourage the engagement of marginalised groups - young women, the disabled, the working classes and ethnic groups – with the 'outdoors', the advances, despite some notable exceptions, have been meager (see for example Cook, 2001; Aitchison, 2003; Anderson and Harris, 2003; Allin and West, 2013). Explanations offered for this relative failure include strong competition from other aspects of youth culture such as the consumption of music and fashion, social media and computer gaming; a lack of trained leaders from the groups concerned; and culturally inappropriate traditions and practices. OAE is no exception. White middle-class males still dominate most spheres of outdoor recreation and education, which may alienate a number of potential users from those groupings (Allin, 2000). Another reason progress may have been so limited is that in recent years society has become increasingly risk averse, so that young people and others deemed vulnerable have become over-supervised and restricted in their access to free play and movement out-of-doors (see for example Furedi, 2006;

Louv, 2009; Griffiths, 2013). These writers and others hold this development responsible for a range of social and health problems such as declining levels of trust within and between generations, increasingly poor judgment as to the levels of physical and social risks, reduced ability to socialise, growth in obesity rates and a higher incidence of mental health problems. Within this context both youth work and OAE have struggled to maintain forms of provision that respond to and reflect the expressed needs of young people. Instead new funding sources have obliged agencies operating in both sectors to deliver specific targeted programmes designed to complement mainstream education, prepare people for work, re-engage young people with their communities, reduce teenage pregnancy, tackle discrete health 'problems' or divert the 'at risk' from deviance (Brookes, 2003). These programmatic targeted forms of intervention are far removed from the Hahnian approaches Brookes uses as a benchmark for the values of outdoor education and citizenship. Equally they have little in common with the Deweyian perspective discussed by Wojcikiewicz and Mural.

Unfamiliar landscapes

OAE places a high value on providing access to and encounters with unfamiliar landscapes or wilderness. In doing so it is an heir to the Romantic tradition of seeking sublime and transformative experiences in rugged and wild places. Mortlock (1984) developed the concept of adventure education from these roots, stressing the inherent value such encounters can have for all young people. Adventure, for him, was about developing the outdoor activity skills needed to explore wild places, especially self-reliance, which made it possible to minimise direct adult supervision and input. For Mortlock and those who shared his views, the landscape to be explored was not only the outer landscape of wild country but also the unexplored inner landscape of the emerging adult. Many have presented empirical evidence that tells of the value placed by participants on being offered the chance to independently explore both unfamiliar and wild landscapes. Amongst the benefits cited are the acquisition of insight and acumen alongside heightened well-being regarding areas of human flourishing such as the spiritual (Heintzman, 2009), moral (Allison et al., 2012), physical (Humberstone, 2011), mental health (Gustafsson et al., 2012) and overall development (Louv, 2009; Becker, 2008). Outdoor youth 'work' traditions, offering these benefits, emerged in many countries influenced by the Romantic Movement - in particular Norway, Germany, the UK and the Czech Republic. In each of these the forms of practice were partially influenced by the landscape, for example, skiing on the snows of Norway, hiking in the forests of Germany and in Britain hill walking on the uplands and sailing on the surrounding seas (Becker, 1998). Each tradition offered differing ways of understanding the 'landscape' of OAE ('scape' derives from the French for cloaking, that is to 'cloak' a place in cultural meaning and story). The development of outdoor youth work therefore took variable paths in different countries for cultural and environmental reasons. The historic axiom of OAE in the UK has been to take young people into new and unfamiliar situations, situations that require them to learn ways of coping and within which they are given the opportunity to make a meaningful journey that will help them to negotiate a successful transition to adulthood. However in each of those nations there were assorted, even competing, traditions. In the UK, for example, Baden-Powell first noticed what he perceived to be the benefits for young people of exploring unfamiliar, even hostile, terrain when observing the rapid development of self-reliance and other traits amongst the young army scouts he commanded during the Boer War (Jeal, 1989). Ernest Thompson Seton, founder of the Woodcraft Indians in 1902 and who with Baden-Powell played a prominent role in the launch of the Boy Scouts in both the United States and Canada, was by way of contrast inspired by a romanticised view of the life of the Plains Indians, a viewpoint that led him to develop programmes within which the environment was perceived as 'home' rather than a hostile terrain (see Wadland, 1978; Rosenthal, 1986). Baden-Powell and Seton were not alone in creating youth movements that provided informal OAE for young people in Britain and North America. Others followed their lead and adapted their founding principles. This resulted in the formation of single-sex organisations such as the Girl Guides and Camp Fire Girls and mixed movements such as the Woodcraft Folk and Youth Hostel Association (Ogilvie, 2012).

Space not place

Baden-Powell and Seton respectively constructed the landscape as simultaneously hostile and homely. This dichotomy continues as various outdoor educators use the landscape for diverse purposes. For example the Forest Schools movement celebrates and makes familiar local woods to young people and their families (Knight, 2009). The John Muir Award encourages groups to discover, explore, do something for and report on natural places both close to home and far away. Meanwhile World Challenge takes young people to exotic, far-flung and challenging destinations to find adventure and to give service. Increasingly leaders are encouraged to take a place-based approach (Wattchow and Brown, 2011). The argument for this is that it fosters a relationship with places as part of the emerging identity of the young person. This in turn leads to knowledge about and a sense of responsibility for the environment that may cultivate pro-environmental behaviours whilst encouraging positive attitudes towards a healthy outdoor lifestyle and a deepening sense of community. The ability to form healthy relationships with places has gradually become an important aspect of youth development. Whilst some (Backman et al., 2014) support this focus on local places, others still opt to advocate visiting unfamiliar spaces in order to help young people better appreciate diversity and subsequently perceive their own neighbourhoods in new ways (Beames, 2010). Wild places have traditionally been exploited by OAE as 'spaces' rather than places, that is landscapes which are unfamiliar to the young person and can therefore be explored adventurously as a rite of passage or hero's journey (Loynes, 2008). Within this construction the young 'hero' learns to deal with the new situation by gaining knowledge, allies, tools and skills to cope before embarking on a quest from which lessons are learned which can be 'taken back home'. This is the archetypal landscape of personal development regarded by some anthropologists and psychologists (for example Campbell, 1968; Maddern, 1990; Norris, 2011; Bell et al., 2012) as critical to a healthy transition to adulthood. In this 'landscape' the historical, cultural and natural histories are of interest only in so far as they support engagement with the unfolding narrative of the hero; the exploits of past adventurers; finding a way in the wild; understanding weather lore; and acquiring the skills to travel and camp in potentially hostile environments.

Programmes

To some degree the notions of place and space in our experiences of the landscape can appear to be in tension one with the other. In their extremes it is difficult to imagine how one can exist alongside the other. One is a blank map on which to write a personal narrative. The other is an already composed story of past and present cultures ready to be told and with which the young person joins in writing the 'next chapter'. However, arguably this is a false dichotomy, for both contribute to important elements within the process of youth development. Perhaps the key message here is that aspects of place and space are different elements of outdoor education programmes. They should be made available but not necessarily at the same time. There is some merit therefore in seeing the conflict of space and place as a productive tension between familiarity and divergence or difference, one which the educator needs to balance and creatively exploit within the context of the outdoor educational experience.

Robin Hodgkin (1916-2003), mountain guide, head teacher of Abbotsholme and Oxford academic, illustrates this when he describes the role of the teacher as one of accompanying young people whilst they explored the intriguing ideas, landscapes and experiences placed before them by an artful facilitator (Perrin, 2003). This approach resonates with the concepts of facilitation held by a number of youth work theorists (for example Jeffs and Smith, 2005; Young, 2006; Ord, 2016). Hodgkin suggests that what he calls a 'semiotic device' is a potentially meaningful experience which should be strange enough to intrigue the young person thereby rousing them to curiosity but not so unfamiliar that they might avoid exploring it. This approach demands that a balance of power operates between the facilitator and the participant that allows for the autonomous and critical development of the latter (Hodgkin, 1976).

By way of contrast, some designers of OAE have developed targeted and systematic approaches, for example those youth organisations that have adopted outdoor development training as an approach (Everard, 1993; Dybeck, 1996). This requires that the corrective, restorative or developmental needs of the young people are identified prior to the formulation of the given programmes which are then designed to achieve specific outcomes. In particular these are constructed for groups deemed to have special 'needs', such as the disaffected, unemployed, excluded or disabled.

This development has pre-eminently been funding driven, a consequence of a desire on the part of governments and some charities to deal with current 'moral panics' and entrenched social problems (see Brookes, 2003; Stuart, 2010).

An intensive one-off 'big experience' – the expedition, long stay residential, gap year or overseas outing – has been and remains a common approach to OAE. However in order to ensure effective interventions, many youth work organisations have integrated OAE with other strategies operating in the community over longer periods of time (Festeu and Humberstone, 2006). Certainly this latter method may better address long-expressed concerns over transference. A key claim of those who advocate this longitudinal approach is that this format engages young people with their peers and leaders in a way that makes it possible to build relationships and trust around shared experiences and understandings not least because the programmes have a grounding in the participants' communities (Mannion et al., 2010), what was earlier referred to as their 'real world'.

How long OAE programmes should be is a topic constantly revisited. Initially the Outward Bound Movement offered courses lasting 29 days. This was because many of the early participants were merchant seamen who had to return home to receive their monthly pay (Arnold-Brown, 1962). Arnold-Brown points out Kurt Hahn advocated a longer time span, having been convinced by his experiences at Gordonstoun School that they had to be of a sufficient length for young people to find pleasure, rather than hardship, in their new physical abilities and fitness. Certainly case study research that has attempted to replicate the outcomes of three-week and ten-day programmes that were compressed into a briefer time span found they were far less effective. Evidence points to young people needing extended continuity as well as specific interventions that allow for the 'space-based' intensive approach to personal development to be integrated with longer term 'place-based' engagement in the community (Mannion et al., 2010).

One recent theory has labeled these approaches as respectively 'wayfaring' and 'dwelling' (Ingold, 2011). According to this model 'wayfaring' equates with such concepts as movement, dynamic engagement, change, transformation, exploring and adventure occurring in unfamiliar 'spaces', whilst 'dwelling' sits with establishing, settling, belonging and participating in everyday 'places'. A German youth work theory proposes a similar duality, this time between 'crisis' and 'routine' (Becker, 2008). Here 'crisis' refers to situations where a person does not have on hand a known response based on previous experience; that is where the individual is obligated to formulate new coping strategies. 'Routine' refers to those situations that are known and where a response has already been devised. Within this model 'transfer' of learning necessitates taking new responses conceived in novel situations and applying these to 'everyday' life or new emerging possibilities that become new routines. For example, new ways of relating to others are acquired in a novel situation such as a residential or expedition experience involving a group of strangers. Upon completion, these previously unfamiliar ways of relating, acquired during the course of these experiences, are then applied to existing relationships located within the context of the social networks to which participants return.

Becker argues people need a balance in life between crisis and routine in order for them to more effectively engage with the dynamic nature of existence. Young people, according to this analysis, disproportionately need 'crises' to help then make a successful transition from youth to adult and that OAE is an ideal way of providing these. The work of Becker and Ingold usefully extend Mortlock's (1984) analysis of adventure education by taking into account the everyday context from which participants depart and to which they subsequently return. Collectively they provide a theoretical analysis which deepens Bacon's (1983) concept of 'Outward Bound' as a conscious metaphor for life.

Body, group and activity

Writings about OAE tend to explore the relationship between the person, the group and the environment, all mediated by the outdoor activity, a model of OAE that emerged in the 1960s (Ogilvie, 2012). Programme aims also tend to centre around one or more of these domains as the intended outcome, for example the acquisition of outdoor skills, personal and social development or environmental awareness. Equally, programme planners consider these as the key elements of the mix with which they orchestrate experiences (Beard and Wilson, 2002). This section explores recent theoretical discussions concerning the possibilities of the body, the group and the activity for OAE.

The body

Widely neglected in formal education, the body is the central means by which a young person engages with an outdoor adventure. Providing experiences that support the development of physical abilities and the diverse use of all the senses is a vital contribution of OAE to youth development (Humberstone, 2014). Learning to perceive landscapes and the elements mediated by different activities, developing the capacity of the body to act skillfully, experiencing the feelings that arise from physical effort, performance and success, learning what it feels like to be fitter and healthier and becoming dexterous and skilful are important contributions that OAE can make. The feeling of engagement, aliveness and agency that come with being able to master skills and overcome physical challenges builds self-esteem and fosters positive 'can do' attitudes that are key strategies for empowerment. Physical achievements are some of the first ways in which young people can express power in the world constructively and, properly facilitated, this can lead to further meaningful pursuits and projects with increasing degrees of self-reliance (Richards, 2003; Leather, 2013).

The group

Recent research suggests that developing relationships, especially in terms of enhancing trust confidence and engagement, is the single most valued outcome of OAE (Williams, 2013; Zink, 2010). It is argued that it underpins enhanced attainment in school, better relationships between child and parent at home and more positive rapport with peers. The ability to sustain social networks is widely seen as key to a successful transition to adulthood and predictor of social mobility. OAE is widely seen as a way of helping this to occur (Williamson, 1997). It is for this reason many leaders use the deliberate construction of the group to help them better tackle social issues around gender, ethnicity, class and disability.

Many commentators have highlighted the vocational (for example Lewis, 2005) and community (for example Mannion et al., 2010) benefits accruing to young people as a result of their learning to function in a group. Predictably therefore the terminology of social psychology is frequently encountered in relation to OAE, especially in the context of the management of group dynamics, the cultivation of social and group development, and the formulation of group roles (for example see Beard and Wilson, 2002; Priest and Gass, 1997). Frequently this 'language' is shared with the participants in order to enable them to explore and reflect on their social experiences more effectively.

Some writers such as Zink (2010) and McCulloch (2013) highlight the importance within the context of OAE of teaching about the other, especially in terms of learning to appreciate, tolerate, support, share and live with others via group residential and adventure experiences. These encounters offer the added benefit of seeing yourself through the eyes of others. There are a number of studies that highlight the importance of the feeling of *communitas* that extended and intensive OAE can bring (for example, Zink, 2010). Sharing achievements is also recognised as an important aspect of building an identity in a peer group. Letting others know who you were and what you did while you are away makes a significant contribution to maintaining the emerging identities of young people and others after an activity or a trip away. These experiences can help peer groups develop, as they lead to the challenging and confirmation of social norms that are unfamiliar or undeveloped in participants. For young people the opportunity to do this away from the social networks of childhood and to encounter new adult role models is also an important aspect of this process (Loynes, 2003). Lastly, knowing that working with others can sometimes achieve more than can be done alone builds an appreciation of community.

The Activity

It seems a simple matter to choose an activity, such as setting off on a camping trip through the mountains or a sailing voyage, yet as McCulloch (2004) points out, the demands of any given one will present differing opportunities for learning and development. McCulloch examined the contrasting experiences afforded by tall ships versus modern sloops and concluded that these provided divergent social experiences in relation to hierarchy and power, and therefore different experiences with regards to the levels of agency afforded the young person. As mentioned earlier, Wojcikiewicz and Mural (2010) suggest that experiential education draws on the potential of the activity to shape the experiences of the participants, which confirms the importance of making the appropriate choices as to what to offer the group. Elsewhere (Loynes, 2004) this author argues that outdoor activities are imbued with a set of values that were associated with them when they originated. For example he describes how navigation techniques refined by army scouts in the Boer War were subsequently developed as a skill by the civilian Scout Movement in ways that intentionally reflected the values of self-reliance and control of movement in unfamiliar space. Furthermore whilst these may still be considered desirable values, it is important that they are understood in relation to their 'origins'. For, as I explain, using the map and compass approach to navigation supports certain values but suppresses others possessing equal educational worth, notably those more relational to being 'in nature', for example utilising the 'natural' signs and symbols of the environment, such as the growth of moss on trees and drystone walls, to indicate a northerly direction (Gatty, 1958; Huth, 2013).

Some OAE organisations have developed the selection process for particular activities into a fine art, for example the employment of low and high rope work and problem-solving tasks that are suited to specific personal or social developmental outcomes (e.g. Rohnke and Butler, 1995). These are typically sequenced to support group development and individual learning as well as being targeted to maximise the possibility of achieving the preordained outcomes of the programme, for example 'building reliance on others' by requiring the participants on a high ropes course to put their trust in their partner who holds the rope as they take a 'leap of faith' from the top of a pole high in the air (Priest and Gass, 1997). Such 'Macdonaldisation' of OAE is almost always counterproductive (Roberts, 2012). For despite the financial pressures to operate in this specific preplanned way it is unlikely that these activities in themselves will meet the Deweyian criteria for an 'educative experience' which requires a more organic, person-centred, complex, open-ended and longer-term encounter such as camps, hikes, voyages and expeditions wherein experiences can develop and participants can flourish.

Facilitation and the outdoor adventure experience

This chapter has emphasised the importance of an intentional approach to leadership and facilitation. Informal education when combined with OAE may appear to be at odds with the apparently more didactic stance usually associated with instruction linked to the acquisition of activity skills. Simplistically the 'instructor' can be contrasted with the more laissez faire 'youth worker'. In reality OAE relies on a wide range of informal and formal educational techniques. Ringer and Gillis (1995) suggest a model that contains three units or sets relevant to informal education practices within OAE. The first are those of the instructor or coach employed to teach the skills required by participants so that they might engage safely and productively with the outdoor experience and wider recreational milieu. Second are the skills needed to transmit knowledge concerning such matters as place, weather and the overall environment. Finally, there are those associated with personal development that will function to help participants understand how experiences in the outer landscape can develop the inner landscape of the mind. This is a rich set of skills that take time to develop in one person. Some programmes opt to divide up the responsibilities by using specialists with different skill sets to deal with discrete elements. Richards et al. (2001), for example, describe using an outdoor instructor, group facilitator and therapist in a programme working with people with eating disorders.

OAE generally places the informal educator in a complex relationship with those they are working with. Heron (1992) models this in his theory of facilitation, suggesting his own three 'levels' of facilitation – content, process and learning – with all three simultaneously in play, although at any given time the emphasis may be placed on one at the expense of the others. Likewise this will also be the case for the outdoor educators. The desire to give experiences of agency and autonomy to participants is essential in order to achieve a worthwhile educational experience. However doing so can appear to be at odds with the need to ensure the safety of the group, especially when some or all of the group members lack the skill, knowledge or experience that, say, a facilitator of a self-guided mountain walk would need to balance the benefits accruing from the freedom devolved to the group to navigate across rough terrain with the self-evident dangers associated with them making navigational errors. In shorter and intensive programmes a careful choice of activity can avoid an overly long expert-novice relationship and undue usage of directive modes of leadership, for example utilising bouldering (low-level climbing, with minimal danger) to introduce novice participants to the experience of climbing as opposed to roped climbing, which requires greater levels of instruction and expert guidance. Some youth work programmes, including the Duke of Edinburgh Award schemes, have addressed this issue by developing progressive models in relation to social service as well as outdoor activities. The Duke of Edinburgh expeditions typically begin with intensive instruction in skills and the teaching of knowledge before proceeding to a self-reliant journey planned and led by the young people (Duke of Edinburgh's Award, 2012).

Ringer and Gillis (1995) also offer a model relating specifically to psychological depth to help facilitators with decisions regarding the appropriate approach. In their view personal development work in the outdoors should focus on five out of the eight levels and therefore implementation requires, on the part of the educator, a range of complex skills and judgment. The first level involves ritual and shallow exchanges with limited meaning. The next, and the first relevant to OAE, is task focused. Facilitation here entails choosing the right task and supporting the group to complete it. This is followed by the encounter level, which relates to the social world of the group and is focused upon helping members relate to each other in constructive ways through the medium of activities. The fourth, the contextual level, involves linking members' experiences with the lives they share with family, friends, colleagues at work, school or college, and their community. Then we encounter the level at which the facilitator intentionally works with group members to explore and develop their identities. Here choice of activity, reflective questioning and conversation are all important. Finally we have the historical/

cultural level in which the current experience helps participants address past issues and change current contexts. This requires great care and judgment if it is to avoid straying into the realms of therapy, especially when the group comprises marginalised and troubled young people. The remaining two levels comprise therapeutic interventions beyond the realms of youth work. The value of the Ringer and Gillis model is that it helps the facilitator decide on the level at which they feel competent to work.

Conclusion

This chapter has reviewed OAE through some of the theoretical lenses used to understand and appraise the field. Whilst OAE is of value for its own sake (Quay, 2013), it is the pragmatic outcomes of personal and social development and, increasingly, environmental relations that are most widely valued. The attribution error, claimed by Brookes (2003), that questions the efficacy of the transfer of learning from the 'escape to the hills' to the 'real world' can be overcome by local, recurring and place based approaches which compliment the one-off big experiences of the wilderness challenge so useful in the transformation of personal narratives in the transition from young person to adult and from marginalisation to inclusion (Loynes, 2010). Well-designed and facilitated OAE offers much potential in supporting young people and others in the social and environmental challenges of the future.

References

Aitchison, C. (2003) 'Venturing into other territories: reflections on theoretical journeys of social and cultural exclusion in outdoor environments' in B. Humberstone, H. Brown and K. Richards (eds.) *Whose Journeys? The outdoors and adventure as social and cultural phenomena*, Penrith: IOL.

Allen, M. and Ainley, P. (2010) *Lost Generation? New Strategies for Youth and Education*, London, UK: Bloomsbury Publishing.

Allin, L. (2000) 'Women into outdoor education: negotiating a male-gendered space' in B. Humberstone (ed.) *Her Outdoors: Risk, Challenge and Adventure in Gendered Open Spaces*, London: Leisure Studies Association.

Allin, L. and West, A. (2013) 'Feminist theory and outdoor leadership' in E. C. J. Pike and S. Beames (eds.) *Outdoor Adventure and Social Theory*, London: Routledge.

Allison, P. (2000) *Research from the Ground Up: Post Expedition Adjustment*, Ambleside: Brathay Hall Trust.

Allison, P., Carr, D. and Meldrum, G. (2012) 'Potential for excellence: interdisciplinary learning outdoors as a moral enterprise', *Curriculum Journal* 23(1), pp. 43–58.

Anderson, J. and Harris, J. (2003) 'Sailing and young people: exclusive or inclusive?' in B. Humberstone, H. Brown and K. Richards (eds.) *Whose Journeys? The Outdoors and Adventure as Social and Cultural Phenomena*, Penrith: IOL.

Arnett, J. J. (2004) *Emerging Adulthood: The Winding Road from Late Teens through the Twenties*, Oxford: Oxford University Press.

Arnold-Brown, A. (1962) *Unfolding Character*, London: Routledge and Kegan Paul.

Backman, E., Humberstone, B. and Loynes, C. (2014) 'Urban nature' in E. Backman, B. Humberstone and C. Loynes (eds.) *Urban Nature: Inclusive Learning through Youth Work and School Work*. Stockholm: Swedish School of Sport and Health Sciences.

Bacon, S. (1983) *The Conscious Use of Metaphor in Outward Bound*, Denver, CO: Outward Bound.

Beames, S. (2010) *Understanding Educational Expeditions*, Rotterdam: Sense Publishers.

Beard, C. and Wilson, J. P. (2002) *The Power of Experiential Learning*, London: Kogan Page.

Becker, P. (1998) 'Some conceptual ideas from the point of the "modernised body"' in T. Lehtonen (ed.) *Adventure for Life*, Jyvaskyla, Finland: Atena Kustannus.

Becker, P. (2008) 'The unfamiliar is all around us always. About the necessity of the element of unfamiliarity in the education process and its relationship to adventure' in P. Becker and J. Schirp (eds.) *Other Ways of Learning*, Marburg, Germany: BSJ.

Bell, B. (2003) 'The rites of passage and outdoor education: critical concerns for effective programming', *Journal of Experiential Education*, 26(1), pp. 41–50.

Bell, B., Beames, S. and Carlson, W. (2012) 'The expedition and rites of passage' in S. Beames (ed.) *Understanding Educational Expeditions*, Rotterdam: Sense Publishers.

Bernstein, B. (1996) *Pedagogy, Symbolic Control and Identity: Theory, Research, Critique*, London: Taylor and Francis.

Brookes, A. (2003) 'Adventure programming and the fundamental attribution error: a critique of neo-Hahnian outdoor education theory' in B. Humberstone, H. Brown and K. Richards (eds.) *Whose Journeys? The Outdoors and Adventure as Social and Cultural Phenomena*, Penrith: Institute for Outdoor Learning.

Bynner, J., Elias, P., McKnight, A., Pan, H. and Gaëlle, P. (2002) *Young People's Changing Routes to Independence*, York: Joseph Rowntree Foundation.

Campbell, J. (1968) *The Hero with a Thousand Faces*, Princeton: Princeton University Press.

Cook, L. (2001) 'Differential social and political influences on girls and boys through education out of doors in the United Kingdom', *Journal of Adventure Education and Outdoor Learning*, 1(2), pp. 43–52.

Dewey, J. (1997) *Experience and Education*, New York: Simon and Schuster.

Duke of Edinburgh's Award (2012) *Expedition Guide 2012*, London: Duke of Edinburgh's Award.

Dybeck, M. (1996) *A Broad River*, Ambleside: Brathay Hall Trust.

Everard, B. (1993) *The History of Development Training*, London: K. B. Everard/Development Training Advisory Group.

Ewert, A. and Yoshino, A. (2011) 'The influence of short-term adventure-based experiences on levels of resilience', *Journal of Adventure Education and Outdoor Learning*, 11(1), pp. 35–50.

Festeu, D. and Humberstone, B. (2006) *Non-Formal Education through Outdoor Activities Guide*, High Wycombe: European Institute for Outdoor Adventure Education and Experiential Learning.

Furedi, F. (2006) *The Culture of Fear*, London: Continuum.

Furlong, A. and Cartmel, F. (1997) *Young People and Social Change: Individualization and Risk in Late Modernity*, Buckingham: Open University Press.

Gatty, H. (1958) *Finding Your Way Without Map or Compass*, New York: Dover Publications.

Griffiths, J. (2013) *Kith: The Riddle of the Childscape*, London: Hamish Hamilton.

Gustafsson, P. E., Szczepanski, A., Nelson, N. and Gustafsson, P. A. (2012) 'Effects of an outdoor education intervention on the mental health of schoolchildren', *Journal of Adventure Education and Outdoor Learning*, 12(1), pp. 63–79.

Heintzman, P. (2009) 'Nature-based recreation and spirituality: a complex relationship', *Leisure Sciences*, 32(1), pp. 72–89.

Heron, J. (1992) *Feeling and Personhood: Psychology in Another Key*, London: Sage.

Hodgkin, R. (1976) *Born Curious: New Perspectives in Educational Theory*, London: Wiley.

Humberstone, B. (2011) 'Embodiment and social and environmental action in nature-based sport: spiritual spaces', *Leisure Studies*, 30(4), pp. 495–512.

Humberstone, B. (2014) 'Embodiment and adventurous activities: to be in the body, in the world' in E. Backman, B. Humberstone and C. Loynes (eds.) *Urban Nature: Inclusive Learning through Youth Work and School Work*, Stockholm: Swedish School of Sport and Health Sciences.

Huth, J. E. (2013) *The Lost Art of Finding Our Way*, Cambridge, Mass.: Harvard University Press.

Ingold, T. (2011) *Being Alive: Essays on Movement, Knowledge and Description*, Abingdon: Routledge.

Jeal, T. (1989) *Baden-Powell*, London: Hutchinson.

Jeffs, T. and Smith, M. K. (2005), *Informal Education: Conversation, Democracy and Learning*, Second Edition, Ticknall: Education Now Publishing Co-operative Ltd.

Knight, S. (2009) *Forest Schools and Outdoor Learning in the Early Years*, London: Sage.

Leather, M. (2013) '"It's good for their self-esteem": the substance beneath the label', *Journal of Adventure Education and Outdoor Learning*, 13(2), pp. 158–179.

Lewin, K. (1951) *Field Theory in Social Science: Selected Theoretical Papers*, New York: Harper and Row.

Lewis, I. (2005) Campaign for Adventure: Risk and Enterprise in Society. Available at: http://www.campaignforadventure.org/ (accessed 26 July 2009).

Louv, R. (2009) *Last Child in the Woods: Saving Our Children from Nature-deficit Disorder*, London: Atlantic Books.

Loynes, C. (2003) 'Narratives of agency' in J. Koch (ed.) *Bewegungs- und korperorientierte Ansatze in der Sozialen Arbeit*. Jahrbuch, Germany: BSJ.

Loynes, C. (2004) 'If you want to learn to navigate throw away the map', *Ecoplus*, 4, 20–39.

Loynes, C. (2007) 'Why outdoor education should get real' in B. Henderson and N. Vikander (eds.) *Nature First: Outdoor Life and Friluftsliv Way*, Toronto: Natural Heritage Books.

Loynes, C. (2008) 'Constancy and change. The hero's journey: a framework for understanding youth transition and for designing youth work interventions' in J. Schirp (ed.) *Abeneuer: ein weg zur jugend?*, Marburg, Germany: BSJ.

Loynes, C. (2010) 'Journeys of transition: the role of narrative within the Stoneleigh Project', *Journal of Adventure Education and Outdoor Learning*, 10(2), pp. 127–145.

Maddern, E. (1990) 'What is it fifteen year olds need?', *Journal of Adventure Education and Outdoor Leadership*, 7(1), 29–32.

Mannion, G., Adey, C. and Lynch, J. (2010) *Intergenerational Place-based Education: Where Schools, Communities, and Nature Meet*, Stirling: University of Stirling Scottish Centre for Intergenerational Practice.

McCulloch, K. (2013) 'Erving Goffman: sail training, interactionism and the "total institution"' in E. C. J. Pike and S. Beames (eds.) *Outdoor Adventure and Social Theory*, London: Routledge.

McCulloch, K. H. (2004) 'Ideologies of adventure: authority and decision making in sail training', *Journal of Adventure Education and Outdoor Learning*, 4(2), pp. 185–198.

Mortlock, C. (1984) *The Adventure Alternative*, Milnthorpe: Cicerone Press.

Nicol, R. (2000) *Outdoor Education for Sustainable Living?: An Investigation Into the Potential of Scottish Local Authority Residential Outdoor Education Centres to Deliver Programmes Relating to Sustainable Living*, Edinburgh: University of Edinburgh.

Norris, J. (2011) 'Crossing the threshold mindfully: exploring rites of passage models in adventure therapy', *Journal of Adventure Education and Outdoor Learning*, 11(2), pp. 109–126.

Ogilvie, K. (2012) *Roots and Wings: A History of Outdoor Education and Outdoor Learning in the UK*, Warwick Bridge: Institute for Outdoor Learning.

Ord, J. (2016) *Youth Work Process, Product and Practice*, 2nd ed, London: Routledge.

Perrin, J. (2003) 'Robin Hodgkin: Educationalist, Quaker and a great mountaineer who ranged from the Caucasus to near-disaster in the Himalayas', *The Guardian,* 30 August 2003.

Priest, S. and Gass, M. A. (1997) *Effective Leadership in Adventure Programming*, Champaign, IL: Human Kinetics.

Quay, J. (2013) 'More than relations between self, others and nature: outdoor education as an aesthetic experience', *Journal of Adventure Education and Outdoor Learning*, 13(2), pp. 142–157.

Rawles, K. (2013) 'Outdoor adventure in a carbon-light era' in E. C. J. Pike and S. Beames (eds.) *Outdoor Adventure and Social Theory*, London: Routledge.

Richards, K. (2003) *Self-esteem and Youth Development* (vol. 1), Ambleside: Brathay Hall Trust.

Richards, K., Peel, J., Smith, B. and Owen, V. (2001) *Adventure Therapy and Eating Disorders: A Feminist Approach to Research and Practice*, Ambleside: Brathay Hall Trust.

Ringer, M. and Gillis, H. L. (1995) 'Managing psychological depth in adventure programming', *Journal of Experiential Education*, 18(1), pp. 41–51.

Roberts, J. W. (2012) *Beyond Learning by Doing*, London: Routledge.

Rohnke, K. and Butler, S. (1995) *Quicksilver*, Dubuque, Iowa: Kendall Hunt.

Rosenthal, M. (1986) *The Character Factory*, London: Harper Collins.

Seaman, J. (2008) 'Experience, reflect, critique: the end of the "learning cycles" era' *Journal of Experiential Education*, 31(1), pp. 3–18.

Stuart, K. (2010) *Issues in Youth Transitions*, Ambleside: Brathay Hall Trust.

Wadland, J. H. (1978) *Ernest Thompson Seton*, New York: Arno Press.

Wattchow, B. and Brown, M. (2011) *A Pedagogy of Place: Outdoor Education for a Changing World*, Monash: Monash University.

White, J. (1997) *Education and the End of Work*, London: Cassell.

Williams, R. (2013) 'Woven into the fabric of experience: residential adventure education and complexity', *Journal of Adventure Education and Outdoor Learning*, 13(2), pp. 107–124.

Williamson, H. (1997) *Youth and Policy: Contexts and Consequences*, Aldershot: Ashgate.

Wojcikiewicz, S. K. and Mural, Z. B. (2010) 'A Deweyian framework for youth development in experiential education: perspectives from sail training and sailing instruction', *Journal of Experiential Education*, 33(2), pp. 105–119.

Young, K. (2006) *The Art of Youth Work*, Second Edition, Lyme Regis: Russell House.

Zink, R. (2010) 'The constitution of outdoor education groups: an analysis of the literature', *Australian Journal of Outdoor education*, 14(2), pp. 21–32.

3

EXPERIENTIAL EDUCATION

The importance of John Dewey[1]

Jon Ord and Mark Leather

This chapter seeks to reconceptualise experiential learning with a focus upon its relationship with outdoor and adventure education. The contribution is premised on a belief that many learning cycles currently in use are problematic and offer little more than oversimplified interpretations of David Kolb's model of experiential learning. We suggest our understanding of experiential learning would be improved by returning to the work of John Dewey, for only by doing so can we begin to more fully comprehend outdoor educational experiences as forms of *lived experience*. Prior to embarking on this task we consider the current conceptualisation of experiential learning so long dominated by the cyclical model associated with Kolb.

Learning cycles

The application of an experiential learning cycle to outdoor and adventure education can be traced to the work of Drasdo (1972) and Parker and Meldrum (1973), both of which borrowed the concept from the work of Lewin (1951). Others followed, especially after the appearance in 1984 of Kolb's text *Experiential Learning: Experience as the Source of Learning and Development*, which contained what subsequently became known as 'Kolb's learning cycle' (see the outer circle of Figure 3.2).

Kolb created this cyclical model specifically to illustrate what he believed Lewin, thirty years earlier, had been seeking to communicate (Kolb, 1984: 21). From that date onwards Kolb's learning cycle almost overnight became embedded within the vocabulary and pedagogy of outdoor education (Brown, 2004; Seaman, 2008; Ord and Leather, 2011), to such a degree, according to McWilliam, that a sizable percentage of practitioners latched onto this model and applied 'it with uncritical evangelical zeal' (2004: 129). This cycle was later abbreviated by writers such as Neill (2004) to become the 'Do–Review–Plan' model (Figure 3.1).

FIGURE 3.1 Do–Review–Plan: three-stage experiential learning cycle (Neill, 2004).

Neill, who acknowledges the origins reside in the work of Kolb, explains that within his simplified model 'Do' equates to 'going forth and having an experience', 'Review' relates to 'reviewing what happened and what can be learnt' and 'Plan' refers to how one may better 'plan a way to tackle the next round of experience'. Sometimes Kolb's cycle is simplified even further in what Ogilvie claims is a 'commonly used shorthand device to aid the memorisation of this [reflective] process: What?–So What?–Now What?' (2005: 261).

A number of detailed critiques of learning cycles *per se* have appeared since Kolb's model surfaced (Beard and Wilson, 2006; Brown, 2004, 2009, 2010; Fenwick, 2000; Seaman, 2008). The authors of this chapter agree with the thrust of those critiques, notably that it is naïve to conceive of experiential learning as conforming to such a simplistic cycle and that doing so is problematic, resulting in an impoverished theoretical conceptualisation of informal educational experiences whatever the setting. Smith (2001) perhaps best summarises the tenor of these critiques when he suggests the idea of stages, or steps, does not sit well with the reality of thinking. Certainly an underlying premise of this chapter is that any framework for understanding experiential learning must take account of the depth and breadth of the experiences that form a part of outdoor and adventure education, not least because conceiving of these in simplistic terms risks curtailing our potential for doing so. For instance a canoe trip or a mountainous trek is much more than merely travelling from point A to point B, not least because the participants bring to the journey their previous experiences. So whilst the journey for one might amount to the greatest challenge of their life, for another it could be so familiar as to be deemed mundane. Consequently the degree of challenge, risk or novelty encompassed within any given journey or activity is something unique to the individual participant, and largely dependent upon their prior life experiences.

It would be fallacious to argue that simplistic models invariably result in simplistic practice, for practitioners are not bound by the simplicity of the model. But as Greenaway cautions, models all too often serve to 'simplify reality', especially when those employing it employ only the 'model's labels' and possess little or no grasp of the 'substance beneath the labels' (2008: 363). Practitioners may, of course, be creative in their use of a given model and move beyond it, and encouragingly research shows some develop 'practice theories' to more accurately explain and interpret the work they undertake (Hovelynck, 2001). That this occurs cannot suffice as an argument against the collective production of better, more meaningful and useful theories or the need for formal theory building. Unfortunately there is little within the simplistic models or theories discussed earlier to encourage practitioners to 'go beyond' them. Therefore they are as likely to constrain as illuminate a practitioner's understanding of experiential learning, and are likely to do little to facilitate a deeper understanding of the complexities of experiential learning. Nor do the simplistic cycles promote a deep exploration of the meaning of informal educational experiences taking place outdoors. For they tend to portray such experiences not in a holistic way that contextualises them in relation to the life of the participants but rather in ways that encourage a compartmentalisation of a given experience (Brown, 2004, 2009), thereby often reducing the learning from the experience to 'practical' outcomes and the identification of how such interventions might be better 'delivered' in the future. For example, if a kayaker capsizes a number of times on the descent of a river it would be realistic using such models to reflect on such aspects as the need to improve the teaching of that particular skill, choose a less difficult passage or apply more careful selection criteria in relation to the formation of the group. These one-dimensional naïve models, however, make it difficult to incorporate the wider implications of learning because they encourage those using them to set aside areas of enquiry that do not easily comply with their criteria. Therefore in relation to the example given they discourage analysis that might ask: how does the participant feel as a result of the proficient rescues undertaken, the care and support of companions and the challenges posed by the journey completed? Such analysis and the resultant knowledge is, of course, never 'decontextualised' (Seaman, 2008: 15), but it will still be better 'situated' within the lives of the participants (Brown, 2009).

Rethinking experiential education

Despite the domination of Kolb's learning cycle, a number of authors do elude to a need for a wider theoretical framework which acknowledges the importance of Dewey's thinking (Kraft, 1990; Barnes, 1997; Martin et al., 2006; Gilbertson et al., 2006; Panicucci, 2007; Quay & Seaman, 2013, 2016). Priest and Gass (2005), for instance, advocate an 'experiential learning and judgment paradigm' which is an extended version of Kolb's model augmented by the addition of a fifth stage linked to 'judgment'. Significantly their approach acknowledges the importance Dewey placed on 'judgment … in the experiential learning process' (2005: 154). Hopkins and Putnam likewise sought to expand upon Kolb's contribution by suggesting 'learning is best conceived as a process, not in *terms of outcomes … [but as]* … a continuous process grounded in experience' (1993: 79). Subsequently Roberts (2008, 2012) applied a more informed understanding of Dewey to experiential education; however, before discussing these developments we need to return Kolb's 1984 text in order to do it justice.

It is important to point out there are marked differences between what is universally referred to as 'Kolb's experiential learning cycle' and both the model he initially published in 1984 and the revised version published in 2014 (see Figure 3.2).

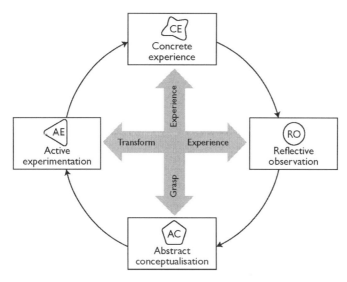

FIGURE 3.2 The 'experiential learning cycle' (Kolb, 2014: 51).[2]

Crucially, as a result of misrepresentations of Kolb's theoretical model, an important element is omitted. Kolb never implied that experiential learning was only to be represented by the outer circle. Alongside this was the interior axis, which Kolb inserted in an attempt to better take account of Lewin's analysis. Kolb set out with the specific intention of developing Lewin's model rather than to replicate it, not least because Lewin had been concerned with how learning occurred within organisations rather than in explaining the process of experiential learning *per se*.

The outer circle, which became synonymous with Kolb's experiential learning cycle, at best tells only part of the story of experiential learning. How much of that story it set out to recount is difficult to assess. For it is not clear from a reading of Kolb's original 1984 work, or its later reworking (2014), the degree of emphasis he wished to put on this outer circle. At times he appears to conceptualise learning in this separate and therefore sequential manner, questioning: 'How can one act and reflect at the same time? How can one be concrete and immediate and still be theoretical? Learning requires abilities that are polar opposites' (1984: 30). However in the same text Kolb also suggests learning is not a sequential process of passing through separate phases or functions but a holistic one, a process he refers to as a dialectic integration of opposing functions. It is this dialectic aspect of learning by experience to which the interior of the circle refers. As Kolb explains:

> …*all the models above suggest the idea that learning is by its very nature a conflict filled process … [for] … experiential learning is also concerned with how these functions are integrated by the person into a holistic adaptive posture toward the world (1984: 30–32).*

Citing Bruner (1966), Kolb claims that at the heart of the creative process of learning there is a dialectic tension between 'abstract detachment' and 'concrete involvement'.

Clearly Kolb's theory must be seen as comprising of far more than its simplistic popularisation as a sequential learning cycle. Indeed in all probability Seaman is right in his conclusion that 'existing cyclic models might be better valued for their historical contribution, rather than as active theories of learning in experiential education' (2008: 3). The authors, however, believe that to understand experiential learning more fully it is essential to revisit the original writings John Dewey (1900, 1916, 1938), not least because it was his work that underpinned much of Kolb's theory as well as the work of Lewin. We also need to do this because, as Greenaway reminds us, Dewey provided a far 'broader vision of "educative experience" than many of his followers do' (2008: 365).

Dewey

Any viable concept of experiential learning requires clarity as to what we mean by experience (Fox, 2008). However the problem with Kolb, and much that followed in his wake, is that experience is conceived almost exclusively as 'doing', as 'concrete experience'. Therefore if we are to fully understand experiential learning we must move 'beyond' this emphasis on 'doing' and similar impoverished conceptions of experience (see Roberts, 2012 for an extended discussion of this point).

Garforth, who edited a collection of his educational writings, concluded Dewey meant something quite specific by experience and did not perceive it as

> the stored up product of the past; nor does he mean simply the immediacy of the experienced present; nor the mere acceptance of environmental impact by a passive recipient; nor does he contrast experience with thought or reason. Experience is continuous from past through present to future; it is not static but dynamic, moving, in process. It is not unilateral but, as Dewey would say, 'transactional, for the experient is modified by his environment and the environment by the experient in a constant reciprocal relationship. (1966: 13)

This concept of 'transaction' was of fundamental importance for Dewey who maintained 'an experience is always what it is because of a transaction taking place between the individual and, what at the time, constitutes the environment' (1938: 43). Underlying this notion of a transaction is what Dewey (1916, 1938) refers to as 'trying' and 'undergoing', the former being the outward expression of the individual's intention or action on the environment, whilst the latter refers to the manner in which the environment impacts upon the individual and the consequences for the individual of that experience. For Dewey this process of 'transaction' is dynamic and always two-way, for the interaction involves an impact on the environment by the individual, as well as in turn an impact on the individual by the environment, as he explains in the following passage:

> *When we experience something we act upon it, we do something; then we suffer or undergo the consequences. We do something to the thing and then it does something to us in return: such is the peculiar combination. The connection of these two phases of experience measures the fruitfulness of experience. (1916: 104)*

In relation to practice, for example, we might opt to clear litter left by others at the site of a regular lunch-stop alongside a river; by doing so we visibly improve the location (a consequence of 'trying') and simultaneously feel good about the deed (a consequence of 'undergoing'). For Dewey experience necessarily contains both these discrete aspects.

Interestingly Kolb does utilise this dual notion of 'transaction' but links it to Piaget's (1951, 1971) concept of 'assimilation' and 'accommodation'. Kolb suggests:

> *In Piaget's terms, the key to learning lies in the mutual interaction of the process of accommodation of concepts or schemas to experience in the world and the process of assimilation of events or experiences from the world into existing concepts or schemas. (1984: 23)*

Accommodation and assimilation for Kolb represent the dialectic tension at the heart of experiential learning, characterised by the degree to which the individual is changed by the environment and the extent to which the environment is changed by the individual. This is what characterises the inner section of his model of experiential learning (Figure 3.2); however this insight is consistently overlooked within subsequent literature that employs Kolb's learning cycle. Importantly the notion of a change to the environment can be interpreted as a reconceptualisation of how we see the environment or the 'world' as much as an actual physical change within it. Thus as a result of outdoor informal educational experiences we are changed but so is the world, or at the very least, and perhaps more importantly, how we perceive and conceive of it. To illustrate let us consider a hypothetical example involving the various dynamics of women's outdoor experiences (Humberstone, 2000; Boniface, 2006). Imagine an all-female backpacking journey which represents for many or all the participants the first time they have had to rely on both themselves and other women to undertake many of the tasks normally performed by the men in their lives. As a result of the challenges undertaken and the relative ease with which they completed such novel tasks as pitching tents, planning routes and carrying rucksacks they begin to see both themselves and the world differently. No longer do they view themselves as being inevitably restricted by their gender; instead now, maybe for the first time, they may comprehend gender as a social construct which they can challenge. Consequently the women may start questioning assumptions about their own perceived 'lack of abilities' and formulate a clearer understanding of how an 'oppressive environment', on the basis of their gender, prescribes their identities, abilities and opportunities. This outdoor experience may therefore result in some beginning to question the status quo; if so, then a fundamental transaction will have taken place. Some or all of them as a consequence of this experience will have been changed, as has the world around them, or at the least how they see the world. Such experiences can therefore be rightly viewed as 'transactional' for those group members who discover they have, at both a micro and a macro level, a choice as to whether they conform or not to the norms imposed upon them (Ord, 2016: 185).

Mere 'doing' or the notion of 'concrete experience' provides an inadequate basis upon which to develop a theory of experiential learning, for activity does not of itself constitute experience nor are all experiences educative. Indeed experience can be mis-educative, much as change can be both positive and negative, as Dewey warns: 'the belief that all genuine education comes about through experience does not mean that all experiences are genuinely or equally educative' (1938: 25). Helpfully Dewey provides two criteria to help us define the educative quality of experience. The first involves what was previously described as 'experience as a transaction' – the essential combination of 'trying' and 'undergoing'– what he later referred to as the

> internal and objective conditions of experience … [the transaction] is an interplay of these two sets of conditions. Taken together or in their interaction, they form what we call a situation. (1938: 42)

This is a necessary ingredient to enable an engagement to be designated an educative experience, but it is not of itself sufficient. The second criterion is the extent to which experience promotes 'growth'. For Dewey all learning by experience occurs within the context of the continual adaptation of the individual to, and within, their environment. So for him it makes sense to judge the quality of educative experience in part by how well it facilitates future experiences given 'every experience is a moving force; its value can be judged only on the grounds of what it moves towards and into' (1938: 38). Dewey refers to this as his continuity principle, which is grounded in the temporal quality of experience – from the past, through the present and into the future. The quality of educative experience is therefore to be judged both in the light of past experiences, and in relation to future experiences. This analysis is integral to Dewey's dynamics of the experiential learning 'situation' wherein 'the ability to learn from experience … [involves] the power to retain from one experience something which is of avail in coping with the difficulties of a later situation' (1916: 36). Greenaway (2008: 365) is helpful here for he reminds us that Dewey's interest was focused on those experiences that are forceful, stimulating and likely to live on within the consciousness of those who encounter them, a point clarified by Pring, who suggests:

> Growth or [the] 'educative process' … involves not just more of the same (like a river which gets bigger) but a 'transformation' of what one previously was. One thinks, experiences and feels differently. 'Experience is transformed'. One's understanding of the world is reconceptualised. (2007: 26)

For Dewey there is an organic linkage between education and experience, therefore 'the concept of education is a constant reorganising or reconstructing of experience' (1916: 59). However, as Pring points out, this reorganisation or reconstruction of experience is partly a search for meaning, an attempt to make sense of the world and our place within it. Hence, Dewey's educative inquiry seeks to 'to make sense' but 'to do so in the light of what other people have concluded in similar circumstances' (Pring, 2007: 65). This means the educative experience is as much about how we understand the world as it is with how we act in it. It is as much about meaning-making as it is with the finding of solutions to 'practical' problems.

The 'social' aspect of experience

In relation to the prior description of experiential education it would be wrong to assume there was a sole focus on the individual. Certainly the 'romantic tradition' which sees experiential learning exclusively as an 'individual phenomenon' was, and maybe still is, the dominant perspective. That dominance has helped ensure much practice is grounded upon a belief in the redemptive powers and unsullied ambiance of nature; the centrality of individual development, fulfillment and self-realisation; and an unquestioned acceptance of the benefits accruing from an immersion in nature. The romantic tradition also generally assumes experience, preferably unmediated, is the best of all teachers. An inherent weakness of this position is that experiences are necessarily social. Even an unsupervised solo expedition is never entirely an individual enterprise. After all, the preparations require the assistance of others (even if it is 'only' in the design, manufacture and supply of equipment); friends, family and colleagues are only physically left behind (and even if not communicated with via a mobile phone or written message remain 'present' in the mind); and the language employed to explain the experience to oneself and others is a social phenomenon. Bill Tillman reputedly replied when asked if he would still climb if he was the last man on earth: 'no, what would be the point?' So without labouring the point it is important to remember that everything we, like Tillman, do in the outdoors is in some respect in 'relation to others' and linked to a 'social' world beyond ourselves.

Recognition of this social dimension is central to Dewey's notion of experiential education. Although in the quotation that follows the focus is on the social life of the school, it nevertheless highlights the emphasis he placed on the centrality of social life in all its aspects. Therefore it can helpfully be transposed to the worlds of outdoor and adventure education.

> *In the first place, the school must itself be a community life in all which that implies.*
> *Social perceptions and interests can be developed only in a genuinely social medium –*
> *one where there is give-and-take in the building up of common experience … [and]*
> *in association with others … we have a social group in which study and growth are*

incidents of present shared experience. … The learning in schools should be continuous with that out-of-school. There should be a free interplay between the two. … Under such conditions, the school becomes itself a form of social life, a miniature community and one in close interaction with other modes of associated experience beyond schools. (1916: 257-258)

The concept of the 'social' also resides at the core of Dewey's notion of a 'learning situation'; therefore he places, as do outdoor informal educators, a premium upon

shared activity, [where] each person refers what he is doing to what the other is doing and vice-versa. That is, the activity of each is placed in the same inclusive situation [within which] each views the consequences of his own acts as having a bearing upon what others are doing and takes into account the consequences of their behaviour upon himself. (1916: 26)

Outdoor and adventure education provides an excellent means to explore the 'social' for it comprises a rich array of activities requiring an almost limitless supply of opportunities for exercising cooperation, negotiation and the skills of associational living. In addition the residential experience which is an integral part of so much outdoor education presents the informal educator with abundant openings wherein they might engage with the 'social' aspects of experiential education (see Chapter 10 for a wider discussion). However if the chances are not to be 'wasted' those same educators must give careful consideration to the question of transferability. Attention must be consistently paid to ensuring what is learnt in the outdoor environment or residential unit is 'transferred' to the home and community environment from which participants come and to which they must return. Dewey again, in a different context, reflects on this issue when he stresses the importance of linking schools and communities and rooting experiential education in the day-to-day lives of participants. Informal educators operating outdoors need to try to ensure that the removal and detachment from the normal social settings, so common to outdoor and adventure education, does not result in the learning being equally detached and isolated from the everyday life experiences of participants. For example, whilst a great many outdoor educators may have supported and encouraged nervous participants to successfully complete an abseil they thought beyond their ability, how many of them have fully maximised the opportunity to transfer the potential learning from the experience? They have achieved something they thought impossible. What other barriers might they also be able to overcome? This is not achieved by the simple interjection, 'wow, look what you have done – think what you could achieve now'. Whilst this may be a start, what is required is the enabling of a deeper conversation about 'what is going on' for the participant in their life and how beliefs about their own abilities might be holding them back.

'Learning situations' according to Dewey must involve thinking and problem solving. As he points out:

> the situation should be of such a nature as to arouse thinking. ... [This] means of course that it should suggest something to do which is not either routine or capricious – something, in other words, presenting what is new (and hence uncertain or problematic) and yet sufficiently connected with existing habits to call out an effective response. ... The most significant question which can be asked, accordingly, about any situation or experience proposed to induce learning is what quality of problem it involves. (1916: 114)

As the plethora of examples offered up in texts attests, it may be fairly straightforward to present those engaging in outdoor and adventure education with meaningful problems to solve (see for example Consalvo, 2009; Neuman, 2007). However these problems should not be selected arbitrarily or disconnected from the lives of participants and the challenges posed by the difficulties that frequently arise from living in a residential setting. Where the relevance of given problems is not immediately obvious, it is incumbent upon the educators to ensure the value of engaging in a particular problem-solving activity is made explicit. The task of selecting and presenting appropriate questions designed to raise pertinent issues that bring to the fore concerns or highlight the conflictual aspects of group living requires careful preparation on the part of informal educators. Selection is not a simple or straightforward task, and will entail sensitivity and knowledge of participants' backgrounds.

'Moral' and 'political' aspects of experience

At the heart of Dewey's thinking resides a conviction that learning does not happen merely for learning's sake but, as Roberts suggests, it 'takes place with the understanding that knowledge has moral consequences that invite (and often demand) social action' (2012: 59). It should take cognizance of and address the needs of the community in ways that will serve to enhance our common life, so that the future is better than the past. Democracy as a guiding principle is central to Dewey's moral commitment to this wider purpose. In relation to this he makes a clear distinction between formal and everyday democracy. The success of the formal structures of democracy, Dewey believed, requires the existence of an educated electorate, but that of itself was not sufficient. For he held that 'democracy is more than a form of government; it is primarily a mode of associated living, of conjoint communicated experience' (1916: 66). This everyday, or what we might call informal or participatory, democracy is grounded in the lived experience of individuals located in communities, and clearly informal education in its many forms has a fundamental role to play in its development and survival. Dewey maintains one cannot teach students the skills required for democratic living in an abstract formalistic way; rather, in order to prepare them to become full citizens, they must be given opportunities to live democratically in the here and now. Accordingly education must be structured and function in ways that foster democracy and enable participants to learn to live a shared life and discover the means to mature into fully fledged citizens via collective participation in the task of solving pressing social issues. Experiential education if it is to effectively foster democracy must itself model democratic processes and participative living. In order to do so it must encourage the recognition of shared common interests and 'the free interaction between social groups' (Dewey, 1916: 65).

Methods of teaching 'in democracy' rather than 'for democracy' need to locate the participants at the centre of the process; their interests and concerns must be considered to be of parallel importance to those of the educator (Dewey, 1900; Pring, 2007). The educational process should therefore be the subject of negotiation involving participants and educators alike. The antithesis of this would be a prearranged programme that participants are taken through and where the authority of the educator is perceived to be beyond question. Such questioning means democratic educators need humility and conviction in equal measure, a balance Novak illustrates during his discussion of musical education:

> *Individuals participate in a developing theme. … Participants are expected to want to be competent, committed and creative. The job of the teacher is to make this metaphorical possibility a creative reality. The role involves, on the one hand, knowing who your students are and where their interests and talents lie. On the other hand, the role means having a solid grasp of what you are teaching and creative possibilities that exist in connecting subject matter with individual student interests and abilities.*
> *(2014: 118)*

Rarely is everything clear at the outset nor is it invariably desirable for outdoor and other educators to work towards narrow pre-specified outcomes. Certainly Dewey believed the unknown and presence of risk are important elements with regards to any 'process of inquiry' (1916: 110).

Dewey's commitment to 'education in democracy' is not without its critics. Johnston for one argues Dewey's ideas on democracy are rather rudimentary and overly concerned with encouraging a 'non-dogmatic, non-authoritarian capacity to enquire' (2006: 155). Others draw attention to what they believe is a failure on his part to appreciate the importance of power and politics in social life, holding that Dewey is wedded to a consensus view of society which fails to acknowledge that social life is riven by structural conflicts emanating from specific power relations (Leonardo, 2004). Certainly Dewey's articulation of the process of experiential education is formulated without detailed reference to a political context where key social divisions create inequality and injustice. Humberstone, Brown and Richards (2003) argue this absence results in experiential learning, as typically encountered, being constructed in ways that fail to take account of the complexities of race, class, sexuality and disability (see also Seaman, 2008). An important critique of Dewey and other social pragmatists was articulated by C. Wright Mills. In summary, Wright Mills held that Dewey had formulated an 'ideology of the Liberal professional man, however much he may have thought about the disadvantaged' and concludes that the writings of those adhering to this ideology 'mask the character and shape of political power' (1974: 167). Dewey was a man of his time whose philosophy encapsulated much of America's early twentieth century opportunist and optimistic spirit. Yet throughout his adult life he was a progressive voice, an advocate of often unpopular liberal and radical causes. Consistently he was someone who, on issues relating to race, gender, the rights of labour and social justice, was ahead of his time (Seigfried, 1998; Ryan, 1995). Whilst issues of oppression, power and politics are not made explicit within Dewey's philosophy of experiential learning, he perceived the process of experiential education and the creation of situations involving interactions across existing social barriers as being fundamental to the establishment of a democratic society, viewing experiential education as a means of securing 'the breaking down [of] the barriers of class, race' and 'a liberation of powers' (1916: 66). Many of the attacks launched since Dewey's death in respect of issues relating to race and gender in part flow from a failure amongst many who make them to fully familiarise themselves with the full range of his writings and a certain nervousness with regards to dealing with his belief that inequalities fundamentally flow from an economic system based upon exploitation rather than co-operation. As Ryan (1995: 369) put it, Dewey was 'a visionary' and at the heart of that vision was a belief that a democracy of free and equal citizens was within our grasp. Dewey's formulation of experiential learning embraces the uniqueness of an individual's experience and acknowledges both the diversity of that experience, as well as issues of power which direct and in part define that experience. As time has moved on, unresolved questions of power, injustice and oppression have been more explicitly acknowledged in relation to experiential education (Ord, 2012: 68). But equally, experiential education as an arena of practice and form of intervention, we would argue, has always been well positioned to acknowledge and confront such issues.

Implications for informal education in the outdoors

Outdoor informal educational experiences inevitably involve 'doing' something but they also entail much more besides. Understanding an experience in the context of the outdoors is best done by appreciating the subtle and often significant differences in why particular 'activities' are undertaken, and what they mean to participants. Clearly Dewey's exposition of experiential learning helps us better understand it than the simplistic learning cycle attributed to Kolb. The notion of reflection contained within it remains a valuable concept, as it did for Dewey, who, at times, suggested reflection was synonymous with 'thinking', as he explained:

> *Reflection is turning a topic over in various aspects and in various lights so that nothing significant about it shall be overlooked … thoughtfulness means, practically, the same thing … in speaking of reflection we naturally use the words weigh, ponder, deliberate … closely related names are scrutiny, examination, consideration, inspection … even reason itself. (1910: 57)*

What needs to be stressed is that implicit in the formulisation of experience as 'concrete' or as 'doing' is a separation of thought and action (thinking and doing). The extent to which Kolb is guilty of failing to do this is debatable. However, it is evident that the unsophisticated models of experiential learning drawn from Kolb's work are guilty of this separation. Dewey's philosophical pragmatism categorically objects to such dualism which he regarded 'as radically false' (1916: 122). For Dewey thought and action are not discrete entities but are unified in experience. Human beings are immersed in the world and their thoughts about it are not separate and removed but products of it. The 'transactional experience' of being in the outdoors cannot be isolated from the thoughts, ideas and ultimately the 'meanings' we make of it, but are a consequence of the interweaving of both 'trying' and 'undergoing'. Meaning is therefore central to understanding any educative experience. It is essential therefore for anyone involved in educating others in the outdoors to grasp what the experience means. To illustrate this, consider what a long-distance walk following the same route might mean for three of the individuals taking part. For one this is their first encounter with the region and they marvel at the unique vistas. For a second it involves revisiting places they were familiar with during childhood and the journey brings back a host of happy memories. Finally for a third walker, who joined the party solely to raise money for a charity as a consequence of the death of a friend, their experience is tinged with sadness and they barely notice either the countryside or presence of their companions as their focus is upon completing the 'sponsored mileage'. These random examples highlight the multifaceted nature of any informal educational experience occurring outdoors and illustrate the need for educators to secure some insight into the motivation and background of participants in order to better facilitate their learning. Understanding what an outdoor experience means to group members, for whom it will be an individual 'encounter', is vital (Brown, 2004; Boniface, 2006).

Conclusion

Within the context of outdoor and adventure education programmes both group members and leaders alike are engaged in an unfolding encounter. However, such engagement ought not to involve a suspension of thought and analysis on the part of the latter, who as an educator and leader may on occasions be 'in the moment'. However, although the experience can be, and often is, characterised by an immersion in the 'hands on' nature of the encounter, this should not lead to them neglecting the constant need to think about the deeper meanings of the experience. Practitioners should therefore reflect-in-action (Schon, 1983) – or in Dewey's words 'think' about what the 'transaction of experience' means to those in each 'situation' – and avoid suspending thought, reflection and analysis until afterwards. Of course, it is usually worth returning *post hoc* to those thoughts, insights or feelings one had during the walk, climb or activity, but equally and perhaps more importantly those thoughts, insights and feelings should be engaged with as they occur. With this in mind, we should heed the advice of Brown (2004) and move away from an exclusive focus upon what he refers to as going 'round the circle' – the post-activity review led by the facilitator which attempts to draw out and acknowledge the learning from the activity. Rather we should prioritise the development of 'other' ways by which participants can reflect on and articulate their experiences throughout the course of the day. These 'other ways' should involve engaging in conversation with participants before and during the experience in an attempt to genuinely understand what it means for them. Such an approach would utilise informal educational processes, a topic which will be explored further in the next chapter.

Notes

1   The origins of this paper lie in an article published previously in the *Australian Journal of Outdoor Education*.
2   Kolb, David A. *Experiential Learning: Experience as the Source of Learning and Development, 2nd ed.* Englewood Cliffs, NJ: Prentice Hall. © 2015 Reprinted by permission of Pearson Education, Inc., New York.

References

Barnes, P. (1997) *Theory into Practice: The Complete Practical Theory of Outdoor Education and Personal Development*, Glasgow: University of Strathclyde.

Beard, C. and Wilson, J. P. (2006) *The Power of Experiential Learning: A Handbook for Trainers and Educators*, 2nd ed. London: Kogan Page.

Boniface, M. (2006) 'The meaning of adventurous activities for "women in the outdoors", *Journal of Adventure Education and Outdoor Learning* 6(1), pp. 9–24.

Brown, M. (2004) 'Let's go round the circle: how verbal facilitation can function as a means of direct instruction', *Journal of Experiential Education* 27(2), pp. 161–175.

Brown, M. (2009) 'Reconceptualising outdoor adventure education: activity in search of an appropriate theory', *Australian Journal of Outdoor Education* 13(2), pp. 3–13.

Brown, M. (2010) 'Transfer: outdoor education's Achilles heel? Changing participation as a viable option', *Australian Journal of Outdoor Education* 14(1), pp. 13–22.

Bruner, J. S. (1966) *Toward a Theory of Instruction*. New York: Norton.

Consalvo, C. M. (2009) *Work Play: 36 Indoor/Outdoor Problem Solving Activities for Leadership, Team Work and Problem Solving*. Amherst, MA: Hardpress.

Dewey, J. (1900) *The School and Society, the Child and the Curriculum*, Chicago: University of Chicago Press.

Dewey, J. (1916) *Democracy and Education*, Teddington: Echo Library.

Dewey, J. (1938) *Experience and Education*, New York: Touchstone.

Drasdo, H. (1972) *Education and the Mountain Centres*, 1997 ed. Penrith: Adventure Education.

Fenwick, T. J. (2000) 'Expanding conceptions of experiential learning: a review of the five contemporary perspectives on cognition' *Adult Education Quarterly* 50(4), pp. 243–272.

Fox, K. (2008) 'Rethinking experience: what do we mean by this word "experience"?' *Journal of Experiential Education* 31(1), pp. 36–54.

Garforth, F. W. (1966) 'Introduction' in *John Dewey Selected Educational Writings*, London: Heinemann.

Gilbertson, K., Bates, T., McLaughlin, T. and Ewert, A. (2006) *Outdoor Education: Methods and Strategies*, Champaign, IL: Human Kinetics.

Greenaway, R. (2008) 'A View into the Future: The Value of Other Ways of Learning and Development' in P. Becker and J. Schirp (eds.) *Other Ways of Learning*, Marburg, Germany: BSJ Marburg.

Hopkins, D. and Putnam, R. (1993) *Personal Growth through Adventure*, London: David Fulton.

Hovelynck, J. (2001) 'Practice-theories of facilitating experiential learning in outward bound: A research report', *Journal of Adventure Education and Outdoor Learning* 1(2), pp. 53–57.

Humberstone, B. (2000) *Her Outdoors: Risk, Challenge and Adventure in Gendered Open Spaces*, Brighton: Leisure Studies Association.

Humberstone, B., Brown, H. and Richards, K. (2003) *Whose Journeys? The Outdoors and Adventure and Social Cultural Phenomenon: Critical Explorations of Relations between Individuals, 'Others' and the Environment*, Barrow in Furness: Institute for Outdoor Learning.

Johnston, M. (2006) 'Mind incarnate: Dewey to Damasio', *Daedalus* 135(3) pp. 46–54.

Kolb, D. (1984) *Experiential Learning: Experience as the Source of Learning and Development*, Englewood Cliffs, NJ: Prentice Hall.

Kolb, D. (2014) *Experiential Learning: Experience as the Source of Learning and Development*, 2nd ed. Englewood Cliffs, NJ: Prentice Hall.

Kraft, R.J. (1990) 'Experiential learning' in J.C. Miles and S. Priest (eds.) *Adventure Education*, State College, PA: Venture Publishing.

Leonardo, Z. (2004) 'Critical social theory and transformative knowledge: the functions of criticism in quality education', *Educational Researcher* 33(6), pp. 11–18.

Lewin, K. (1951) *Field Theory in Social Sciences*, London: Harper Row.

Martin, B., Cashel, C., Wagstaff, M. and Breunig, M. (2006). *Outdoor Leadership: Theory and Practice*, Champaign, IL: Human Kinetics.

McWilliam, A. (2004) 'Learning theory and experiential education' in P. Barnes and B. Sharp (eds.) *The RHP Companion to Outdoor Education*, Lyme Regis, UK: Russell House Publishing.

Neill, J. (2004) *Experiential Learning Cycles: Overview of 9 Experiential Learning Cycle Models*, online. Available at: http://wilderdom.com/experiential/elc/ExperientialLearningCycle.htm (accessed 9 Sept 2009).

Neuman, J. (2007) *Education and Learning through Outdoor Activities: Games and Problem-Solving Activities, Outdoor Exercises and Rope Courses for Youth Programs*, EU: International Young Naturefriends.

Novak, J. M. (2014) 'Teaching lemocracy for life', in D. A. Breault and R. Breault (eds.) *Experiencing Dewey: Insights for Today's Classroom*, 2nd ed. Oxon: Routledge.

Ogilvie, K. C. (2005) *Leading and Managing Groups in the Outdoors*, 2nd ed. Penrith: Institute for Outdoor Learning.

Ord, J. (2016) *Youth Work Process, Product & Practice: Creating an authentic curriculum in work with young people,* (2nd Ed) London: Routledge.

Ord, J. (2012) 'John Dewey and experiential learning: developing the theory of youth work' *Youth & Policy* 108, pp. 55–72.

Ord, J. and Leather, M. (2011) 'The substance beneath the labels of experiential learning: the importance of John Dewey for outdoor educators', *Australian Journal of Outdoor Education* 15(1), pp. 13–23.

Panicucci, J. (2007) 'Cornerstones of adventure education' in D. Prouty, J. Panicucci and R. Collinson (eds.) *Adventure Education: Theory and Applications*, Champaign, IL: Human Kinetics.

Parker, T. M. and Meldrum, K. I. (1973) *Outdoor Education*, London: J.M. Dent & Sons.

Piaget, J. (1951) *Play, Dreams and Imitation in Childhood*, New York: W. W. Norton.

Piaget, J. (1971) *Psychology and Epistemology*, Middlesex: Penguin.

Priest, S. and Gass, M.A. (2005) *Effective Leadership in Adventure Programming*, 2nd ed. Champaign, IL: Human Kinetics.

Pring, R. (2007) *John Dewey: Continuum Library of Educational Thought*, London: Continuum.

Quay, J. and Seaman, J. (2013). *John Dewey and Education Outdoors: Making Sense of the 'Educational Situation' through More Than a Century of Progressive Reforms*, Rotterdam: Sense.

Quay, J. and Seaman, J. (2016) 'Outdoor studies and a sound philosophy of experience' in K. A. Henderson, H. Prince and B. Humberstone (eds.) *Routledge International Handbook of Outdoor Studies*, Abingdon, Oxon: Routledge.

Roberts, J.W. (2008) From Experience to Neo-Experientialism; variations on a theme in *Experiential Education* 31 (1) pp. 19–35

Ryan, A. (1995) *John Dewey and the High Tide of American Liberalism*, New York: W. W. Norton.

Schon, D.A. (1983) The Reflective Practitioner: How Professionals Think in Action, USA: Basic Books.

Seaman, J. (2008) Experience, reflect critique: the end of the learning cycles era in *Journal of Experiential Education* 31 (1) pp. 3–18

Seigfried, C. H. (1998) 'John Dewey's pragmatic feminism' in L. A. Hickman (ed.) *Reading Dewey: Interpretations for a Postmodern Generation*, Bloomington: Indiana University Press.

Smith, M. K. (2001) 'David A. Kolb on experiential learning' in *The Encyclopedia of Informal Education Online*. Available at: www.infed.org/b-explrn.htm (accessed 4 Nov 2010).

Wright Mills, C. (1974) *Power, Politics and People: The Collected Essays of C. Wright Mills* (edited by I.L. Horowitz), New York: Oxford University Press.

4

INFORMAL EDUCATION AND THE OUTDOORS

Tony Jeffs

Observant readers will notice one word is common to each of the following: 'outdoor education', 'adventure education' and 'informal education'. This chapter examines what this mutual concern with education entails by asking:

1. What is education?
2. What is informal education?
3. What is informal learning?

Responding to the first question necessitates delving into the origins of education as an idea and as an arena of practice; hence this will be the first topic to be discussed. The reply to the second question, besides considering what informal education is, discusses how it can and does relate to outdoor and adventure education. The third is addressed in part because it is repeatedly confused with informal education, so consideration is given to what distinguishes these two before moving on to discussing the role informal learning can play within outdoor and adventure education.

What is education?

Education is a word frequently combined with others to explain a policy area or domain of activity. Some examples include 'primary, secondary and adult education', which relate to specific age groupings. Another category contains titles such as 'outdoor, health, music, business and art education', sectors identified according to subject matter. Finally we have groupings such as 'special, liberal and informal education', describing discrete modes of educational intervention. Predictably overlap arises between the categories. For instance, activities central to outdoor education, such as walking and aerobic exercise, appear within both health and physical education. Likewise a balanced primary or secondary education ought to incorporate elements found within outdoor education. Linkages and crossovers are legion but cannot eradicate the diversity, for each educational 'sub-species' has claim to a distinctive history, unique formats and theoretical foundation underpinning its identity. The golden thread connecting each one is the concept of education as a process of learning designed to equip people and groups with the knowledge and skills to enable them to flourish, socially, spiritually and economically, and to learn autonomously throughout their lifetimes either alongside others or as individuals. Primarily this is what unifies disparate entities such as adventure, special and adult education, for, as Hopkins and Putman point out, they are like all educational pursuits 'concerned with overall development' (1993: 3), not the mere teaching of a skill or the training in a technique.

Etymologically 'education' derives from the Latin 'educere' or 'educare' which translates to 'leading or bringing out'. Although Latin words provide our root, the ideas incorporated within them emerged not in Rome but Ancient Greece. There many citizens believed we are born with immortal souls which following our death return to a 'world' inhabited by the gods wherein all things become known to it. Afterwards the soul is reborn in a new body; however during the trauma of birth this knowledge and wisdom is forgotten but not erased. Thereafter learning becomes a process of recollecting. Articulated by Plato, Socrates and others, this theory held that acquiring knowledge and wisdom entailed 'bringing out' what is immemorially lodged in our souls. Presumably few reading this chapter share Plato's and Socrates' belief in the transmigration of souls or espouse the theory of 'recollection' outlined above. However before dismissing 'recollection' out-of-hand and moving on it is worth pausing to ask why so many have long found the teaching methods it cultivated to be attractive. One who did was Jerome Bruner, author of two of the twentieth century's most influential education texts, *The Process of Education* and *The Relevance of Education*. Bruner in the latter argued for a method he designated 'discovery teaching' involving 'not so much the process of leading students to discover what is "out there", but rather their discovering what is in their own heads' (1971: 72). So why do individuals who reject the beliefs on which the methodology resides still believe it relevant? First, because it furnishes an alternative to the dominant view that education amounts to nothing more than the pouring of 'knowledge' and 'facts' into empty heads. Instead here is a model inviting us to contemplate an alternative to what we encounter in schools, wherein students are force-fed a curriculum and drilled to pass tests with preordained answers force-fed to pupils deemed ignorant of the approved responses. Plato (1941) long ago warned this tactic consistently proved futile as nothing 'learned under compulsion stays in the mind' (*Republic*, 536d; if Plato seems old-fashioned some recent research buttresses the fundamentals of his position; see Grove, 2014; Jones et al., 2015; Jones, 2010). 'Recollection' remains alluring because it bids us to view those we teach as possessing knowledge and talents we can help 'lead out' and nurture, to set aside deficit views of those arriving at the outdoor centre as blank sheets upon which we must imprint correct answers; instead it asks us to appreciate their hidden unexploited talents and expertise and as educators unlock and learn from them. Second, the concept of 'leading out' suggests we sidestep narrowly didactic approaches and turn to dialogue, conversation and discussion. Again this technique has a substantial protracted history, for we know it was employed by Socrates; known as *elenctic* or *elenchus*, it entails posing probing questions to help our partners in dialogue reveal what they know. *Elenchus* necessitates individuals interrogating their beliefs and embarking via dialogue on a search for truth. Skilful educators still cultivate learning by applying this method. Barrow is surely correct in suggesting the approach of Socrates and Plato still 'strikes a radical blow against any view of education that sees it ultimately in terms of facts to be stored, the mindless accumulation of *obiter dicta* and the passive reception of unquestionable fiats' (1976: 42).

Dialogical education may struggle to co-exist with a national curriculum, SATs and examination league tables, but it is congruent with the world beyond the classroom, not least that of outdoor and adventure education where the process generally concentrates less on 'the end result' and more upon encouraging participants 'to think for themselves' (Barnes, 2004: 9). This technique urges us to shun, for instance, telling groups or individuals the best route up a mountain or what to take on a trek; instead it commences by posing questions such as 'What route would you take?' or 'What do you think we will need?' Respondents may tender a competent answer, even one superior to our own, but some answers may, in our professional opinion, be unhelpful, even dangerous; however these are not worthless for they can provide a point of departure for a dialogue during which adroit questioning will allow all to collectively unearth 'better' answers. Embracing this procedure will, as stated by Herbert Read, who held it was the preeminent way to teach art, ensure 'the education of the pupil is always the self-education of the teacher' (1943: 285). Being interactive helps educators avoid becoming fusty and bored by allowing them to escape the tedium of dispensing the same 'old script'. The foundations upon which the concept of education as 'leading out' rests may be improbable, but as a guiding principle for how outdoor and adventure educators might function it remains an attractive methodology, not least because it helps all parties acquire some mastery of the arts of reasoning and the making of sound judgements.

What to teach?

Whatever approach we adopt as a teacher or outdoor educator, the question always arises regarding what it is you wish to teach. Sometimes it will be something specific, perhaps how to set up camp, or sometimes a less precise outcome, maybe how to operate as a team. Be it narrow or broad an educator's intervention signals an ambition to achieve change. Indeed why would one wish to become an outdoor educator if not to help others change themselves for the better? It is surely inconceivable that one would become an outdoor educator in order to make people more stupid or evil, or to foster contempt and hatred for the things you teach and the values you hold dear. Hirst and Peters remind us how in this respect education, as opposed to training or instruction, proceeds on the basis that what it seeks to foster in someone 'is valuable but also that it involves the development of knowledge and understanding', not a mere skill. Therefore whatever else educated persons are, they are 'individuals possessing an understanding of something', not merely 'know-how or knack' (1970: 19). Ownership of a package of skills and itemised knowledge, although beneficial, is never of itself sufficient. Hirst and Peters' perspective by implication highlights the dividing line between an instructor, for example acquainting a group as to the 'correct' way to mount a horse, and an educator, who whilst superficially doing the same thing, is drawing upon a well of experience and theory that allows them to explain this 'skill' and contextualise and locate it within a conceptual framework. Possessing that framework means if the opportunity arises they can exploit it to reflect upon equine physiology, the design and manufacture of saddles or animal psychology. Equally the conversation accompanying the task might be nurtured by the educator so as to enable the group to reflect upon the moral and ethical issues relating to the 'exploitation' of horses for human enjoyment by drawing upon the ideas of writers and philosophers such as Singer (1975) or Regan (1983), or alternatively to a consideration of the aesthetics of horse-riding and say a consideration of the paintings of George Stubbs (1724–1806), Edwin Landseer (1802–1873) and Alfred Munnings (1878–1959). The range of topics that might arise from this ostensibly straightforward task are boundless, yet utilising them via the mediums of conversation and dialogue requires the outdoor educator to possess a deep appreciation of the theory and history of what they are teaching plus the facility to foster dialogue. In this context conversation must not be mistaken for idle chatter or banter which tends to manufacture winners and losers. Rather it is what Michael Oakeshott calls 'an unrehearsed intellectual adventure' involving individuals freely coming together to share their thinking and experiences who are content to let thoughts 'take wing' (1991: 198). It is this form of conversational adventure that accomplished outdoor educators are equipped to nurture and nourish.

Education, unlike instruction and training, always 'implies something worthwhile is being or has been intentionally transmitted in a morally acceptable way' (Peters, 1966: 25). This means if, say, an outdoor educator is teaching climbing or sailing they will do so in ways that do not imply an acceptance of morally reprehensible behaviours such as selfishness, cruelty or greed. Consequently outdoor educators, like all educators, must pay due regard to what and how they teach. Sports coaches, for instance, have been known to become so fixated on training their charges to be winners that they jettison all normal moral values and inculcate dishonest techniques and excessive aggression, even *in extremis* encouraging usage of performance-enhancing drugs (Coulomb-Cabagno and Rascle, 2006; Savulescu et al., 2004). This may generate champions, but society often pays a price as research highlights a disturbing correlation between male, and to a lesser extent female, involvement in organised and professional sports and overly aggressive behaviour, including sexual violence and bullying outside of that context (Forbes et al., 2006; Steinfeldt et al., 2012; Gage, 2008). Interventions that risk generating these outcomes are self-evidently antipathetic to the model of education set out by Hirst and Peters. Being an educator obligates one to work at all times in 'morally acceptable ways', and this is why numerous forms of coaching, training and instruction cannot be deemed educational. Outdoor and adventure educators endeavour to teach people to say climb, camp, sail or traverse a wilderness to the best of their ability, but as educators such ambitions will always be subservient to the need to create good citizens and morally responsible persons.

No teacher or educator would be wise to commence a session without a grasp of what it is they wish to impart; however indentifying their objective is seldom a straightforward task. Two examples must suffice to exemplify the challenge with respect to this task. First, you may prioritise teaching the group a single or range of activities, but a majority may be fearful and nervous regarding the strange environment they now find themselves in. Faced with this situation, the primary task now becomes allaying those fears. This reminds us outdoor and adventure educators, like colleagues in adjacent fields, must eschew rigidity and be confident about when it is necessary to change tack in order to address the 'here and now'. Second, are you certain as to what it is you actually wish to teach on a given day? For example, is it how to handle a canoe or foster a love of the outdoors, encourage empathy with others or increase self-esteem, teach transferable skills to improve employability or create independent self-confident thinkers? Readers will happily append additions to the inventory. Many will be compatible, some not. One way to escape this conundrum is to ask if an overarching aim can be unearthed. Ancient Greeks, although disagreeing as to specifics, broadly shared a belief that education was primarily concerned with refining the capacity for wise judgement. Plato held the preeminent aim was to foster self-mastery so that an individual cares 'only for the right ... and above all justice' (Plato, 1941, *Republic,* vii 540, p. 256). Aristotle similarly maintained education should focus upon producing good persons and citizens along with the capacity to make skilled judgements-*phronesis* (Ord, 2014; Natali, 2013). Others followed in their wake, especially those sharing the Ancient Greek love of democracy or 'government by the people'. Thomas Jefferson, who in 1779 drew up the legislative framework for the earliest universal state system of education, and three years before much of the American Declaration of Independence, believed educational institutions must prioritise teaching students to 'think for themselves' and how to 'participate as equals in political democracy' (Staloff, 2009: 129). Jefferson, like other democrats living in a world that was then ruled by tyrants and princes, shared Epictetus' opinion that 'only the educated are free' (Epictetus, 1904: 291). So therefore, Jefferson held that education must place a sustained emphasis upon preparing all to be capable of fulfilling the role of a free citizen in a free society.

Such viewpoints are probably always in a minority. For how many of us nowadays believe learning to become an independent thinker or acquiring a love for a subject is more important than passing exams or getting a 'good degree'? Not that many one suspects. The mainstream opinion that learning for employment should take precedence has a long history, emerging in its present form around the same time as Jefferson outlined his plans. Articulated here by Robert Owen in 1812, founder of probably the earliest primary school and first community centre opened in Britain, it advocates schools above all else should inculcate 'habits of obedience, order, regularity, industry and constant attention, which are to them of more importance than merely learning to read, write and account' (quoted in Tomlinson, 2005: 131). Here is an early expression of the belief that education's primary role is the training of productive and docile workers. This long-running divergence as to role and purpose will not go away because, as Freire explains, 'all educational practice implies a theoretical stance on the educator's part' that assumes 'sometimes more, sometimes less explicitly – an interpretation of man and the world' (1985: 43). These profound debates apply as much to outdoor and adventure education as mainstream schooling. Therefore, although much educational policy may be decided in public forums, all educationalists must to an extent choose what their own over arching aims are as well as what it is they really wish to teach. Ultimately doing so is not a responsibility a professional can entrust to others, but something they are obligated to take unto themselves. In particular they must select what values they seek to foster and what are those that they seek by deed and word to discourage.

Schooling and education

Public debates relating to education regularly run into the sand because we conflate schooling with education. Principally this occurs because the formal education sector comprising schools, colleges and universities consumes a vast array of resources. In the UK it is the third biggest item of government expenditure, teaching eight million students and employing three and a half million. Understandably politicians and the electorate focus on this sector. Schooling's primary purpose is to prepare students for adult life, as Harrison puts it, to age young people 'exponentially – to make them hundreds, if not thousands of years older than when they entered the classroom' by passing on knowledge and skills that have been acquired by our forebears (2014: 142). Profound disagreements, as we have seen, exist regarding what that entails, yet whatever the dominant current stance, surely a balanced schooling would embrace in part both the arts of industry and humanity, the first providing the knowledge and skills required to thrive in the labour market and the second those needed to live a fulfilling life as a member of a family, community and democratic society. The equilibrium between these two is never a given but always a matter of dispute, hence the re-occurring debates as to whether school pupils should receive outdoor and adventure experiences or music lessons or sex education. Of course they are not mutually exclusive for, as Beames et al. suggest, the two can complement each other and there are good reasons for linking the two, for 'the outdoors brings curricula alive' (2011: 1). Shifts in emphasis may be arbitrarily imposed on a whim but generally surface following public discourse, therefore educationalists must usually live with the outcomes. In some countries such debates do not occur. Schooling in such societies can focus solely on training and indoctrinating pupils to be compliant functionaries or unthinking adherents of particular religious or political codes. This warns us schooling is always a double-edged instrument, one as capable of serving as a vehicle for oppression as it is for liberation. Comparative evidence also warns us it can either entrench social inequality or erode it, the outcome being a matter of political preference (Green et al., 2006; Sherman and Poirier, 2007). Therefore schooling's history is best understood as a tale 'of changing circumstances, not ... of inevitable progress' (Hamilton, 1990: xiii). Schooling is of itself neither inherently bad nor an unalloyed good for either students or society. Yet Dewey, like others, was surely correct in thinking 'education is the fundamental method of social reform', but it is always essential to append the caveat that this will only occur if those responsible for managing our schools and colleges 'insist' it is a priority (1897: 78). Currently the formal sector in Britain and some other countries seems to be less concerned with social reform, or for that matter educating students, and their learning than it is with credentialising them via tests and examinations (Labaree, 2010). This has meant that value sets and subjects that are not formally credited such as PE and outdoor education are marginalised (Siedentop, 2002). Or as Ogilvie, the leading historian of outdoor education put it, 'We have ended up teaching subjects not people' (2013: 3). Whilst an overarching tendency to play safe and 'teach to the test' has led to activities and subjects not impacting directly on league table positions or exam outcomes being squeezed out (Fee, Greenan and Wall, 2009). Hence the decline during the last two decades in the time allotted to outdoor and adventure activities in English and Welsh schools with even low cost pursuits such as walking and hiking being pushed aside (DforE, 2013). The imbalance between the relative size of the different sectors means that outdoor and adventure education, like adult education and youth services, are ominously susceptible to internal shifts in the structures of schooling leading to wide fluctuations in demand (Lynch, 2003; Higgins, 2005; Dillon et al., 2005; Tillings and Dillon, 2007). Pressure on schools, and latterly colleges and universities, to meet measured outcomes on diminished budgets has resulted in the prioritisation of standardised teaching, good order and discipline and rigid managerial hierarchies to secure economies of scale and 'eclipse' external rivals. The resulting ambience means they neither foster democratic discourse nor collaborative behaviour and ineffectually prepare students to be 'interlocutors later in life, that is to give them the foundations on which they may find something meaningful to say to one another' (Harrison, 2014: 141). Because these attributes cannot be tested, formal educational bodies display scant interest in helping students acquire a sense of the aesthetic, a love of nature or respect for their fellows. Hence the crucial need for provision of outdoor and adventure education, informal education, youth work and liberal adult education to compensate for the failings of an increasingly dysfunctional school system.

Taught or practiced?

Kant (1900), two centuries ago, helpfully distinguished between what can be didactically taught and what must be practiced. Itemising what we cannot solely or to a substantive degree teach in a classroom or online is a helpful starting point. In lieu of a definitive listing, a few examples of what cannot be taught exclusively in this way might include medicine, leading an expedition, climbing, counseling, caving, social work and animal husbandry. Besides 'activities', one would find it difficult, even impossible, to teach solely in a classroom are an assortment of valuable traits that make for human flourishing – for instance citizenship, courage, empathy, respect for others and sound judgement. Albert Camus, the novelist, existentialist philosopher and French Resistance fighter, once told an interviewer 'everything I know about morality and the obligations of men, I owe to football' (Martin, 2012). Camus confirms what many of us believe, namely that sports, like outdoor and adventure activities, can teach morality and much besides by placing individuals in circumstances which oblige them to make decisions for which they find themselves accountable and collaborate with others. However it would be injudicious to make exaggerated claims for outdoor and adventure education (or sport) as hoped for outcomes are never a given. As Alexander (1995) in relation to American football and Fine with respect to both Little League Baseball (Fine, 1987) and chess (Fine, 2015) discovered, each of these impacted on participants in disparate ways. Sports, cultural activities and outdoor and adventure education are, like schooling, double-edged. Outcomes are rarely predictable, partly because the educators' or coaches' variable techniques shape the 'lessons' learnt. Also the activities function within social contexts that wield in an influence which may negate any values the educator sought to impart. Camus was fortunate his football experience was positive. Maybe it was because the coach operated according to a moral code and possessed a set of moral values Camus came to admire, or possibly he was repelled by those prevalent amongst his coaches and teammates and this motivated him to uncover better alternatives. It is unlikely we shall ever know, but asking the questions reminds us that all those whom outdoor and adventure educators work with possess what sociologists call 'agency' – a capacity to adopt or reject the behavioural models on offer. Educators in outdoor and adventure settings or elsewhere can never exercise more than partial control over what others take from what they teach, for much 'gets passed on silently or unknowingly during the education process [and] germinates discretely, slowly, and often unpredictably, especially when it comes to the realm of spirit' (Harrison, 2014: 141). Be that as it may, outdoor and adventure education still holds out a special promise that it can teach important ethical and social values thanks to the special environment it operates in and the opportunities it offers for dialogue and the modelling of morally desirable behaviours.

What is informal education?

Josephine Macalister Brew's *Informal Education* (1946) was the first text to consciously employ the term 'informal education'. From 1940 until her death in 1957, the author served as education officer with the National Association of Girls' Clubs and Mixed Clubs. Previously she had variously been a community worker, adult educator and youth worker, which perhaps helps explain why she identified informal education as a golden thread permeating all three (Smith, 2001). *Informal Education* advocated taking 'education' into places where people congregate. Schoolteachers, for instance, were encouraged to perceive the playground as somewhere educational conversations and dialogue with pupils might prosper and the school gate as a venue where they might converse creatively with parents. Outdoor educators might similarly try relocating to the back of the mini-bus to cultivate dialogue and social workers might do the same with clients lingering on the office doorstep. Brew's reasons for urging these and others to 'reach out' was not for 'professionals' to go into the community in order to regale those they encountered with a pre-rehearsed script, but to partake in dialogue and conversation that might help everyone discover the knowledge within themselves and learn from each other. Doing this, and acting as an informal educator, would entail the professional being disposed to take part in the exchanges that arose from the concerns and interests of others. It would also display a willingness to listen, to let others set the agenda and allow the conversation to flow rather than assume what they held to be important should dictate content. Before scrutinising what informal education encompasses, it must be noted Brew, and most subsequent writers on the topic, never wished for it to be the preserve of trained specialists (see Jeffs and Smith, 2016, ; Richardson and Wolfe, 2001). Rather, as the forgoing examples imply, this is a mode of intervention those operating in assorted settings can usefully embrace. For that to happen what is needed is for them to redefine themselves for a segment of their working day as informal educators and seize the opportunities open to them to attend to dialogue and educative conversations. The openings are legion. Be they an instructor at an outdoor centre, a social worker in a family centre, a sports coach at a leisure centre, a lecturer in a FE college, a volunteer running a village youth club, a care worker in a residential home or a shop-floor worker training apprentices, it matters not as long as each is predisposed to nurturing in themselves the skills required to foster mutual learning.

Brew may be the first author to embrace the term, but as this chapter has implied, informal education had a prehistory. She conceded this by commencing with a passage by Joseph Addison, a seventeenth-century essayist:

> It was said of Socrates that he brought philosophy down from heaven to inhabit among men, and I shall be ambitious to have it said of me that I have brought philosophy out of closets and libraries, schools and colleges, to dwell in clubs and assemblies, at the tea-tables and coffee houses. (1946: 6)

Dialogical education, of which informal education is a part heir, possesses an honourable pedigree. It prospered in Athenian society, the era of Addison and subsequently in places and times when a vibrant democracy and civil society encouraged people to congregate and partake in the uninhibited exchange of ideas (Jeffs, 2001). The obverse is that when civil society is weakened and freedoms of speech and assembly curtailed, informal education retreats and *in extremis* is driven underground. So in part it functions as a barometer gauging the health of democracy at any given time within a given locale. Informal education is a delicate bloom requiring a sympathetic soil and climate to thrive, something which explains why at a micro level it rarely flourishes in settings such as schools or workplaces where power is unevenly distributed and workers lower down the pecking order cannot openly express opinions for fear of the repercussions.

What makes informal education unique?

Informal education differs in notable aspects from training, instruction and school-ing, and it is what makes it unique that now attracts our attention. First, informal educators preeminently operate via the mediums of conversation and dialogue. Unlike the formal sector where a set curricula and syllabi sculpt the educational encounter, or much of the outdoor education sector where participants are offered pre-ordained programmes, the content of informal education primarily materia-lises from open-ended conversational encounters. Informal educators consciously engage in these to foster learning by helping others to clarify their thinking, for-mulate ideas and better articulate their learning needs. Doing so tends to involve a number of stages best summarised as follows:

1. Assess – Making an assessment of what may be going on around us and our possible role
2. Engage – Engaging in conversation
3. Question – The raising of questions
4. Discern – Consideration of these in relation to what we discern as making for human flourishing
5. Develop – Proceeding to the development of a response (Jeffs and Smith, 2016: 74)

Second, informal education emerges from voluntary relationships. Even within institutions such as prisons, residential units or schools, where the attendance or presence of one party is legally enforced, informal educators will strive to ensure those they connect with choose freely to do so. Often problematic and requiring careful planning nevertheless, as the example of chaplains operating in prisons and the armed forces confirms, it is possible to manufacture physical and intellectual space wherein dialogue and unfettered conversations can flourish. Outdoor educa-tors may work with parties and individuals who have been 'sent', but similarly they can consciously create openings for dialogue to arise on a voluntary basis.

Third, informal education usually takes place where people freely assemble so practitioners must simultaneously be 'around' and 'accessible'. Often in settings controlled by others such as schools, colleges, prisons, hospitals, leisure centres and the 'street' this means the educators must be able to adroitly read the environment and gauge the mood of the spaces they operate in if they are to make contact with the assorted groups co-existing within these settings. Informal educators must study the ever-changing 'geography' and the 'written and unwritten timetables' of, say, a leisure centre, school, outdoor centre or college in order to ascertain when and where to make contact. That means being *au fait* with such details as where specific sub-cultural groups 'hang out' or the nooks and crannies 'loners' and the bullied retreat to. This kind of intelligence is crucial in order for informal educators to work with those outside the mainstream, who may be most in need of their help. Informal education requires space to breath, so practitioners allocate time between and within activities for dialogue and conversations to flourish (Hirsch, 2005).

Outdoor and adventure educators can likewise build into programmes space for this to occur and exploit meal times, journeys to and from activities and 'rest periods' to engage with users. Like 'street workers', they can adjust their pace to walk alongside an isolated member of the group or to allow those who are detaching themselves to 'catch up' with them. Equally they need to know when to let conversation run its course on the mini-bus, during breaks or over lunch and when to interject to exploit a chance to test an opinion or raise a question when the conversation is flowing. Social spaces in outdoor centres, notably canteens and dining rooms, lounges and outside seating provide promising venues where conversations can burgeon. MacKenzie in his account of setting up an outdoor centre recalled the importance of the 'stray words' that predicated thoughtful conversations, recounting how he consciously read a newspaper where youngsters gathered, a ploy which frequently prompted enlightening conversations on current issues (1965: 17). Sustaining and initiating conversations and exploiting the openings created by those 'stray words' is an art form in itself. The skills equipping one to do so are essential for any informal educator, but thankfully like many craft skills, these can be acquired by study, observing skilful practitioners in action and seeking their advice, and reflection upon your own performance.

Fourth, in a majority of the settings where informal educators operate, dialogue can be curtailed by time constraints, distractions and the ebb and flow of activities, resulting in educators finding it hard to close down and follow up conversations. Consequently they have long invested resources on outings, camps and residential events for clientele. In part, the function of these is to focus on teaching via experience, hence the tendency to take parties to unfamiliar locales with urban dwellers transported to rural settings and rural compatriots to cities. Visits to foreign destinations are similarly justified on the grounds they advance cultural awareness. 'Taking groups away' is also perceived as worthwhile because it allows informal educators to plan holistic educational encounters, presenting them with the space to develop sustained dialogue and generate conversation to a degree rarely possible elsewhere. Journeys, walks, meal times, joint activities and rest periods usually taking place in unfamiliar surroundings where existing hierarchies can 'dissolve or be put aside' (Priest and Gass, 1997: 21). All create entrees wherein conversations can flourish, conversations that it would be difficult, even impossible, to generate in other settings or circumstances. Shared experiences of living together, albeit as transitory communities, present unrivalled openings for educators to nurture dialogue and teach via the medium of modelled behaviour (see chapter 10, this volume, for a further discussion of this topic). Leaders may, however, have divergent agendas to those of party members, the former anxious to exploit the residential as a vehicle for learning can find themselves at odds with party members seeking relaxation. When this occurs the outdoor and adventure educator can be trapped between factions, neither of whom have an authentic commitment to learning from them. Some may even resent them as interlopers thwarting their differing ambitions. When this arises the outdoor educator's first task may be to convince some or all the party that what they offer has an inherent value and comprises more than a menu of activities.

Fifth, informal educators must pay careful attention to the presentation of self, including being accessible and approachable but not 'in your face', friendly without being gushing, companionable but not obsequious and so on. Rarely is it easy to get the right balance, especially when, like outdoor and adventure educators often do, they find themselves working with groups they have neither selected nor know. Irrespective of the operating environment, informal educators must, to be effective, draw upon a repertoire of skills equipping them to make contact with strangers, manage group dynamics and sustain productive relationships. Such skills are not the exclusive property of informal or outdoor educators, but both rarely prosper without them. Informal education is a craft and as such must be studied and proficiency honed. Expertise in this field is, as Kant pointed out, something acquired in part via practice and constant reflection upon that practice. That means becoming what Schon calls a 'reflective practitioner', someone who permits themselves to 'experience surprise, puzzlement or confusion' throughout their professional lives and 'reflects on the phenomenon' encountered by relating this 'to prior understandings' of their practice. Crucially such reflection leads to the formulation of 'theory in action' which will sustain their professional development (Schon, 1983: 68). Books and training help, but only partially. For once the basics are acquired via that route, knowledge and theory need to be sharpened by usage and reflection, a process made easier by engagement with what Lave and Wenger (1991) label a 'community of practice'. This entails getting together with others who share your concerns and passion for outdoor and informal education. Membership of a community of practice is an intrinsic part of being fully professional. Making such a commitment to join a 'community of practice' is one reason why becoming an outdoor and adventure educator is more than 'doing a job'. It is, as Steiner reminds us, like all branches of teaching, a calling, a craft more privileged than most because it seeks 'to awaken in another human being powers, dreams beyond one's own; to induce in others a love for that which one loves; to make one's inward present their future; this is a threefold adventure like no other' (2003: 183–184). Within the context of outdoor education, to teach is a transcendental opportunity to share your love of nature and the activities you hold dear; it is a privilege beyond calculation. If you do not truly love nature and the outdoors, are indifferent to the activities you share with others, and do not delight in associating with people from many and varied backgrounds, ultimately no amount of play-acting will conceal those truths from your companions. Authenticity is the bedrock upon which good teaching resides. Consequently not all are fitted for it. The narcissistic individuals obsessed with status and wealth and those afraid to confront truth and defend it against all comers are amongst the many unlikely to make good educators.

Finally informal educators must, as Brew (1946) stressed, be of themselves interesting, not boring or dull, and trustworthy people whom others will freely spend their time. Sensitivity to shifts in the social and cultural environment they operate in is essential for others to respect their judgement and opinions. Simply being 'around' is never enough, nor is the random dispensing of experiences, information and activities. Being an informal educator requires one to study the lived experiences of those they work with and alongside. They must be conscious of the influences of race, sexuality and gender. For example, in the case of the latter Estes and Ewert (1988) found women engaging with outdoor education typically looked for spiritual development, whereas males more often sought challenge and adventure. Witman reported that women valued 'trust activities', whereas males valued those related to 'power and dominance' (1995: 134). Such variations are not set in stone, but practitioners must always be sensitive to the possibility of their presence. Also practitioners should be aware, as Brown and Mitchell caution, that when individuals join an outdoor programme they do not leave all their 'troubles and social ills behind' but often bring with them 'a baggage of problems and tensions' (1991: 1). For outdoor and adventure educators, for example, this means constantly 'making themselves ready' for the next group; if it comprises young carers, they need to know something about how that responsibility impinges on the young person's lifestyle and life chances. Some young carers may have no desire to discuss what this involves, but others may wish to unburden themselves to a relative stranger. Either way, the outdoor educator must be prepared. If the party is from Neath, Nottingham, Nigeria or Newry, the outdoor educator should find out something of the history and socio-economic background of the place to unearth points of shared reference and to ensure they respond appropriately during the conversations that will invariably arise. Failure to undertake basic research may result in irreparable offence occurring which will make it difficult, even impossible, to work effectively with the party. At every level outdoor and adventure educators, like colleagues in other settings, must pay meticulous attention to the presentation of self in order to be taken seriously. Much as they will seek to convey the appropriate demeanour and arrive correctly attired for an activity, so equally they must arrive intellectually equipped if they wish to be listened to and their opinions respected.

What is informal learning?

Earlier the origins of 'education' were reviewed but no definition of 'learning' offered. So before discussing informal learning a brief definition of 'learning' may be helpful. In essence learning is the process by which we 'come to know ourselves and the world around us' (Oakeshott, 1991: 35). It comprises both doing – learning for ourselves – and receiving – learning from others including teachers and professionals such as outdoor educators. Learning takes many forms, but whatever the setting, the act of learning requires individuals to actively engage with the process for, as Berry (2011) explains, in the outdoor setting, as much as elsewhere, it is ultimately done by people themselves, rather than for them. Oakeshott sought to capture something of the variegated nature of learning by reminding us it included

> *looking, listening, overhearing, reading, receiving suggestions, submitting to guidance, committing to memory, asking questions, discussing, experimenting, practising,*

taking notes, recording, re-expressing, and so on – anything which does not belie the engagement to think and to understand. (1972: 26)

Although we learn via these and other means as a consequence of the planned actions of professional educators such as schoolteachers and outdoor educators, we also learn from non-professionals such as parents, friends and neighbours as well as from experiences that are random and accidental. We also learn ceaselessly, if often unconsciously, from being part of the world around us and from solving the problems that beset us. Yet mistakenly we all too readily assume learning 'has a beginning and an end; that it is best separated from the rest of our activities; and that it is the result of teaching' (Wenger, 1998: 3). One survey found just a quarter of adults described themselves as a 'current learner' (Sargant, 1997). What this ridiculous but understandable response tells us is that most of us only recognise formal inputs as learning and fail to credit the colossal volume of informal learning experiences shaping our lives. It is crucial practitioners grasp that people will be informally learning from the moment they join an outdoor and adventure education programme until they depart, albeit many, perhaps most, will not consciously be aware this is the case, perceiving only the formal instruction as 'learning'.

Much learning may be unintended and accidental, 'serendipitous or coincidental with some activity, and largely buried in the context of other tasks' (Sommerlad, 1999: 16). However it is not always so straightforward. For individuals purposely seek out encounters they believe may proffer a chance to learn. Wordsworth for one walked daily for hours in the countryside partly because he knew that doing so often inspired his writing. Most of us similarly seek out places and people we believe will stimulate reflection and aid our learning. Informal and other educators understand that process, which is why they organise visits to the countryside, museums, galleries, the theatre and places of social and architectural interest. And it is why outdoor and adventure educators plan their routes so a party might encounter a special vista or building. All this tells us informal learning may be the hoped for product of deliberate planning. This scattergun approach underpins the insertion of specific storylines into soap operas in the hope they will heighten public awareness of an issue as much as it does the placing of public art and information boards in public spaces. Similarly it is held good architecture, like beautiful scenery, can change people for the better, much as bad architecture degrades. It is a concept encapsulated in that wonderful phrase, coined by an Outward Bound worker, that 'mountains speak for themselves', educating us whether or not we know it without the need for an intermediary (James, 1980). Henry Morris, who planned the Cambridgeshire Village Colleges, which inspired a minor revolution in school architecture, similarly explained how

competent teachers and beautiful buildings are of equal importance and equally indispensible. ... We shall not bring about any improvements in standards of taste by lectures and preachings; habitation is the golden method. ... [B]uildings that are

> *well-designed and equipped and beautifully decorated will exercise their potent, but unspoken, influence on those who use them from day-to-day. (1945: 103–104)*

Buildings and the environment are, for good or ill, silent educators. This was why many nineteenth-century educationalists and social reformers, including Octavia Hill, John Ruskin and William Morris, devoted themselves to protecting the countryside, historic buildings and places of natural beauty for future generations, for they believed their destruction equated to the loss of the best of all our teachers. As Ruskin explained:

> *My own belief is that the best study of all is the most beautiful; and that the quiet glade of forest, or the nook of a lake shore are when once you pass the multiplication table worth all the schools in Christendom. (1865: 82)*

It is always important to remind ourselves that much of what we enjoy in the world around us survives not through an accident of fate but because reformers founded bodies like the National Trust and Society for the Preservation of Ancient Buildings and fought for effective planning regulations to protect our environment from despoliation by the greedy, ignorant and selfish. Safeguarding our heritage remains essential because in part because it creates informal routes to knowledge.

Learning by chance

Clearly informal learning has much in common with informal education, but they are not one and the same. The key difference is that the former involves no individually focussed premeditated intervention by an educator let alone conversation and dialogue. Informal learning emanates from random fortuitous encounters. MacKenzie deliberately taking his newspaper into the lounge of the outdoor centre to read it and thereby encouraging young people to pick up on his 'stray words' is an example of informal education. He purposefully behaved as an informal educator. If he had simply left newspapers scattered around the centre for party members to either read or ignore we would classify that as an example of facilitating informal learning. Similarly informal learning may result from a health education poster on the side of a bus, leaflets left in a waiting room or the work of a painter, landscape gardener or architect who hopes what they create may serve to educate, inform and inspire. Whatever the mechanism, the information or vision is communicated indiscriminately and without additional interpretation; no advisor, mentor or informal educator is on hand sharing, supporting or sustaining the educational journey. Individuals may gain an insight and debris will be left behind (Smith, 1994), but that is all that can be hoped for. Informal learning may be a 'silent random educator', but the outcomes can be profound. Therefore outdoor and adventure educators, knowing this, should exploit all the fertile openings for informal learning available to them, employing wall space for posters, artwork, maps, photographs and other material for visitors to view, read and study; leaving newspapers, magazines and books to be picked up and borrowed; carefully choosing what music to play; providing well-stocked bookshelves conveniently located with users invited to take home half-read volumes; sourcing local food for meals and including the appropriate details on menus; labeling the plants and trees in gardens; and leaving information sheets relating to local history, flora and fauna, places of interest, writers and artists, geology, farming practices and folk customs scattered about the building to read and take away. As the foregoing list indicates, the potential for informal learning in this context is boundless.

Conclusion

Outdoor and adventure educators are blessed with abundant opportunities to fulfil their role as educators not least because where they are based is usually, of themselves, special places. Locations that Wordsworth had in mind when writing

> *Come forth into the light of things,*
> *Let nature be your teacher. (The Tables Turned – 1798)*

Combined with the excitement and challenge of the activities the venues themselves are often places that will conjure up exceptional gateways for informal education. Moreover the daily routine gives staff close proximity to individuals and groups, thereby presenting a rich array of openings for conversation and dialogue. Although outdoor educators may be fulfilling a leadership role, they are rarely obliged to operate within the constraints of the fixed hierarchy, which makes conversation in many other settings artificial and guarded. Yet to seize these possibilities outdoor and adventure educators must be able to first make effective formal presentations to groups in classrooms and beyond. For at times they will be called upon to teach to a set curriculum and present information, ideas, complex procedures and theories in an erudite, accessible and precise manner to others who may be nervous arrivals adjusting to an unfamiliar world. Second, they must be capable of embarking on an educational journey via conversation and dialogue with individuals and groups irrespective of the locale. Whether in the midst of crossing a mountainside, standing on a riverbank, in the depths of a cave or sitting by a campfire, they must possess the vocabulary and knowledge to enable them to express themselves with lucidity and enter into conversation with others on topics not always of their own choosing. That means being sufficiently well educated to help explain the world they are entering and passing through in ways that stimulate the interest of newcomers to it. Finally, as a music teacher must have mastery of their instrument so the outdoor and adventure educator must be similarly skilled and proficient, to a degree that conveys an easy reassuring confidence to those around them, a confidence that confirms to others they are in the presence of someone competent to teach via the medium of outdoor and adventure activities. Their demeanour must speak of this innate ability. Korn captures just how this often-invisible process works in relation to the art of fine furniture making.

He explains how over many years he learned about being a maker not just from what people communicated purposely, but also from what they did, how they went about doing it, and the attitudes and beliefs that informed even the most casual conversations (2015: 77).

To teach any subject or craft in that way, including those embedded in outdoor and adventure education, requires dedication and professionalism. Fostering in others confidence on water demands the educator possesses a special belief in their capacity to operate in that environment; similarly to teach the importance of health and safety calls for a demeanour which conveys one's own belief in its value. Simply put, one must believe in the inherent value of what you are doing before you can hope to persuade others to treat it with a similar degree of reverence. As Csikszentmihalyi explains:

> Creative persons differ from one another in a variety of ways, but in one respect they are unanimous. They all love what they are do. It is not hope of achieving fame or making money that drives them: rather, it is the opportunity to do the work that they enjoy doing. (1996: 107)

Few educational sectors guarantee more openings for creative endeavour than outdoor and adventure education, and the same can be said of informal education; therefore to join the ranks of those who work in these fields is to embark upon a magnificent journey of self-discovery that, if you wish, will last a lifetime.

References

Alexander, C. (1995) *Battle's End: A Seminole Football Team Revisited*, New York: Knopf.

Barnes, P. (2004) 'Debate and cliché: a philosophy for outdoor education' in P. Barnes and B. Sharp (eds.) *The RHP Companion to Outdoor Education*, Lyme Regis: Russell House Publications.

Barrow, R. R. (1976) *Plato and Education*, London: RKP.

Beames, S., Higgins, P. and Nicol, R. (2011) *Learning Outside the Classroom*, Abingdon: Routledge.

Berry, M. 'Learning and teaching in adventure education' in M. Berry and C. Hodgson (eds.) *Adventure Education: An Introduction*, Abingdon: Routledge.

Brew, J. M. (1946) *Informal Education: Adventures and Reflections*, London: Faber and Faber.

Brown, D. and Mitchell, I. (1991) *A View from the Ridge*, Glasgow: Earnest Press.

Bruner, J. (1971) *The Relevance of Education*, New York: Norton.

Coulomb-Cabagno. G. and Rascle, O. (2006) 'Team sport players' observed aggression as a function of gender, competitive level and sport type', *Journal of Applied Social Psychology* 36(8), pp. 1980–2000.

Csikszentmihalyi, M. (1996) *Creativity*, New York: HarperPerennial.

Department for Education (2013) *Evidence on Physical Education and Sport in Schools*, London: Department for Education.

Dewey, J. (1897) 'My pedagogic creed', *School Journal* 54, pp. 77–80.

Dillon, J., Morris, M., O'Donnell, L., Reid, A., Rickinson, M. and Scott, W. (2005) *Engaging and Learning with the Outdoors – The Final Report*, Slough: NFER.

Epictetus (1904) *Discourse of Epictetus,* New York: H. M. Caldwell.

Estes, C. and Ewert, A. (1988) 'Enhancing mixed-gender programming: Considerations for experiential educators', *The Bradford Papers Annual* [Indiana University], 3, pp. 10–19.

Fee, H., Greenan, K. and Wall, A. (2010) 'An investigation into secondary school exit standards. Implcations for university lecturers', *International Journal of Management Education* 8(2), pp. 43–52.

Fine, G. A. (1987) *With the Boys: Little League Baseball and Preadolescent Culture,* Chicago: University of Chicago Press.

Fine, G. A. (2015) *Players and Pawns: How Chess Builds Community and Culture,* Chicago. University of Chicago Press.

Forbes, G. B., Adams-Curtis, L. E., Pakalka, A. H. and White, K. B. (2006) 'Dating aggression, sexual coercion, and aggression-supporting attitudes among college men as a function of participation in aggressive high school sports', *Violence Against Women* 12(5), pp. 441–455.

Freire, P. (1985) *The Politics of Education,* London: Macmillan.

Gage, E. A. (2008) 'Gender attitudes and sexual behaviour: comparing center and marginal athletes and non-athletes in a collegiate setting', *Violence Against Women* 14(9), pp. 1014–1032.

Green, A., Preston, J. and German Janmaat, J. (2006) *Education Equality and Social Cohesion: A Comparative Analysis,* Basingstoke: Palgrave.

Grove, J. (2014) 'New students have forgotten bulk of A-level knowledge', *Times Higher Education Supplement,* 25 June.

Hamilton, D. (1990) *Learning about Education: An Unfinished Curriculum,* Milton Keynes: Open University Books.

Harrison, R. P. (2014) *Juvenescence: A Culture History of Our Age,* Chicago: University of Chicago Press.

Higgins, P. (2005) *Written Evidence Submitted to Select Committee on Education and Skills* (10 February), London: House of Commons.

Hirsch, B. (2005) *A Place to Call Home: After-School Programs for Urban Youth,* Washington: American Psychological Association.

Hirst, P. H. and Peters, R. S. (1970) *The Logic of Education,* London: RKP.

Hopkins, D. and Putman, R. (1993) *Personal Growth through Adventure,* London: David Fulton Publishers.

James, T. (1980) *Can the Mountains Speak for Themselves,* Denver: Colorado Outward Bound School.

Jeffs, T. and Smith, M. (1990) *Using Informal Education,* Milton Keynes; Open University Press

Jeffs, T. (2001) 'First lessons: historical perspectives on informal education' in L. D. Richardson and M. Wolfe (eds.) *Principles and Practice of Informal Education,* London: Routledge.

Jeffs, T. and Smith, M. K. (2016) *Informal Education: Conversation, Democracy and Learning,* Salop: Education Now Books.

Jones, H. (2010) *Bioscience Learning and Teaching Case Study UEA,* London: The Higher Education Academy.

Jones, H., Black, B., Green, J., Langton, P., Rutherford, S., Scott, J. and Brown, S. (2015) 'Indications of knowledge retention in the transition to higher education', *Journal of Biological Education* 49(3), pp. 261–273.

Kant, I. (1900) *Kant on Education,* Boston: D. C. Heath.

Korn, P. (2015) *Why We Make Things and Why It Matters: The Education of a Craftsman,* London: Square Peg/Random House.

Labaree, D. F. (2010) *Someone Has to Fail: The Zero-Sum Game of Public Schooling,* Cambridge, MA: Harvard University Press.

Lave, J. and Wenger, E. (1991) *Situated Learning: Legitimate Peripheral Participation*, Cambridge: Cambridge University Press.

Lynch, P. (2003) 'Participation in outdoor education – the challenge of quantification', *Journal of Physical Education New Zealand* 35(1), pp. 25–33.

MacKenzie, R. F. (1965) *Escape from the Classroom*, London: Collins.

Martin, A. (2012) *The Boxer versus the Goalkeeper: Sartre versus Camus*, New York: Simon and Schuster.

Morris, H. (1945) *Buildings for Further Education*, paper delivered to Royal Institute of British Architects.

Natali, C. (2013) *Aristotle: His Life and School*, Princeton: Princeton University Press.

Oakeshott, M. (1972) 'Education: the engagement and its frustration' in R. F. Dearden, P. H. Hirst and R. S. Peters (eds.) *Education and the Development of Reason*, London: Routledge and Kegan Paul.

Oakeshott, M. (1991) 'The voice of poetry in the conversation of mankind' in M. Oakeshott *Rationalism in Politics*, Indianapolis: Liberty Fund.

Ogilive, K. C. (2013) *Roots and Wings: A History of Outdoor Education and Outdoor Learning in the UK*, Lyme Regis: Russell House Press.

Ord, J. (2014) 'Aristotle's phronesis and youth work: beyond instrumentality', *Youth and Policy* 112, pp. 56–73.

Peters, R. S. (1966) *Ethics and Education*, London: Allen and Unwin.

Plato (1941) *The Republic* (trans. F. M. Cornford), Oxford: Oxford University Press.

Priest, S. and Gass, M. A. (1997) *Effective Leadership in Adventure Programming*, Champaign, IL: Human Kenetics.

Read, H. (1943) *Education through Art*, London: Faber and Faber.

Regan, T. (1983) *The Case for Animal Rights*, Berkeley: University of California Press.

Richardson, L. D. and Wolfe, M. (2001) *Principles and Practice of Informal Education*, London: Routledge.

Ruskin, J. (1865) *Sesame and Lilies*, London: Smith, Elder and Co.

Sargent, N. (1997) *The Learning Divide: A Study of Participation in Adult Learning in the United Kingdom*, Leicester: NIACE.

Savulescu, J., Foddy, B. and Clayton, M. (2004) 'Why we should allow performance enhancing drugs in sport', *British Journal of Sports Medicine* 38, pp. 666–670.

Schon, D. (1983) *The Reflective Practitioner*, London: Temple Smith.

Sherman, J. D. and Poirier, J. M. (2007) *Educational Equity and Public Policy: Comparing Results from 16 Countries*, Paris: UNESCO

Siedentop, D. (2002) 'Content knowledge for physical education' *Journal of Teaching in Physical Education* 21(4) pp. 368–377.

Singer, P. (1975) *Animal Liberation*, New York: HarperCollins.

Smith, M. K. (1994) *Developing Youth Work*, Milton Keynes: Open University Press.

Smith, M. K. (2001) 'Josephine Macalister Brew: youth work and informal education' in R. Gilchrist, T. Jeffs and J. Spence (eds.) *Essays in the History of Community and Youth Work*, Leicester: Youth Work Press.

Sommerlad, E. (1999) *Informal Learning and Widening Participation: A Literature Review*, London: The Tavistock Institute.

Staloff, D. (2009) 'The politics of pedagogy: Thomas Jefferson and the education of a democratic citizenry' in F. Shuffelton (ed.) *The Cambridge Companion to Thomas Jefferson*, Cambridge: Cambridge University Press.

Steiner, G. (2003) *Lessons of the Masters*, Cambridge, MA: Harvard University Press.

Steinfeldt, J. A., Vaughan, E. L., LaFollette, J. R. and Steinfeldt, M. C. (2012) 'Bullying among adolescent football players: role of masculinity and moral atmosphere', *Psychology of Men and Masculinity* 13(4), pp. 340–353.

Tillings, S. and Dillon, J. (2007) *Initial Teacher Education and the Outdoor Classroom*, Shrewsbury: ASE and FSC.

Tomlinson, S. (2005) *Head Masters: Phrenology, Secular Education and Nineteenth-Century Social Thought*, Tuscaloosa: University of Alabama Press.

Wenger, E. (1998) *Communities of Practice: Learning, Meaning and Identities*, Cambridge: Cambridge University Press.

Witman, J. P. (1995) 'Characteristics of adventure programs valued by adolescents in treatment', Monograph on Youth in the 1990s [Center for Research on Youth and the Youth Leadership Council, Dalhousie University] 4, pp. 127–135.

5

THE LIVING LANDSCAPE

Being in place

Jean Spence

> *Great interest was given to girls who had to walk a long way to work by telling them
> something about architecture; they began to observe with interest whether the capitals of
> the columns they passed were Doric, Ionic or Corinthian. (Stanley, 1890)*

In 1890, when Maude Stanley advocated the inclusion of architecture in the educational content of club work, she was addressing pragmatically the problem of tedium experienced by young women who had a long walk to work. Her broader, educational purpose was to use the everyday reality of that walk to improve the observational skills of the young women. Stanley understood that the ability both to *see* and to appreciate the world we inhabit in our everyday lives can transform the experience of the mundane. She also understood such interest did not necessarily develop organically; it required the stimulus of information and an appreciation of the *process* of walking to work as well as the goal of arriving. Laying aside the class prejudices which beset her reasoning for developing observation as a means of attending to life's 'duties', her insight touches upon the underemphasised potential of informal education to find inspiration in the outdoor landscapes and travails of daily routine.

Similar circumstances to those which exercised Stanley informed the promotion of outdoor activities in early club work. At least one thread of the outdoor educational tradition emerged in response to the difficulties of life in nineteenth-century British industrial towns and cities. Through holiday clubs, residential opportunities, and the organisation of healthy pursuits in the 'open air' of the countryside, club workers and philanthropists sought to offer working people at least temporary relief from the tedium of poverty, overcrowding and the 'vitiated atmosphere' of daily life (Montagu, 1904: 250). In the emergent boys clubs in the late nineteenth and early twentieth centuries, the additional imperative of training boys to be 'men' fit for the demands of nation and the empire added dimensions of character training to the diet of fresh air and exercise, in ways which inevitably drew upon the experiences of the pioneers of such work in the public schools and the army – including camping and scouting incorporating ideals of adventure and challenge (e.g. Pilkington, 1896; Baden-Powell, 1908; Russell and Rigby, 1908).

Escaping from the problems and depredations of urban poverty into the 'unspoiled' and 'healthy' pre-industrial countryside continues as an outdoor educational ideal. Time spent in proximity with 'nature' remains a practical and sympathetic response to the pressures of urban life. Yet the ideal retains a pastoral romanticism symptomatic of the post-Enlightenment dualism that unequally divided nature and science, country and town in ways that were validated by the material conditions of rapid industrialisation. Late twentieth-century habits of referencing the rural in the new urban developments named as 'villages' and 'cottages' in post-industrial landscapes have emerged as a new, ideological version of such dualism. Thus have the virtues of the rural been contrasted with the depravity of the urban; the wild 'unspoiled' and 'natural' places pitted against the soft, demoralising luxuries of civilisation, the green of the field set against the soot and smoke of industry. Outdoor education adopted uncritically and implicitly perpetuates these binary and value-laden concepts, thereby elevating the benefits of the outdoors as 'elsewhere' and inscribing the specific educational qualities of the outdoors in the contours, the air and the wildness of the rural landscape itself.

In contemporary conditions, the horizons of elsewhere have expanded. In a world saturated with communications networks, for those who can afford the time and money, there are readily available opportunities for travel to what were once faraway places. Being mentally or physically 'elsewhere' has entered the realm of the everyday and the idea of 'escaping from the pressures' of the mundane physicality and habits of everyday life has become ubiquitous. Ever present and insistent media images of the novelty of the exotic elsewhere create a dissatisfaction with present place and time that is essential to the passive consumption habits of late capitalist growth. Legitimating such consumption, a moral discourse promotes travel as a route not just to elsewhere, but to personal development, to new and better selves. New experiences in other places are claimed to enrich our understanding, 'broaden our horizons', and teach us about ourselves. Moral benefits are held to be inherent in the experience of travel itself. Invitations to consume travel frequently combine imagery of wilderness and unspoiled landscapes with opportunities to engage in outdoor activities. Travellers can even win further virtue points by engaging in challenging activities in faraway places 'for charitable purposes'. When we cannot travel physically, we are exhorted and tempted to travel mentally. We can escape through a screen when we cannot pit our bodies against the teeth of the wind and the waves or a mountain ridge, losing ourselves in virtual challenges and adventures. When we cannot board an aeroplane to a strange and distant land, we can run to the solace of Google Earth. We can reach for the stars and travel intergalactically through virtual space and time, always with the solace that therein lies enlightenment and a more knowing self.

The successful promotion of the consumption of elsewhere depends partly upon a delineation of 'here' as 'lacking' or even actively problematic. We can only be convinced that we need a 'weekend break' if there is something from which to break! This implies a persistent devaluation of the processes of everyday lives which are sometimes transformed simply into a means of achieving the goal of reaching the next excursion, holiday or activity elsewhere.

Outdoor education has not been immune to such instrumentalism, frequently directing informal educational processes associated with outdoor activity, such as fundraising and organisation, towards the goal of being elsewhere. Yet there are other countervailing tendencies within its remit. In particular, when outdoor education embraces environmentalism it is more likely to observe and operationalise the connections between 'here' and 'there'. Although environmentalism is not immune to romanticising the 'natural' environment, it nevertheless locates responsibility in local lives and settings. Early examples of this can be found in the woodcraft traditions which were incorporated into the pioneering enthusiasm for outdoor pursuits and camping in the early twentieth century. In some youth organisations, such as the Scouts, Guides and Woodcraft Folk, there has always been an enthusiasm for working in and with the 'nature' in local environments (Rosenthal, 1984; Mills, 2014). Whilst this does not entirely escape the dualism of wild and civilised, it nevertheless recognises that the wild is continuously present. In the woodcraft tradition, close observation within urban as well as rural space was a means of inspiring care for and interest in the qualities of nature in the everyday environment. That 'woodcraft' was not fully embraced by outdoor educational approaches and largely confined within its organisational parameters during the mid-twentieth century speaks of the dominance of 'activities', the pitting of self against nature, in the pursuit of health, companionship and the development of character (Davies, 1964).

It was not until the later years of the twentieth century that what had been latent in woodcraft blossomed into the environmentalism that accompanied a growing consciousness of the risks associated with the unconsidered exploitation and despoliation of the earth and its resources. Romanticism within environmentalism is countered by very material calculations and scientific predictions about the condition of the planet. The growing insistence of the environmental message has permeated all levels of social policy and practice, including education, and has implications for indoors as well as outdoors, for architecture as well as fields. Interconnectedness between the local and the global, between town and country, between nature and science has given birth to a range of initiatives of global relevance, but pursued in local landscapes, whether urban or rural. Within environmentalism, here and elsewhere cannot be separated. The call of the local has informed a localised 'place-based' educational approach which has been characterised as capturing 'the ancient idea of "listening to the land" and living and learning in harmony with the earth and with each other' (Woodhouse and Knapp, 2000: 6). Significantly, although it is articulated mainly within the USA and with reference to schooling, it concerns attending to and interconnecting global as well as the local responsibilities of citizenship.

In the post-industrial conditions characteristic of many of the UK's regions not only has there been a 'turn' to the rural but also a renewed recognition of the benefits of outdoor leisure activity in relation to the new work cultures that are predominantly sedentary for a growing number of employees. Awareness of the benefits of accessible opportunities for exercise has combined with the influence of environmentalism to inform urban planning and 'regeneration' initiatives. In my own locality, particular examples of this include the landscaping of the slag heaps scarring the landscape after a century of deep mining, including opportunities for outdoor activity, in one case a dry ski slope. Anthony Gormley's now famous 'Angel of the North' sculpture stands on one such site, indicative of the re-integration of culture and nature, evident within this 're-greening' process. By the river and on the coast, abandoned shipyards and dockland have become marinas and centres for water sports. Sculpture trails referencing the region's industrial and pre-industrial history highlight the transformation of the industrial into creative, cultural skill. Most ex-industrial districts have their own examples of such developments. It is perhaps worth noting that many desolate and destroyed places remain, and that the privatisation of public land has resulted in the sale of urban open spaces, including playing fields. That this has not noticeably impacted upon the discourses of 'outdoor education' is perhaps indicative of the original limitations of the concept. Nevertheless post-industrial greening does provide local opportunities for outdoor pursuits and for informal educational opportunities in a local, outdoor space, even if that space is no longer 'everyday'.

Within outdoor education, environmentalism both softens distinctions between here and there and at the same time opens the possibility of pursuing interconnections in practice (Smith, 1987). In a special issue of the journal *Youth and Policy* dedicated entirely to the question of 'Young People and the Environment' in 1993, a County Durham youth worker employed by Groundwork Trust to work with young people in local post-industrial landscapes explored the relationship between youth work, environmentalism and outdoor activities. His informal educational work drew directly upon awareness of the meaning and significance of local place for participants whilst at the same time deploying a more traditional approach to outdoor activities, including the process of preparation, planning and fundraising as a means to going elsewhere, in order to intensify the learning for the young people involved. The outdoor activities element included

> *a day canoeing at Cragside, a National Trust estate in Northumberland where the group were struck by the beauty of the natural environment and decided to arrange to stay there a second weekend. This provided the first opportunity for the group to become involved in practical conservation work as they were able to strike a deal for free accommodation in return for one day spent clearing rhododendrons on the estate.* (Connelly, 1993: 45)

Here environmental youth work was driving a shift towards a more holistic view of informal education in the outdoor context. Environmentalism, beginning in the everyday, and outdoor activities elsewhere by stages can merge to contribute to a more fully integrated learning experience. The 'beauty' of Northumberland is significant in this account. It was this, rather than the canoeing, that encouraged the interest and desire for furthering the experience at Cragside.

The idea of 'beauty' in a landscape tends to be associated with open, rural and wild spaces such as those experienced by the young people in Connelly's project, and clearly encounters with such beauty are not only part of the attraction of working in such settings but also part of the educational influence. Perceiving beauty provokes emotional responses that can lead to reflection and a sense of commonality with others and with nature. There is beauty too in towns and cities – in the lie of the land, in a view from a tower block, in architecture and in parkland, as Maude Stanley recognised. Every place has its own aesthetic, to be found in the quality of our experience of it and our emotional relationship with it, but often it is an aesthetic that does not lie on the surface, in our immediate experience, but rather, as Stanley understood, it needs educational interventions to begin the process of revelation. Despite such insights it is seldom the potential to perceive beauty that informs our educational thinking about local spaces and places. In Connelly's article, any beauty that might be withheld in the County Durham landscape was submerged beneath attitudes deriving from the trauma of de-industrialisation:

> attitudes towards the local environment are extremely hostile and negative, 'shithole' being the most commonly used description. Most of the young people with whom the project has developed relationships express a strong desire to live elsewhere and feel no sense of pride in the village. One evening when I asked where the nearest public toilets were I received the reply 'piss in the street, man, it's only Doggie'. (ibid.: 48)[1]

Such negative attitudes are rooted in an instrumentalism of place, where being in a particular environment is considered only to be relevant to the opportunities it offers for other necessities, such as work, and other pleasures, such as 'things to do'. Informal educational practices which address such negativity, not by attempting to help employment prospects, or by offering pleasurable distractions, but by seeking to create interest in place itself can transform the experience of being in place. However, this cannot be accomplished without a widening not only of the application of 'outdoor education' to such matters but also a more developed understanding of the relevance of space and place within informal educational approaches.

Space and place

Within education, questions of space and place have received attention as a consequence of the changing landscapes and technologies of everyday life related to global shifts in industry, economy and people. Especially since the 1980s the effects of geo-physical changes upon social relationships have seemed increasingly pertinent to informal educational practice. For example, sociologists of youth and youth workers have highlighted the ways in which local space is contested between young people and adults, and between different identity groups. Different places have been shown to have different meanings associated with territoriality, social structural inequalities and questions of risk (e.g. Pearce, 1996; Scott, 2000; Crawshaw, 2001). Such matters can inform the positioning of facilities, the targeting of work and the underlying aims and objectives of informal educational interventions, as well as the positioning of particular practices. For example, spatial knowledge is intrinsic to the art of detached youth work, insofar as the worker must locate and understand the meaning of the places young people inhabit. However, having located the young people, detached workers are likely to be working on agendas other than space or landscape except in relation to territorial boundaries and conflict. This is not the equivalent of focusing upon and utilising the features of outdoor spaces and the landscape as the means of stimulating a consciousness of the value and meaning of everyday places.

Similarly, geographical knowledge is essential to the establishment of facilities for specific outdoor activities in local spaces. It would be fruitless to construct a skate park in an area that was out of reach of transport, or that was seen by some as a 'no-go' area. Local place and boundary knowledge, and understanding the surface patterns of movement, conflict and harmony must be integrated into any planning that seeks to achieve successful facilities for encouraging outdoor activities. In campaigning or planning for outdoor facilities, sensitivity to local environmental matters can be achieved through conversation with local people whose involvement in the processes of development can facilitate a deeper level of understanding of the relevance of local space and place in people's lives. However, it is unlikely to move in this direction without an objective to do so on the part of the planner or outdoor educator, without an understanding that the goal of providing a facility can be only the end part of the action.

Politicians, especially those associated with the administrations of New Labour, have not been immune to the social policy and practice implications of debates about space and place in local settings, but they have been concerned about the significance for targeting services rather than with a care for the local environment as a space for informal educational practice. Thus the development of the Connexions Service for young people considered the potential role of detached youth work in making contact with those who were located 'outside' the reach of formal institutions but did so with the purpose of including them within such institutions not with interventions relevant to the young people themselves in space and time (Crimmens et al., 2004). In the policy document *Youth Matters,* there was a recognition of the value of providing 'things to do and places to go' for young people, but again, the emphasis was upon 'provision' rather than appreciation of local space and place (Barton and Barton, 2007). Most comprehensively, the planning for 'Myplace' centres in the last years of the New Labour government paid attention to the relationship between outdoor and indoor activities, to questions of accessibility and territoriality and to environmental issues associated with building design, construction and sustainability, but even here there was a predetermination to create a particular type of facility on the landscape (Durham University and YMCA George Williams College, 2011).

The different ways in which different social groups inhabit the same landscape and the ways in which objective, physical places and boundaries delineate subjectivities (Scott, 2000; Smith, 2001) have implications at all sorts of levels and this includes the possibility of moving beyond the mechanics of location, of 'managing' problematic spaces or of making suitable provision in suitable places. A more holistic approach requires an integration of 'being' in the landscape and a revelation of the complex meanings of space and time that can be read within and written into that landscape.

If informal education begins with conversation and dialogue grounded within the spaces and rhythms of everyday lives, then the geographical insights that apply to the places in which people spend their lives are highly relevant to the processes of such education (Jeffs and Smith, 1999; Smith, 1994). Insights about the significance of space and place do not come 'ready-made' or clearly labelled, but through conversation and dialogue lived-in spaces and places, the landscapes of everyday lives, can become matters of observation, enquiry and interpretation. Spatial awareness thus becomes more than a tool for other interventions, but a condition of life itself. However it can only do so if locality is perceived and experienced not only as a place where we 'are' but also as a place where we might 'want to be' and in which we might want to act. If we recognise our potential as actors within our local environment then we can move beyond passively accepting it as 'a shithole' from which all we can hope is escape (Connelly, 1993).

To fully explore the potential of informal education within spatial lived realities, and in so doing to further broaden the remit of 'outdoor education', involves us in a search for an aesthetic of place in the sense that Dewey understood it, as an aspect of everyday experience (Dewey, 1958, see also Bourassa, 1988). This demands as a first principle an understanding that lives are 'situated' on and in landscapes which contain complex dimensions of meaning. It involves a willingness to explore further, below the surface, to interrogate the layers and depths of landscapes in time as well as place. That implies valuing the features of local landscapes as spaces for the fulfilment of creativity, activity and joy. This can involve a determination, and action to change what is undesirable, as much as a recognition of what is valuable in itself.

Being in place

Not many miles north of the village nicknamed 'Doggie' mentioned earlier.

Late yesterday afternoon, in weak spring sunshine, I walked to the top of a hill near my home. The hill is a landscaped pit heap. A thin layer of soil exposes slag in patches and on the lower reaches. The busy A19 bounds its steep eastern slope, and the hill drops gently towards old allotments and the ex-mining village of Murton in the west. A post-modern retail outlet, an arc of white, tent-like domes, sits at the base of its northern edge, with an entrance road, car park and scattered signage that spans the space between the indoor retail experience and the outdoor opportunity for exercise offered by the hill. Parked cars glint in the sunshine. On the eastern perimeter of Murton, a new housing estate has been tightly packed into a corner of a field that was once within the boundaries of the mine. At the eastern side of the retail outlet, a constructed lake sports a fine sculpture consisting of metal rods that move like reeds with the wind. Newly positioned earth-moving equipment and pipes near the lake bear the slogan 'improving bathing water quality', presumably of the sea which is about two miles further east. The lake is the culmination of a series of ponds linked by a stream that runs across the hill from west to east on a flat ridge halfway to the summit. To the south, a new road, laid down before the financial crash, remains unopened. It leads to a roundabout at another slag heap marking the entrance to an industrial estate that has never been built. Effectively, the road leads to somewhere that is considered nowhere. I cannot see it from the hill, but I perceive it because I have walked the unused road. Beyond the road, a moor glows with strong yellow patches of gorse. The original village derived its name from the moor – Moor-town.

Climbing the wooden steps constructed on the north side of the hill, my ears are assailed with lark-song. Two larks take off from the scrub land as I approach the ridge. Larks sing above me for the duration of the walk.

One protruding part of the hill to the north has been landscaped in the shape of a ziggurat. From its summit, five adolescent boys on bicycles career gleefully at great speed over its edges. Few people pass: a middle-aged turbaned man taking a walk, a young woman with a retriever whose back has been shaved for an operation, struggling to fetch the ball she throws, a young man in trainers with two Pomeranian dogs. A cyclist in luminous green pedals furiously eastwards along the centre of the unopened road.

The view from the summit is varied and beautiful. Yesterday it was slightly misty, but a wide sweep reveals countless features. These include, on the southern horizon, the eleventh-century church at the centre of Easington village. Nearer, towards the sea, stands a radio tower used for early-warning purposes during the Second World War. The concrete block on which it sits is a favourite spot for racist graffiti. Beyond the A19 a small group of nineteenth-century agricultural labourers' cottages front an ancient wooded plantation that can be seen for miles around in this district, and was a favourite destination for my childhood wandering. Below the cottages stands the buildings associated with the original waterworks. Renovation began about eight years ago to create a wine bar and restaurant, but this work has long ceased. They remain partially derelict. A small, dilapidated but still used industrial estate built in the 1970s replaced a Victorian terrace of houses. To the north, in the distance, I see a house that was once owned by my great uncle, our richest known relative, attached to whom there are stories about how he dealt with his poorer relatives. In every direction, there are banks of windmills that have become as common in this landscape as the pits once were.

By the lake, I notice two moorhens running to the water. Sometimes there are swans here. It is impossible not to notice the litter that has accumulated amongst the reeds and blossoming kingcups, but from a viewing platform I spy a toad hanging onto a cut reed. It dives and swims away when it sees me. There is a memorial plaque on the platform to a child who bore my name – Spence.

She died two months before the landscaping work here was completed twelve years ago. Past the dried bed of the stream, where cowslips are blossoming, trees planted in plastic tubes are becoming established. Two brown butterflies are carried north on the breeze; the occasional bumblebee moves into and out of view. At the first pond, by a large patch of yellow kingcups in a thickly reeded place, an unusual movement stops me. First a small fish, and then a large toad comes into view. Soon there are three toads in my gaze, involved in what seems like a mating ritual in the reed beds. Imperceptibly, below the water beetles skimming the surface, the pond comes alive with toads. I take out my phone camera but like crows, toads are camera-shy. I need better equipment and a long lens to stand a chance. The pictures are very poor. I decide just to watch, and remember a lake by the Second World War tower. As a child a group of us, with a local father, tramped there to find mating toads, fish, tadpoles, unnamed water insects, pond weeds, common newts, and the glory of the lake, beautiful large black and dark brown crested newts with all manner of pattern and yellow to orange shades on their bellies. That 'lake', effectively just a large pond, has been filled in for farming purposes. Perhaps these new ponds and lakes constructed as part of post-industrial land reclamation will once again recover what was lost in that act of agricultural reclamation.

I describe yesterday's walk as an illustration of the richness of place and its inherent potential for informal educational conversation. It was a sunny spring day. I needed to escape from writing this chapter. I went for a walk. It was not a new walk. I know the terrain well because it is part of my local landscape and because I enjoy walking. Every walk in that same place is different – affected by the time of year, the time of day, the weather, my mood and state of health, the presence or absence of other people, of building and agricultural developments in the surrounding landscape, the state of the economy, whether or not I have with me a camera. I might perhaps have undertaken the walk simply for the sake of the exercise, moved quickly towards my goal of reaching the summit and noticed very little other than my pounding heart and struggling limbs. I might have taken the SLR camera with the specific intention of photographing the wild flowers beginning to establish themselves on the hill. These would have been different walks in the same space and my attention would have alighted upon different objects of interest. Whatever walk it was, I was an actor in my own landscape, and I went into that landscape with a certain amount of knowledge about its situation and history. All else was contingent upon circumstances. Nevertheless, there emerged from the walk a whole series of moments that might have been the stuff of an informal educational conversation had others been present to share the observations and the knowledge that they brought with them. The conversations could have ranged over economic, social and family history, politics, social policy, equality and discrimination, ecology, transport and the nature of memory. Had I been undertaking youth work, I might have categorised the visit to the hill with a group of young people as an 'outdoor activity' involving walking, photography, or even cycling. Certainly exercise and fresh air would have been involved, and potentially the development of skill, but more significant educationally would have been the use of the activity to observe and name the features in the landscape to which the excursion gave access.

This is a very particular and personal example, but it indicates the potential layers of meaning in any landscape. Observing and naming landscape features, places in local spaces, can stimulate reflection, memory, creative activity and further investigation. There is no reason in principle why this might not be incorporated into an outdoor educational perspective. It has been claimed, and not without justification (e.g. Smith, 1987), that particularly within well-designed outdoor education programmes, the experience of new and different environments can stimulate self-reflection and heighten awareness of personal and group identities as participants work to acclimatise themselves, to make sense of the new and to articulate the meaning of their unfamiliar experience (e.g. Barratt and Greenaway, 1995). Yet if we think of the spaces of everyday life as being more than surface phenomena, it is possible to provoke different experiences in even the mundane, unnoticed places of habit. Most, if not all of those things claimed as emanating from the 'outdoors' in 'other' places, including 'challenge' and 'adventure', can also emanate from 'this' place, in the here and now. To attempt 'seeing' and 'experiencing' in these terms can begin to transcend the inherent dualism of aspects of the outdoor educational tradition.

If we consider outdoor education in the situation of the everyday, and attend to the value of 'excavating' the layers of knowledge and meaning in local landscapes, then it is possible to consider 'environment' in terms of buildings and structures as much as to open places. There is no reason why landscape should not include the cultivated as much as the wild, why beauty should not be encountered in the vista from a tower block as much as that from a mountain or a reclaimed pit heap. Similarly, there is no reason in principle why the 'challenge' inherent in the learning associated with outdoor education should not include the challenge of discovery, rather than that of 'conquering' nature, or why the 'skills' developed should not be those consonant with the pursuit of an aesthetic of place rather than be restricted to restricted conceptions of employment or 'responsible citizenship'.

Whilst recognising that for some people, home places are so insecure, volatile, dangerous, restricted or impoverished that they cannot be the subject of place-based informal education, for the remainder, the space of everyday life offers rich material for learning bearing traces of everyday lives in the past, present-day meanings and potential for shaping in future. The skills needed to tap into this involve nothing more than the ability to use our senses, to perceive the qualities of our surroundings to stimulate further enquiry and to make connections with the knowledge we bring. In order to begin, it is necessary to cultivate the art of observation, and to begin to 'name' the features and places that delineate the contours of everyday lives.

Seeing and naming

Like learning from doing, seeing and naming do not necessarily come automatically. We need to begin with an intention to observe, to put ourselves in the way of observation. If we cannot differentiate types of column in city buildings, columns, and probably buildings, will fail to excite our interest. They will be simply 'columns'. Indeed, we might not even notice them at all. Similarly, if we are unaware of the names of different wild flowers, we are likely to fail to recognise their individual features and sometimes we might even fail to see them at all. In countryside or town, all yellow flowers with a flat head are simply categorised as dandelions. Thus do we miss the richness of the family of flat-headed yellow flowers. Thus do we fail to notice a patch of land on which fleabane is growing and obstruct the possibility of learning about the quality of the land on which fleabane might thrive. Whilst the notion of naming a type of flower might not seem too important, the act of naming in itself, as most informal educators recognise, is an important precursor to action. If we can name a Doric column or a fleabane, we are more likely to appreciate its beauty in itself and beneath its surface, more likely to appreciate the place in which it resides, and ultimately more likely to act in its defence or otherwise. Ultimately, naming is a political act which contributes to human agency. Observation is integral to the possibility of naming, but observation often requires guidance, purpose and focus in order to overcome the superficial.

In 1963, my first year at secondary school, the biology teacher instructed the class to collect, press and present eighty wild flowers. We were to provide common and Latin names and family classifications for each specimen and to record the date when and place where the flower was found. Everyone in the class was intimidated by the task, believing it to be impossible in our industrial locality. Yet not only did we find them, but most of us exceeded the number significantly. Often we were helped by older peers who had previously completed the task. They directed us to the best pickings which frequently encouraged us to visit local places that might otherwise have remained beyond our range. Of course some flowers were discovered in other places, during family holidays and excursions, implying a particular focus in those places. Subsequent conversations with ex-classmates suggest that none of us ever forgot what we learned in that process about the flowers, about the quality of our local landscape and about the similarity and differences in flora between places.

In 2014, I took two teachers and a group of primary school children to the place where most of the local flowers could be found. It is a cliff top of magnesium limestone lying immediately next to where the local colliery had stood until 1990. This place has become a treasured part of my favoured outdoor activity of walking and photography, and the flowers are the main object of that photography which in its own terms has revealed floral images that might have been beyond my unaided observation. The children were armed with phone cameras and iPads and photographed every flower that I named. They found one flower that I had never previously seen, and could not name. Our conversations included the knowledge of the place that they had derived from parents and grandparents, relating mainly to the mining past, and the despoiled beach below. Identifying flowers added to their understanding of the meaning of the place and they were enthralled, particularly by the orchids, which became the subject of an art project for them. Continuing to the beach, they made sculptures from the stones and rocks that remain from the history of quarrying and mining.

In this story, the first important moment was to be given an objective for observation. But just as important to the outcome of the story were the original conversations between children, the exchange of information between peers that expanded horizons in the search for a particular landscape rich in wild flowers. Now there are intergenerational conversations, and different meanings emerging, including the use of photographic technology to photograph the flowers, rather than the picking, collecting and pressing which characterised the activities of the older generation.

Mainly we live on the surface of landscapes punctuated by features and places that we may or may not notice, that might or might not be of significance in our lives. Before the wild flower project, that place was to me nothing other than a place of work for local men. That knowledge was not invalidated by the discovery of a place of flowers, but it took on different dimensions and meanings. In particular it provoked ambiguity about a beautiful wild place obscured and despoiled by the source of income and security. On the surface of that landscape, the absence of the mine is now the source of a different complexity of emotions about the lost aesthetic of mining, experienced despite the squalor that accompanied it, and that can perhaps only be recognised in absence.

Different groups and different individuals create their own patterns of behaviour and knowledge in response to what they experience and encounter. The magnesium limestone cliffs and the despoiled beach have been opened up to visitors since the closure of the mine. The paths are used by dog-walkers, by people (mainly men) fishing and hunting rabbits, by photographers and other artists, by cyclists and walkers on the designated coastal footpath, and by one man who lives in a cave and is unable to live in a house. This is a place to find coal and wood, to hunt for treasure with metal detectors, and to scavenge the 'found objects' beloved of local art. It is a place of detritus where dead seabirds were washed up after the storms of the spring of 2013, and the place where industrial dumping once covered the sands and suffocated all life in rock pools. It is also a contested place, where the greening intentions of land management which help the unique flora to flourish, and the regulators of public health and safety, are constantly thwarted by the night hunters, by unregulated summer partying and camping, by people who in the mining past claimed this as their own domain and whose identities are bound up with it. The physical place contains within it transitional identities, conflicting interpretations of 'ownership' and different layers of meaning.

What becomes meaningful to us in our everyday and visited landscapes is contingent upon our life experiences and the opportunities we have to observe, name and develop our understanding of their qualities. It is also to some extent dependent upon the quality of the landscape itself. Some places are problematic. They might, for example, hold physical danger, be subject to intense surveillance, be enclosed and secret, hold negative memories, be volatile or war-torn. Some are identified with particular ethnic groups, some unsafe or out-of-bounds for women or LGBT groups (Filemyr, 1997; Webster, 1996). Others, such as the beach in my story above, are inaccessible to people with disabilities. Such matters inform the decisions that people make about everyday and distant journeys. Consciously and unconsciously they prescribe the physical movement of everyday life. Thus Carol Ann Scott described the journey home from school of 'young metropolitans':

> For many students of schools sharing city space, the logic of practice is grounded in mutual territorial acknowledgement and informal peace agreements. So they may follow part of a street, but then cut over walls, car-parks, gardens, churchyards and back onto streets or back lanes, if these elements of the city landscape lie in their 'path'. Students widely mentioned that bollards were 'there' but they moved them, or gates were locked but they went over or round them, or that something was fenced but they managed to squash through somewhere, or they took a diversion to avoid the 'Hillers' (a nearby school cohort) who went along 'there'. (2000: 29)

Mapping the habits of movement can be a method by which we begin to identify the features in our landscapes which are of relevance us. Pearce (1996) used such a method within research to signify the gendered nature of young people's space. To undertake this exercise for ourselves would be of some interest in beginning a personal journey of awareness, but to undertake it and share it in a group situation could be a moment of enlightenment and a provocation for discussion and dialogue for all involved. What patterns do we trace in our landscapes? Which places do we visit most frequently? Which do we avoid? Which places have most meaning for us? Are there places in our map to which we pay no attention? What constrains and enables our journeys? What do we not see, or ignore? What disturbs us? What happens when our maps are overlaid? And, of course, 'why?' With the aid of technology and returning to the possibilities offered by Google Earth, such mapping can be undertaken now in ways that are much more detailed than anything that could be drawn by Pearce's students in 1996. Moreover, this is a process that might take place in an indoor environment, interweaving what might be considered 'indoor' and 'outdoor' education.

Self-conscious mapping is a means whereby we might begin to observe, name and allocate meaning to the features of our local spaces. However, furthering our appreciation of the aesthetics of local space requires more intensive observation and interrogation than mapping itself allows. It involves being in place and developing the art of using our senses more intensively: looking and seeing, listening and hearing, touching and feeling, sniffing and smelling, and even picking and tasting can all be of relevance in the places and in the features of the landscape that we might identify as being of significance. All experiences through the senses stimulate emotional responses, essential to the development of an aesthetic of place, as well as presenting the raw material for further investigation and the discovery of layers of meaning that can contribute further to that aesthetic.

We can all be empiricists of the local by simply engaging our senses more fully. Using contemporary technology, empirical data can be gathered and represented for discussion and conversation without the necessity of interfering with what is there. We can, in particular, identify the features of relevance in our own landscapes by using the recording and photographing facilities of mobile phones and tablets. Such tools are already widely used in the context of our personal routines. To direct the focus more fully on those features of our daily lives that enclose us, that attract us, that frame our relationships and that disturb us can facilitate a level of observation that has the potential to move beyond the superficiality of data. In this way, through a combination of the recording process and the social relationships mobilised in the conversational mode of informal education, we might travel beyond the fleeting, the taken-for-granted, the mundane of our being in place, to engage in what Foucault might have called an 'archaeology' of knowing our local places in order to become not just responsible citizens but knowing actors.

Conclusion

In arguing for the potential of developing informal educational practices through the prism of everyday outdoor space and place, this chapter has necessarily presented a critique of the limits of the dominant perspectives within outdoor education. Mainly, the problems lie in the dualism and the related romanticism of traditional approaches. Whilst such romanticism persists, the influence of environmentalism has drawn attention to the potential of the local landscape to facilitate outdoor educational activity in a way that begins the process of overcoming the inequalities of 'here' and 'there'. In pointing to the possibilities of generating an aesthetic of the local, the intention is not to imply that the local and everyday life are superior to the landscapes of elsewhere in the opportunities they offer for informal education, and the development of a commitment to and responsibility for place. Rather, it is to suggest that by focusing on the local it might be possible to begin to address some of the negative effects of dualistic thinking, not least that which in promoting the consumption of 'elsewhere' delineates everyday places as worthless, as places from which we must be ever and always escaping.

The suggestion for using contemporary technologies in the process is one which might be further developed. Indeed, if we are to be successful in our informal educational approach in contemporary conditions, it is essential that we integrate without valourising modern technologies. Again the purpose would be to press such technologies into educational service in ways that are meaningful to participants, and to help move away from the mode of consumption in which fantasies of 'elsewhere' dominate.

Using photography to define landscape features, to represent those features, to offer the images as a focus of discussion, and even to play with the focal properties of cameras to suggest different ways of 'seeing' can not only develop skill, creativity and art with reference to the local landscape but has meaning in other places. Using technologies in this way enables us, again, to become actors and creators in place, rather than merely passive consumers.

90 Jean Spence

Ultimately, the practices of the informal educational adventures in landscape must lead towards a more holistic understanding of outdoor education in terms of its location and its range of activity, highlighting the independence between places, the interdependence between the indoor and the outdoor and most importantly, the interdependence of people. The purpose of such an endeavour is to bring greater meaning, understanding and activity, and thus joy, to our lives.

Note

1 'Doggie' is a nickname for the village derived from the fact that it used to work with dog iron.

References

Baden-Powell, R. (1908) *Scouting for Boys*, London: Horace Cox.
Barratt, J. and Greenaway, R. (1995) Why Adventure? The Role and Value of Outdoor Adventure in Young People's Personal and Social Development: A Review of Research, commissioned by the Foundation for Outdoor Adventure. Available at: http://reviewing. co.uk/wad.htm (accessed March 2014).
Barton, A. and Barton, S. (2007) 'Location, location, location: the challenges of "space" and "place" in youth work policy', *Youth and Policy* 96, pp. 41–50.
Bourassa, S. C. (1988) 'Toward a theory of landscape aesthetics', *Landscape and Urban Planning* 15, pp. 241–252.
Connelly, D. (1993) 'Environmental youth work: making connections', *Youth and Policy* 42, pp. 44–50.
Crawshaw, P. (2001) 'Negotiating space in the risky community', *Youth and Policy* 74, pp. 59–72.
Crimmens, D., Factor, F., Jeffs, T., Pitts, J., Pugh, C., Spence, J. and Turner, P. (2004) *Reaching Socially Excluded Young People*, Leicester: NYA and JRF.
Davies, B. (1964) 'The outdoor myth', *Challenge Magazine* [Journal of the National Association of Boys' Clubs] (no page nos. or detailed date).
Dewey, J. (1958) *Experience and Nature,* New York: Dover Publications.
Durham University and YMCA George Williams College (2011) *Myplace Evaluation: Final Report*, Myplace support team and DfE. Available at: www.gov.uk/government/uploads/ system/uploads/attachment_data/file/181645/MYPLACE-FIN-REP.pdf.
Filemyr, A. (1997) 'Going outdoors and other dangerous places', *Frontiers: A Journal of Women Studies* 18(2), pp. 160–177.
Jeffs, T. and Smith M. K. (1999) *Informal Education: Conversation, Democracy and Learning*, Ticknall: Education Now.
Mills, S. (2014) '"A powerful educational instrument": the woodcraft folk and indoor/ outdoor "nature"' in S. Mills and P. Kraftl (eds.) *Informal Education, Childhood and Youth: Geographies, Histories, Practices*, Basingstoke: Palgrave Macmillan.
Montagu, L. (1904) 'The girl in the background' in E.J. Urwick (ed.) *Studies of Boy Life in Our Cities*, London: Dent and Co.
Pearce, J. (1996) 'Urban youth cultures: gender and spatial forms', *Youth and Policy* 52, pp. 1–11.
Pilkington, E. M. S. (1896) 'An Eton playing field' reprinted in F. Booton (ed.) (1985) *Studies in Social Education*, Vol. 1, 1860–1890, Hove: Benfield Press.

Rosenthal, M. (1984) *The Character Factory: Baden-Powell's Boy Scouts and the Imperative of Empire,* New York: Pantheon Books.

Russell, C. E. B. and Rigby, L. M. (1908) *Working Lads Clubs,* London: Macmillan.

Scott, C. A. (2000) '"Going home with the chaps": concerning the degradation of young urbanites and their social space and time', *Youth and Policy* 69, pp. 17–41.

Smith M. K. (1994) *Local Education: Community Conversation Praxis,* Buckingham: Open University Press.

Smith, M. K. (2001) 'Place, space and informal education' in L. D. Richardson and M. Wolfe (eds.) *Principles and Practice of Informal Education,* London: Routledge/Falmer, pp. 138–147.

Smith, P. R. (1987) 'Outdoor education and its educational objectives', *Geography* 72(3), pp. 209–216.

Stanley, M. (1890) 'Clubs for working girls' reprinted in F. Booton (ed.) (1985) *Studies in Social Education,* Vol. 1., 1860–1890, Hove: Benfield Press.

Webster, C. (1996) 'Local heroes: violent racism, localism and spacism among Asian and white young people', *Youth and Policy* 53, pp. 15–27.

Woodhouse, J. L. and Knapp, C. E. (2000) *Place-Based Curriculum and Instruction: Outdoor and Environmental Education Approaches,* ERIC Digest, ED448012, Washington. Available at: http://files.eric.ed.gov/fulltext/ED448012.pdf.

6

WILDERNESS AND INFORMAL EDUCATION

The importance of wild places and spaces

Jon Ord and Liz Mallabon

As Cronon reminds us, 'Wilderness gets us into trouble only if we imagine that this experience of wonder and otherness is limited to the remote corners of the planet, or that it somehow depends on pristine landscapes we ourselves do not inhabit' (1995: 18). Wilderness is a much more 'human concept' than we might initially think, and before considering the educative potential of wild places and spaces we must consider its meaning.

What is wilderness?

Wilderness for many offers the quintessential experience of the outdoors. Here apparently is a 'natural' environment promising emersion in 'nature' free from the impact of human activity. Taken for granted, notions such as these belie a hidden complexity, for hard and fast definitions of wilderness are elusive and what is meant by it can never be taken as self-evident or unambiguous. Wilderness is a far from straightforward concept. As Rossiter reminds us, here we are encountering a 'word whose meaning has morphed throughout human history' (2006: 83). Yet there are certain key phases during this historical development of the concept or 'word' which for our purposes deserve special attention. These are biblical notions of wilderness, the Romantic movement's usage of the term during the late eighteenth and early nineteenth centuries, and finally the American wilderness movement which amongst its many achievements must be included the passing of the Wilderness Act of 1964. Which, apart from being in all probability the earliest piece of legislation to employ the concept, created the need to construct a legal definition of 'wilderness' to sit alongside the existing dictionary and social classifications (McCloskey, 1966, 1995).

Biblical notions of wilderness

Within Western societies our understanding of wilderness has been to a significant degree fashioned by Judeo-Christian representations of it encountered within the Bible where, according to Gilmore, 'wilderness occurs 245 times in the Old Testament and 35 times in the New Testament' (2006: 44). However these representations are not clear-cut for, as Nash points out, wilderness is initially juxtaposed with paradise so that it 'has no place in the paradise myth' (2014: 9). Gilmore also notes wilderness is employed within the Bible variously to describe a place of renewal and 'of deliverance' (2006: 46). Wilderness in the Bible therefore embodies elements of ambiguity which combine a barren, inhospitable and alien environment with the spiritual qualities of rejuvenation and realisation. Nash suggests this diverse usage is best viewed as a multilayered rather than contradictory interpretation of wilderness, perceiving it as offering both 'a sanctuary from a sinful and persecuting society' as well as signifying an environment in which one may 'find and draw close to God' (Nash, 2014: 16). It is important to recognise that within this representation, although the hostile wilderness might be imbued with unique spiritual qualities derived from spending time within it, there is nothing inherently valued about the wilderness *per se*. So it may be portrayed as a means to a 'spiritual' end but within this context the wilderness environment itself is not an entity that is perceived as either precious or overly significant of and for itself.

Romantic notions of wilderness

The representation of wilderness altered with the emergence of the Romantic Movement in the late eighteenth and early nineteenth centuries. Wilderness was henceforth not predominately viewed as a place of privation and hardship, the endurance of which might for some lead to spiritual rejuvenation. Rather writers in and followers of the Romantic tradition saw wilderness as a setting which had unique and distinctive qualities. This is exemplified by Estwick Evans, a lawyer who in the winter of 1818 commenced a solitary walk of over 1,000 miles from his home in New England to Detroit dressed mostly in buffalo skins in order to experience the solitude of the wilderness. The following quotation taken from his account of that journey conveys something of this shift in attitude:

> How great are the advantages of solitude! – How sublime it is the silence of nature's ever-active energies! There is something in the very name of a wilderness, which charms the ear, and soothes the spirit of man. There is religion in it. (1819: 6)

Jean-Jacques Rousseau was also a precursor to birth of the Romantic Movement with his rejection of religious dogma and doctrine, replacing it with a commitment to the importance of nature and the natural world as guides to spiritual truth. Wokler captures something of the essence of Rousseau's thinking in the passage below, by asking us to consider if

> *confronted by the great spectacle of nature which addresses our eyes, our heart, our judgment, and our conscience, it seems strange that any other religion should be required at all. (1995: 87)*

Within the Romantic Movement, besides painters, philosophers and writers, were to be found poets, such as Byron, Coleridge and Shelley, who sought out the 'wild places' of the English Lake District and the European Alps and then wrote about how moved they were by the intensity of the encounter. Collectively their poetry and prose communicated to the public 'a new found love of wild places, thus reversing earlier trends' (Bromley, 2006: 2). But it is perhaps Edmund Burke in his *Treatise on the Philosophical Basis of Our Ideas on the Sublime and Beautiful* who best captures this change. The book was not solely devoted to the topic of the wilderness or countryside, but in discussing the former from a fresh perspective it had a marked influence upon the attitude of many of Burke's contemporaries to the wilderness. In the *Treatise* Burke suggests 'that sublime and beautiful are built on principles [that are] very different' (1767: 310). Whilst notions of beauty, he argues, are based entirely on pleasurable feelings, the sublime 'operates in a manner analogous to terror ... [this] is a source of the sublime' (1767: 58). By way of contrast the sublime produces awe and wonder, and it was this experience the Romantic poets found intoxicating. Thus landscapes previously depicted by 'solitude, deathliness, sterility, barrenness, inhumanity' now acquired the qualities 'which Romanticism had made so appealing' (Macfarlane, 2003: 136). This new appreciation of wilderness emerged during an era which depicted wild places as having an inherent value.

Aesthetics played an important part in fostering this reconfiguration, but so did changes in the social structure. For the value placed on wilderness was also rooted in a critique of 'civilised' society, the origins of which can also be traced to a large degree to the writings of Rousseau who, as Nash points out, 'argued in *Emile* that modern man should incorporate primitive qualities into his presently distorted civilised life' (2014: 49). The Romantic Movement was similarly critical believing it to be ruled by 'selfishness ... [where] individuals seek to control, dominate, and use others for their own self aggrandizement' (Gutek, 1988: 71). The solution for Rousseau (1762), and the Romantics who came after him, was a return to nature which would provide a 'primitive and original state ... [whereby] human life was guided by pure motives arising from the person's unspoilt instincts' (Gutek, 1988: 74). It is clear to see why wilderness would provide such a backdrop for Romantic sensibilities, as nature in its pristine, untouched, unspoilt condition might afford the perfect antidote to human beings distorted by a civilised existence.

American wilderness movement

Although not entirely distinct from the Romantic Movement that preceded it, the American wilderness movement led to an important modification in how we think about wilderness. Nash argues the latter grew out of the War of Independence and its aftermath, an era when the citizens of this new nation were searching for something uniquely American; consequently 'in the early 19th century American nationalists began to understand that it was in the *wildness* of its nature that their country was unmatched' (2014: 69). As such nature was gradually perceived by many American citizens to be a cultural and moral resource, even for some the basis upon which national self-esteem might be constructed. It was this viewpoint which underpinned the creation of Yellowstone National Park in 1872, and the designation thirteen years later of 715,000 acres of the Adirondacks as a 'Forest Preserve' (Keiter, 2013). The creation of Yellowstone National Park had a significance that resonated way beyond the confines of the USA, for this was the first time a nation state had enacted legislation to protect what was perceived to be a wilderness area. There was however a 'downside' as the legislation resulted in the forced removal and exclusion of the Native Americans who were already 'residents' of this particular 'wilderness' (Spence, 1999), a point returned to later.

Predictably the American wilderness movement was never a homogeneous entity, not least because leading figures within it were frequently at odds with each other regarding their attitudes towards the 'wilderness'. Some viewed the 'wilderness' as a frontier to be overcome, others as land and resources awaiting exploitation. A key figure in these debates was John Muir, who was born in Scotland in 1838 but arrived in America in 1849. Immersed in frontier life from an early age, Muir came to see something different and unique about the natural environment. Rejecting his father's austere Calvinistic religious views, Muir sought instead to find God in nature. The following 'meditation' offering advice to those panning for gold exemplifies many of his beliefs:

> *Keep close to nature's heart, yourself; and break clear away, once in a while, and climb a mountain or spend a week in the woods, wash your spirit clean from the earth-stains, of this sordid, gold seeking crowd, in god's pure air. It will help you in your efforts to bring to these people something better than gold. Don't lose your freedom and your love of the earth as God made it. (quoted by Highland, 2001: 109)*

Muir undertook a series of solitary expeditions into the American wilderness, especially in the Californian Sierras, recording these in his writings, which recounted his embrace of nature, extolled the virtues of the wilderness, the wonders of the natural world and were full of geological and botanical information gleaned from his studies. His essays and books were widely read, and the many meetings he addressed attracted large audiences. He was both a solitary man and a public figure who promoted at every opportunity a belief that the human race had a 'oneness' with the earth and nature (Worster, 2008). According to Nash, Muir's life's mission was to educate 'his countrymen in the advantages of wild country' (2014: 129). Therefore it is perhaps no accident that Muir's lifespan coincided with the birth of the American conservation movement, given his leading role in many early campaigns to preserve wilderness areas. His final foray involved an unsuccessful attempt to prevent the construction of a dam in the Hetch Hetchy Valley in Yosemite National Park. Despite his achievements and the advances made during his lifetime, Muir by the time of his death in 1914 was depressed as to the ability of conservationists to protect the American wilderness from despoliation (Worster, 2008). Nevertheless there can be no doubt he was a central figure in the formation of a movement to preserve the American wilderness, one which inspired the growth of similar pressure groups elsewhere.

Designation and protection of wilderness areas

A part of Muir's legacy is surely the Wilderness Act of 1964, which created the 'national wilderness preservation system' in the United States. More than half a century on from its enactment it is still considered fundamental to the protection of nearly 110 million acres of wilderness and more than 750 designated wilderness areas spread across 44 states. According to its supporters the 1964 Act still offers 'the highest form of land protection [with] no road, vehicles or permanent structures permitted '(Wilderness Society, 2014).

European interest in wilderness protection has grown over the last few decades, but the most prominent advocates of preservation are often based in the United States. In part this may be due to the variation in spatial scale between the two localities (Carver et al., 2002). However there remain areas of Europe, for instance large tracts of northern and eastern Finland, that are viewed as relatively untouched wilderness (Symington and Dunford, 2009). Similarly McNeish, who holds that the word 'wilderness' has been somewhat overused and misapplied, nevertheless claims the deer forests of Strath na Sealga, Fisherfield and Letterewe are perhaps rightly described by Scottish hill-goers as 'The Great Wilderness'. He also suggests Rannoch Moor should likewise be viewed as 'one of the true wilderness areas of Scotland' (McNeish, 2009: 79). However others in recognition of the retreating wilderness within Europe, including Britain, have adopted phrases such as 'wild land' or 'wild-landscape' to describe what others still designate a 'wilderness' (McMorran et al., 2008). Here Hendee, Stankey and Lucas's (1978) concept of a continuum may be helpful when discussing wilderness. For it encourages us not to think of wilderness as a single entity defined by a lack of human infringement, but rather as a continuum thereby helping us to envisage a spectrum of 'wilderness' or wild landscapes, ranging from 'pristine wilderness' devoid 'of human habitation and … other human related influence to at the other end totally urbanised environments' such as 'the shopping mall or office' (Carver et al., 2002: 25). Carver, Evans and Fritz (2002) adapted Hendee, Stankey and Lucas's (1978) approach to plot wilderness areas of the UK and produce maps that grade land according to degrees of wilderness using the following criteria:

- Remoteness from UK local population
- Remoteness from national population
- Remoteness from mechanised access
- Apparent naturalness
- Biophysical naturalness
- Altitude

Such exercises offer useful insights, but we should be aware notions of naturalness are highly subjective as well as culturally and historically specific. For example the appearance, and the economic and social structure of much of the Scottish Highlands, was transformed by the highland clearances of the late eighteenth and nineteenth centuries, which all but destroyed the crofting way of life that had existed for centuries (Richards, 2000).

The Knoydart Peninsula, on the west coast of Scotland facing the Isle of Skye, provides an insight into how our conceptualisation of 'wilderness' can alter over time. McNeish notes how Knoydart is 'generally perceived to be a wilderness' and was frequently described by the media as 'Scotland's last great wilderness' during the 1980s when the Ministry of Defense expressed an interest in purchasing it for training purposes (2009: 147). Yet as Richards points out, in 1745 over one thousand young men were working the land there, and an etching from the nineteenth century shows 40 to 50 trading ships moored in Barrisdale Bay located at the heart of the peninsula. Likewise the wide-open spaces of Dartmoor were once tree covered (Keene, 2001). Contrasts such as these remind us that what we currently identify as 'natural' environments may have been radically reshaped, relatively recently, by human intervention.

It is also important to stress that wilderness is in some respects a Eurocentric concept, and that many areas now regarded as quintessential wilderness environments were for millennia home to indigenous people. Most, if not all, of the environments which we are quick to refer to as natural, untouched and devoid of human habitation were, and in certain places still are, quite the reverse. The tracts of northern Finland are home to the Sami people, Aborigines have lived for thousands of years in the Australian Outback, and the designated wilderness areas of the United States (where the law usually prohibits permanent human habitation and the construction of new dwellings) were long home to various Native American tribes (Spence, 1999). The dominance of this Eurocentric perspective has resulted in the imposition of legal restrictions upon indigenous populations that threaten both their traditional way of life and economic survival. For instance Native Americans have been prosecuted for using motorboats to fish in the 'Boundary Waters' wilderness area in the United States (Freedman, 2002).

By now it should be apparent that twenty-first century notions of wilderness are never simply about physical characteristics and geographical locations.

Rather wilderness should be viewed as a 'place' that is a complex – culturally constructed – concept (McMorran et al., 2008). Our understanding of wilderness is largely founded upon preconceived ideas shaped by policy as well as tradition, customs and social mores (Cronon, 1995; Sharp and Strack, 2007) all which sit alongside an expectation that the area so designated is one minimally modified by human activity (Carver et al., 2002; Willis, 2011). Therefore we find that what wilderness 'means' is invariably complex, seemingly always, once we look beneath the surface, dependent upon a range of frequently competing and multilayered perspectives.

Wilderness as a 'linguistic' concept

Given the potential for confusion that emerges whenever we seek to clarify our thinking in relation to what 'wilderness' means, there is real merit in examining at this stage the notion of wilderness as a linguistic concept. Too often considerations about the idea of wilderness presupposes its ontology – its existence in the world – when it should be remembered that it is a word, one used to describe aspects of the world and not as it is often, at least implicitly, suggested 'an aspect of the world' itself. To explore this idea further it is helpful to turn to the ideas of the linguistic philosopher Ludwig Wittgenstein (1953, 1958, 1969). One of his achievements was to offer a potential solution to the philosophical problem presented by sceptical empiricists such as Descartes (Monk, 1990; Kenny, 1973), who argued there was no absolute foundation to knowledge; in other words one could never be sure of knowing anything, because one might always entertain doubt. Wittgenstein's innovative resolution to this problem, which had long engaged philosophers, was to approach it from a different angle. Rather than focusing on the logic of the argument, Wittgenstein's approach centred on the use of words and importantly on 'the occasions in which we use them, [and] the contexts which give them their sense' (Monk, 1990: 578). He analysed, for example, the concept of doubt in relation to notions of certainty, suggesting that it makes no sense to doubt everything; he argued that 'our doubts depend on the fact that some propositions are exempt from doubt, [they] are as it were like the hinges on which those turn' (Wittgenstein, 1969: 341), and concluded that 'doubting itself, presupposes certainty' and that scepticism was in itself flawed by its own logic, pointing out that 'If you are not certain of any fact, you cannot be certain of the meaning of your words either' (Wittgenstein, 1969: 114–115).

So what has this got to do with the problem of wilderness in outdoor education? A great deal is the simple answer, because for Wittgenstein meaning is centred on 'use', as he makes clear, 'the use of the word in practice is its meaning, (1958: 69). Or, as he suggests, we should 'think of words as instruments characterised by their use' (Wittgenstein, 1958: 67). Importantly the use of words and the meaning we derive from them, as we have seen with his analysis of what it means to both 'know' and 'doubt', can only be understood by appreciating their juxtaposition. By adopting a Wittgensteinian perspective in our analysis of the concept of wilderness we reveal some useful insights. First there will be no absolute notion of wilderness; consequently attempts to assemble an exhaustive definition are futile. It is not surprising therefore that many writers have over the years struggled with this insurmountable challenge (Callicott and Nelson, 1998; Nelson and Callicott, 2008). Second the use of the concept of wilderness will always be relative to some notion of civilisation. The two ideas, like doubt and certainty, operate in tandem. Therefore these two words ultimately have no meaning in isolation from each other, a fact that did not elude Milton, who argues 'the very concepts of wilderness and civilisation require each other to have real meaning' (cited in Nash, 2014: 246).

Millar is therefore surely correct when suggesting that 'wilderness unlike mountains, canyons and forests is a perceived reality, a quality. It has more to do with the geography of the mind than of the land' (2014: xiv). Likewise Nash tentatively asks whether we should not 'accept as wilderness those places people call wilderness' (2014: 5). Nash is, however, wrong to dismiss his own suggestion, on the grounds it leads to the random designation of wilderness, for in doing so he fails to realise that words and concepts cannot be used arbitrarily. For as Wittgenstein points out, words can never be 'entirely' subjectively employed, just as words cannot be 'used' idiosyncratically. The use of the word wilderness, like all words in a language, is made within what Wittgenstein calls 'language games' (Wittgenstein, 1953, 1958), a characteristic of which are patterns of informal rules governing their use. For example, Wittgenstein argues: 'If anyone utters a sentence and means or understands it he is operating according to definite rules' (1958: 38). It is these rules which give words their currency within a given language. This is not to say certain words are any less contested. But whilst the language game might set specific parameters – for example, it can never make any sense to refer to, say, a shopping mall as a wilderness – the notion of wilderness will, like certain other words and concepts, for example, the concept of art, remain essentially contested but within boundaries. This contestation is inevitable with regards to the notion of wilderness because it is a perceived reality relative to both one's notion of 'wild' and understanding of a 'tamed or civilised existence'. For example, the tracts of Dartmoor may well feel like a wilderness to the sightseer from the city who has not encountered such open spaces before, but to a regular visitor who is aware of its fluctuating human influences from prehistoric hut dwellings to contemporary cattle grazing and who is familiar with its landscapes and byways it may well not be perceived as wilderness at all.

Informal education and the wilderness

When we grasp Dewey's notion of experience as a transaction between the individual and their environment (see Chapter 3), we are far more likely to appreciate that encounters with physical environments such as rivers, lakes, forests and mountains amount to much more than the sum total of the physical tasks and activities that take place within them. Dewey's conception is much richer and more nuanced than what Storry terms the mere 'experience of doing' (2003: 136). Dewey's stance is one that equates more fully to what might be termed a lived experience, and requires an appreciation of the place of the individual in the totality of their social, physical and cultural 'setting'. Integral to Dewey's notion of experience is the 'principle of continuity' (1938: 35), a principle Breault summarises as follows:

Continuity in education means that any learning experience that is organised for the student should take into consideration the experience the child brings to the learning activity and should prepare the child for future experiences. (2014: 49)

Continuity appreciates the past – where one has come from – as well as the future - where one is going to. Of course this thought process is not envisaged merely in terms of physical destinations but existentially with regards to what 'is going on' in one's life at that particular time what is pertinent to the individual. Ultimately to appreciate Dewey's notion of experience one needs to accept that it is built upon an understanding of the 'meaning' of experiences (Dewey, 1916; Pring, 2007). For Experiences to be educative therefore the educator must be aware of and engage with what the experiences mean to individuals, which involves appreciating why they are there and for what purposes.

Experiences of places, especially those we wish to describe as wilderness, will necessitate therefore an appreciation of what those environments mean to the individuals venturing into them. The meaning of wilderness as we have seen may be highly personal and relative to an individual's background, but it still cannot be understood in isolation from what one regards as 'civilisation' – what is normal, taken for granted, and everyday – in other words, one's sense of 'place'. Essentially what the wilderness as an informal educational tool provides is a disruption, a challenge or at the very least a contrast to one's existing sense of place. It therefore promises a route whereby learning for many young people and adults can be accelerated in relation both to a better understanding of self and the environment.

It is certainly possible, particularly for participants in outdoor education programmes who originate from inner-city localities, that their experience of the outdoors will be limited. They may well, for example, never have seen a night sky unpolluted by artificial lighting, walked on unpaved tracks, or been out of sight or sound of roads and houses. Increasingly it is also unlikely they have been more than momentarily without access to a mobile phone and the internet. The extent to which each or all these is the case will fundamentally affect how participants regard the environment they are venturing into and whether or not they might classify it as a 'wilderness'.

But such limited experience of the outdoors does not necessarily produce predictable or standardised responses amongst participants. For some it may induce feelings of foreboding akin to those associated with early biblical representations of wilderness where no value is placed on anything connected with it, resulting in those group members merely thinking it is something that must be endured – an inconvenience – the privations of which must be overcome. Alternatively the encounter may promote feelings of awe and wonder, prompting the onset of romantic sensibilities, and despite the unfamiliarity instil a desire to experience such places in the future. The outdoors may at times be experienced as 'wild', but in truth there will be a multitude of reactions, responses and attitudes towards what maybe a novel environment for some people.

It is essential for outdoor and informal educators to ascertain what the environment means to the participants. The best way to do this is to study their reactions to what they encounter, listen to what they say to each other, and talk to them. By engaging in conversations and dialogue with party members about what this place means to them, and to you as an educator, it becomes possible to deepen both their and your appreciation of the environment.

It is always likely there will be a gulf between the participants' and the educators' experience of wilderness. Those able to take responsibility for others in wilderness environments, or wild places, will inevitably have more experience of such conditions. Such familiarity may breed indifference, even disdain, towards those new to this world, to a degree that they may fail to appreciate what responses an initial encounter with remoteness may elicit in others. Indeed some outdoor educators may well prefer wilderness environments to the alternatives and feel more comfortable and 'at home' in them, whereas participants may feel the reverse and long for a return to the 'civilised' comforts and the securities of electric light and locked doors. Such a divide can mean that educators fail to grasp the full educative potential of less wild places, making it difficult for them to engage in conversation and dialogue with party members. Those with limited experience of the outdoors may not necessarily need to undertake a weeklong wilderness expedition to have their sense of place challenged. One night in the woods, maybe even in a log cabin rather than under canvas, might arouse the kind of responses that the educator initially seeks to bring about. Clearly the further one goes into 'the wilderness' in terms of distance and time, and metaphorically, the greater the contrast it provides in relation to the participants' existing sense of place, is what counts. For the sense of wilderness is relative to the participants and not simplistically determined by the educator or programme. Therefore the educator must be reflexive and reflect on their attitudes towards wilderness and be prepared to reassess and reconfigure their own definitions in the light of their experiences and those whom they are engaging with it. The educative potential of wilderness like wilderness itself will always be in a state of flux. That is what helps to make it such a precious educational resource.

Use of the wilderness

So how can we employ wilderness as an educative vehicle? What follows cannot hope to be an exhaustive response to that question, for wilderness, like experience itself, is multifaceted and offers a myriad of possibilities. First as we explored earlier with the contrast between notions of civilisation and wilderness, and between one's sense of 'place' and the impact of 'wild places', the idea of going into the wilderness has a sense of **parting or departing**, of leaving something behind. Acknowledging this is important, and the implications of taking this step need to be scrutinised by the educator, for what is being left behind will be unique to each participant. Similarly unique will be their attitude towards the process of departure. One party member, for example, may be glad to leave behind troubling circumstances, whilst another may be apprehensive about being away from familiar people and places. For many, the attraction of wild or wilderness locations will be that it is not the place where they live, but somewhere one step removed from their normal social environment, hence they embrace the potential it has to catapult them into a world of entirely different social realities (Schmid and Buechler, 1991). Wilderness can, therefore, for some participants in outdoor and adventure education programmes provide a freedom from social pressures, and from the restrictive norms and values of a particular community or social setting. In this sense it may offer 'an antidote to the strains of modern living' (Kelly cited in Nash, 2014: 213). Wilderness can also promise a contrast to the accepted ways of understanding the world, one less constrained by the trappings of the social boundaries that hold us back in other settings; thereby it can enable us to reflect anew upon how we lead our everyday lives. This 'release' may be particularly important for those belonging to oppressed groups who find that in this setting they are temporarily liberated from embedded stereotypes and granted a measure of freedom to define themselves on their own terms.

Second, it can impart **simplicity**, especially if one spends a sufficient amount of time in a wilderness environment. For example, all the schedules, tasks and demands of day-to-day life are likely to diminish as the reality of the environment we occupy alters. No longer is the format of the day dictated by the routines of work and home life, but by the challenges posed by the landscape and the weather. By stages, perhaps even without being conscious of the process, a realignment may occur wherein it is now the sunrise and sunset that sets the schedule for the day, not the diary, watch and mobile phone. Now it is our interactions with the immediate environment that structures the daily round. As Schmid and Bucheler's research into weeklong wilderness journeys found after the first day, these expeditions seemed to rapidly 'acquire their own particular rhythm' (1991: 37).

The 1980s and 1990s saw an increase in the number of wilderness programmes, both as a setting for an experience and as an experience in itself (Dawson et al., 1998). This expansion appears to have continued unabated and it has been accompanied by the emergence of a growing volume of research undertaken into the content, style and outcomes of wilderness programmes. Some notable examples include studies on the emotional responses to involvement in wilderness expeditions (Cashel et al., 1996); the impact of 'rites of passage' programmes (Beames, 2004; Norris, 2011); reactions of participants to solo experiences (Smith, 2005); the diverse organisational formats of these expeditions (Klein, 1997; Allison and Beames, 2010); the effectiveness of wilderness programmes for at-risk youth (Sklar et al., 2007); and their outcomes in relation to the promotion of health and well-being (Louv, 2012). A recurring theme encountered in much of this research is the focus upon solitude, with its echo of Romanticism, within many wilderness programmes. Solitude, it seems, is often regarded as a key attraction for many who embark on a wilderness experience (Sharp and Stracke, 2007).

Linked to solitude, but not bound to it, is the similarly contentious notion of '**spirituality**' (Nash, 2014; Williams and Harvey, 2001). Knecht (2004) describes how participants often characterise their wilderness experiences as 'spiritual', even though in most cases they did not self-identify as being religiously inclined. Marsh's research relating to backcountry skiers, telemarkers and snowboarders in Wyoming revealed a strong spiritual element, with a high proportion reporting their engagement fostered a 'connection beyond the self, a heightened sense of clarity and self-awareness … [and a] … sense of rejuvenation and fulfillment' (2008: 292). For many it seems the concept of wilderness aligns closely with that of spirituality and transcendence. Carter describes the experience of wilderness as 'confronting yourself with [your] own uniqueness' (cited in Nash, 2014: 253). Of course this is not a new phenomenon as John Muir a century or more ago claimed that wilderness had a transcendent quality (Browning, 1988; Highland, 2001).

The simplicity, solitude and possibly the spiritual components of the wilderness experience, it is claimed by some, have unique healing qualities (Davis-Berman and Berman, 1994). Beringer and Martin (2003) are certainly not alone in emphasising the healing or therapeutic effects of wilderness environments. The question of whether or not it is possible, as Mackaye claims, 'to recharge depleted human batteries directly from mother earth' (cited in Nash, 2014: 245), is beyond the scope of this chapter. Whilst it is possible to claim wild places demand dependency on self rather than on society, there are a number of writers and researchers who make stronger claims for their beneficial impact. The Wilderness Foundation for instance claims on its webpage that

> *Our research on our recent wilderness therapy programmes has demonstrated that people can change naturally when they are removed from the environments that are filled with negative events and influences that may trigger self-defeating thoughts, feelings and behaviour. (2012)*

Whilst it appears to be a well-argued case that wilderness environments have the potential to produce feelings which participants associate with spiritual or therapeutic qualities, the authors would not wish to overstate this aspect in terms of informal education, not least because it may not accord with the feelings, needs or experiences of all participants; we must also accept there are other, more mundane, but perhaps equally important aspects of the wilderness environment informal educators may wish to work with. For example, as suggested in Chapter 10, the residential experience can provide a powerful medium for informal education. However it may be the case that the residential experience has even greater potential for developing opportunities for dialogical and informal learning when the living together occurs in a wilderness environment, one where the distance, both in time and space, from the familiar may be more pronounced than is normally the case.

Our role as informal educators is so often twofold. First we foster environments for learning or, put another way, create learning opportunities. These will often be environments conducive to what Rogers (2003) termed 'acquisition' learning. However, perhaps it is more often the case that informal educators are obliged to foster 'incidental' learning in settings that are not theirs to control (Jeffs and Smith, 2005). Settings where the learning is indirect, and occurs as a consequence of engaging in conversation and dialogue in order to foster a 'process of learning' (Smith, 1988; Ord, 2016). The informal educator's second role is to bring new insights to situations, both familiar and unfamiliar. People may have experiences in wilderness settings, regardless of anyone else's presence, purely as a result of being in that setting. That is to be welcomed, but it still leaves the informal educator with the task of offering different perspectives and posing those questions that will help others explore the experience at a greater depth and which induce additional learning. As the above implies, wilderness environments of themselves can have a special role to play in fostering reflection and awareness, for example, in relation to **sustainability** as a political and social issue. Wilderness and similar environments minimally impacted on by humans have, as Spurr points out, two distinctive qualities. First, they offer 'a reservoir or holding ground for biotic [communities]' (2008: 120), for it may only be possible to maintain essential forms of genetic diversity if sufficient environments free from human interference are preserved and remain 'uncivilised' (Schonewald-Cox and Stohlgren, 1989). Second, Spurr argues these environments offer a 'standard of comparison for measuring and evaluating those other biotic communities which are much more influenced by man' (ibid.). In relation to both of these qualities, wilderness, as an educative setting, has a unique role to play in fostering learning about and for sustainability (see Chapter 11 for a wider discussion of this).

Wilderness can so often enable us to see the bigger picture, especially to conceive of humans as a part of nature not detached from it. As Zahniser reminds us, 'We need wilderness to get away from technology that gives us the illusion of mastering rather than belonging to the environment' (cited in Nash, 2014: 254), because wilderness can serve to reduce life to the basics – the bare necessities – of food and shelter and so:

> *Wild country has the power to remind civilised people that out there is a different world, older and greater and deeper by far than ours, a world which surrounds and sustains the little world of men. (Abbey cited Nash, 2014: 255)*

Conclusion

This chapter has argued that, in addition to the earlier discourses created by biblical notions of wilderness, Romanticism during the eighteenth and nineteenth centuries and the subsequent transcendentalism of writers such as John Muir, it is advantageous for us to comprehend why wilderness is best seen as a linguistic concept, one which can only be grasped when juxtaposed to notions of civilisation. And so it follows wild places are best understood when contrasted with one's own notion of place – the familiar. The use of wilderness in informal education has great potential, not least because of its capacity to disrupt participants' own unique sense of place. In part because wilderness is a relative concept, the starting point for the use of wilderness environments as a locale for informal education must be an appreciation of what wilderness means to those one is seeking to educate. Informal educators must not for this reason set out to superimpose their understanding of wilderness environments and wild places onto those of the other participants who may well be encountering them for the first time via the medium of an outdoor or adventure education programme.

White and Hendee in their discussion of the relationship between naturalness, solitude and the wilderness summarise the benefits of wilderness environments in terms of three categories: (1) development of self, (2) development of community, and (3) spiritual development (2000: 224). We would also at this late stage like to add a fourth – the potential of wilderness environments to facilitate education for sustainability. It may be helpful to close by presenting the typology of wilderness experience composed by Dawson et al. (1998), which talks of wilderness as teacher, wilderness as classroom and wilderness as both. In truth it is all these things and so much more. For the contrasts wild places produce cannot fail but supply a limitless inspiration for creative conversation and learning, which is perhaps why it may be the perfect setting wherein informal and dialogical education can flourish.

References

Allison, P. and Beames, S. (2010) 'The changing geographies of overseas expeditions', *International Journal of Wilderness* 16(3), pp. 35–42.

Beames, S. (2004) 'Overseas youth expeditions with Raleigh International: a rite of passage', *Australian Journal of Outdoor Education* 8(1), pp. 29–36.

Beringer, A. and Martin, P. (2003) 'On adventure therapy and natural worlds: respecting nature's healing', *Journal of Adventure Education and Outdoor Learning* 3(1), pp. 29–39.

Breault, R. (2014) 'Active learning' in D. A. Breault and R. Breault (eds.) *Experiencing Dewey*, Abingdon: Routledge.

Bromley, P. (2006) *Countryside Management*, Abingdon: Taylor and Francis.

Browning, P. (1988) *John Muir in His Own Words*, Lafayette, CA: Great West Books.

Burke, E. (1767) *Philosophical Enquiries into the Origin and Ideas of the Sublime and the Beautiful*, London: New Oxford Library.

Callicott, J. B. and Nelson, M. (1998) *The Great New Wilderness Debate*, Athens, GA: University of Georgia Press.

Carver, S., Evans, A. and Fritz, S. (2002) 'Wilderness attribute mapping in the United Kingdom', *International Journal of Wilderness* 8(1), pp. 24–29.

Cashel, C. M., Lane, S. W. L. and Montgomery, D. (1996) 'Emotional response patterns of participants during wilderness experience', *Wilderness and Environmental Medicine* 1, pp. 9–18.

Cronon, W. (1995) 'The trouble with wilderness, or getting back to the wrong nature' in W. Cronon (ed.) *Uncommon Ground: Rethinking the Human Place in Nature*, New York: Norton.

Davis-Berman, J. L. and Berman, D. S. (1994) *Wilderness Therapy*, Dubuque, IA: Kendal Hunt Publishing.

Dawson, C. P., Friese, G. T., Tangen-Foster, J. and Carpenter, J. (1998) 'Wilderness experience programs in the United States: dependence on and use of wilderness', *USDA Forest Service Proceedings RMRS-P-4*: 99–104.

Dewey, J. (1916) *Democracy and Education*, Teddington: Echo Library [reprinted 2007].

Dewey, J. (1938) *Experience and Education*, New York: Touchstone [reprinted 1997].

Evans, E. (1819) A Pedestrious Tour of Four Thousand Miles through the Western States and Territories during the Winter and Spring of 1818, New Hampshire: Concord.

Freedman, E. (2002) 'When indigenous rights and wilderness collide: prosecution of Native Americans for using motors in Minnesota's Boundary Waters canoe wilderness area', *American Indian Quarterly* 26(3), pp. 378–392.

Gilmore, A. (2006) 'Wilderness in the Bible and the wild places of the earth', *Journal of European Baptist Studies* 7(1), pp. 44–57.

Gutek, G. L. (1988) *Philosophical and Ideological Perspectives on Education*, Boston, MA: Allyn and Bacon.

Hendee, J. C., Stankey, G. H. and Lucas, R.C. (1978) *Wilderness Management*, Washington, DC: US Forestry Service.

Highland, C. (2001) *Meditations of John Muir: Nature's Temples*, Birmingham, AL: Wilderness Press.

Jeffs, T. and Smith, M. K. (2005) *Informal Education, Conversation, Democracy and Learning* (3rd ed.), Ticknall: Education Now.

Keene, P. (2001) 'The evolution of a Dartmoor landscape', *Dartmoor National Park Publications*, Online. Available at: www.dartmoor-npa.gov.uk/__data/assets/pdf_file/0017/41039/au-burrator.pdf (accessed 16 September 2014).

Keiter, R. B. (2013) *To Conserve Unimpaired: The Evolution of the National Park Idea*, Washington, DC: Island Books.

Kenny, A.K. (1973) *Wittgenstein*, Harmondsworth: Penguin.

Klein, D. (1997) 'Beyond the wilderness', *About Campus*, January–February, pp. 18–22.

Knecht, C. (2004) 'Urban nature and well-being: some empirical support and design implications', *Berkeley Planning Journal* 17, pp. 82–108.

Louv, R. (2012) *The Nature Principle: Reconnecting with Life in a Virtual Age*, Chapel Hill, NC: Algonquin Books.

Macfarlane, R. (2003) *Mountains of the Mind: A History of a Fascination*, London: Granta Books.

Marsh, P. E. (2008) 'Backcountry adventure as spiritual development: a means-end study' (SEER 2007, Abstract), *Journal of Experiential Education* 30(3), pp. 290–293.

McCloskey, M. (1966) 'The Wilderness Act of 1964: its background and meaning', *Oregon Law Review* 45, pp. 288–321.

McCloskey, M. (1995) 'What the Wilderness Act accomplished in the protection of roadless areas within the National Park System', *Journal of Environmental Law and Litigation* 10, pp. 455–472.

McMorran, R., Price, M. F. and Warren, C. R. (2008) 'The call of different wilds: the importance of definition and perception in protecting and managing Scottish wild landscapes,' *Journal of Environmental Planning and Management* 51(2), pp. 177–199.

McNeish, C. (2009) *The Munros: Scotland's Highest Mountains* (fully revised and updated), Broxburne: Lomond Books.

Millar, C. (2014) 'Foreword' in R. Nash, *Wilderness and the American Mind* (5th ed.), New Haven, CT: Yale University Press.

Monk, R. (1990) *Ludwig Wittgenstein: The Duty of Genius*, London: Vintage.

Nash, R. (2014) *Wilderness and the American Mind* (5th ed.), New Haven, CT: Yale University Press.

Nelson, M. and Callicott, J. B. (2008) *The Wilderness Debate Rages On: Continuing the Wilderness Debate*, Athens, GA: University of Georgia Press.

Norris, J. (2011) 'Crossing the threshold mindfully: exploring rites of passage models in adventure therapy,' *Journal of Adventure Education and Outdoor Learning* 11(2), pp. 109–126.

Ord, J. (2016) *Youth Work Process, Product and Practice: Creating an Authentic Curriculum in Work with Young People* (2nd ed.), London: Routledge.

Pring, R. (2007) *John Dewey: Continuum Library of Educational Thought*, London: Continuum.

Richards, E. (2000) *Debating the Highland Clearances*, Edinburgh: Edinburgh University Press.

Rogers, A. (2003) *What Is the Difference? A New Critique of Adult Teaching and Learning*, Leicester: NIACE.

Rossiter, K. (2006) 'Keeping the "wild" in 'wilderness', *International Coalition of Outdoor Recreation and Education Conference Proceedings*, Boise State University, Idaho.

Rousseau, J J. (1762) 'Emile, or on education' in W. Boyd (ed.) *Emile for Today*, London: Heinemann.

Schmid, T. J. and Buechler, S. M. (1991) 'Crossing boundaries: sociology in the wilderness', *Teaching Sociology* 19, pp. 39–41.

Schonewald-Cox, C. M. and Stohlgren, T. J. (1989) 'Wilderness and the protection of genetic diversity', *Wilderness Benchmark 1988: Proceedings of the National Wilderness Colloquium*, Asheville, NC: USDA Forest Service, Southeastern Forest Experiment Station.

Sharp, R. L. and Strack, J. A. (2007) 'Beyond traditional ideas of wilderness in outdoor recreation programs', *Association of Outdoor Recreation and Education Conference Proceedings*, Asheville, NC – Crown Plaza Resort.

Sklar, S. L., Anderson, S. C. and Autry, C. E. (2007) 'Positive youth development: a wilderness intervention', *Therapeutic Recreation Journal* 41(3), pp. 223–243.

Smith, M. K. (1988) *Developing Youth Work*, Milton Keynes: Open University Press.

Smith, T.E. (2005) 'Going outside to go inside: frameworks for the solo experience' in C. Knapp and T. Smith (eds.) *Exploring the Power of Solo, Silence and Solitude*, Boulder, CO: Association for Experiential Education.

Spence, M. D. (1999) *Dispossessing the Wilderness: Indian Removal and the Making of the National Parks*, Oxford: Oxford University Press.

Spurr, S. H. (2008) 'The value of wilderness to science' in M. Nelson and J. B. Callicott (eds.) *The Wilderness Debate Rages On: Continuing the Great New Wilderness Debate*, Athens, GA: University of Georgia Press.

Storry, T. (2003) 'Ours to reason why', *Journal of Adventure Education and Outdoor Learning* 3(2), pp. 133–143.

Symington, A. and Dunford, G. (2009) *Finland*, Lonely Planet: London.

White, D. D. and Hendee, J. C. (2000) 'Primal hypotheses: the relationship between naturalness, solitude and the wilderness experience benefits of development of self, development of community and spiritual development' in *USDA Forest Service Proceedings RMRS-P-15*, 3: 223–227.

Williams, K. and Harvey, D. (2001) 'Transcendent experience in forest environments', *Journal of Environmental Psychology* 21, pp. 249–260.

Willis, A. (2011) 'Re-storying wilderness and adventure therapies: healing places and selves in an era of environmental crises', *Journal of Adventure Education and Outdoor Learning* 11(2), pp. 91–108.

Wilderness Foundation UK (2012) 'Wilderness Therapy'. Available at: www .wildernessfoundation.org.uk/what-we-do/wilderness-therapy/ (accessed 24 Oct 2014).

Wilderness Society (2014) 'Wilderness Act'. Available at: http://wilderness.org/article/ wilderness-act#sthash.h9fCbfaB.dpuf* (accessed on 15 July 2014).

Wittgenstein, L. (1953) *Philosophical Investigations*, Oxford: Basil Blackwell.

Wittgenstein, L. (1958) *The Blue and Brown Books*, Oxford: Basil Blackwell.

Wittgenstein, L. (1969) *On Certainty*, Oxford: Basil Blackwell.

Wokler, R. (1995) *Rousseau*, Oxford: Oxford University Press.

Worster, D. (2008) *A Passion for Nature: The Life of John Muir*, New York: Oxford University Press.

7

MOUNTAINS, CLIMBING AND INFORMAL EDUCATION

Jon Ord

Journeying through mountains and climbing to their summits is understandably viewed as a fundamental ingredient or a cornerstone of outdoor and adventure education. This long-standing presence has contributed towards the formulation of a number of 'taken for granted' notions amongst practitioners and others in outdoor education about the inherent worth of mountains and climbing. This chapter critiques some of these assumptions and in particular reflects on what it is we learn as a result of educational encounters that occur in mountainous environments. Mountains may well be a quintessential medium for informal, outdoor and experiential education, but reflecting critically on our preconceptions of what mountains mean to us, both as individuals and as educators, as well as for those we are taking into such environments, perhaps for the first time, is essential if we are to maximise their educational potential.

The changing meaning of mountains

Mountains themselves have not been given a great deal of attention by the authors of the more popular outdoor and adventure education textbooks. For instance, in the widely read student text *The RHP Companion to Outdoor Education* (Barnes and Sharp, 2004) there is scant mention of mountains per se apart from a brief discussion relating to risk assessments and climbing. Equally, a second widely used text, Beard and Wilson's *Experiential Learning*, makes only a passing reference to mountains when they are discussed in a chapter on various environments as 'spaces' for experiential learning. Indeed Beard and Wilson (2002) devote more attention to climbing walls, which they cite as an example of the growing convergence of outdoor and indoor learning milieus, than mountains themselves. Hopkins and Putnam (2012) do identify mountaineering, climbing and abseiling as essential activities in relation to adventure programmes designed to foster personal growth, but once again little is said about what assumptions are being made about the mountains themselves or how they might be best utilised. Nevertheless irrespective of these oversights mountains and climbing are linked to an implicit discourse relating to outdoor and adventure education. In particular many, probably most, outdoor educators hold that:

- Mountains are places that possess a distinct and significant value.
- The value placed on them outweighs that allotted urban environments.
- Engaging in activities such as walking and climbing in mountain environments has a potentially transformative power.
- This transformative power results both from specific activities, such as rock climbing, abseiling and climbing to a summit, as well as walking in their midst and encountering the vistas they afford.

We may well wish to maintain that the beliefs listed above relating to mountain locations are valid, but it should be acknowledged these are judgments of relatively recent origin. In this respect it is helpful to recall that mountains have not always been held in such high esteem. During earlier times in our history they were regarded somewhat differently, as they still are within some cultures. As Macfarlane (2003: 145) reminds us, little evidence exists of widespread aesthetic appreciation of the mountains in Europe prior to the eighteenth century. Indeed rather than looking forward to the encounter it was commonplace for travelers to choose to be blindfolded before navigating Alpine passes to prevent them seeing the 'terrifying' panoramas awaiting them. Such a response can be linked in part to the fact that for many centuries within Europe, mountains were treated as dangerous, inauspicious unwholesome entities, hence the uncomplimentary names given to so many Alpine peaks, for example, Eiger (Ogre), Mount Maudit (Accursed Mountain) and Teufelsberg (Devil's Mountain) (Cleare, 1980). Throughout Europe large swathes of the population long held that mountains were the haunt of monsters, trolls, demons and dragons, hence they were places to be avoided rather than sought out. A similar absence of any appreciation of mountains can be encountered within British literature well into the eighteenth century, including Samuel Johnson's *A Journey to the Western Islands of Scotland* published in 1785. This is an account of a tour undertaken with his biographer James Boswell which entered the 'bosom of the highlands' after departing St. Andrews and proceeded via Loch Ness to the Isle of Skye, a journey that took them through Glen Shiel and on to Glenelg, where they embarked for Skye, a route that meant they passed by the Five Sisters of Kintail, now regarded as 'one of the great picture postcard views of Scotland' (McNeish, 2009: 162). Johnson, however, seems to have been totally unimpressed by the scenic grandeur that has enthralled subsequent generations of visitors. He perceived no 'value' in the surrounding mountains, compared to the cultivated lowlands he was familiar with, commenting

> *Of the hills… They exhibit very little variety; being almost wholly covered with dark heath… An eye accustomed to flowery pastures and waving harvests is astonished and repelled by this wide extent of hopeless sterility. The appearance is that of matter*

incapable of form or usefulness, dismissed by nature from her care and disinherited of her favours, left in its original elemental state, or quickened only with one sullen power of useless vegetation. (1785/1924: 55-56)

Johnson was in no way unique in adopting a stance of indifference. Daniel Defoe (1748) writing in 1724 of the Yorkshire Dales, so beloved of contemporary walkers and tourists, judged that although 'they had a kind of an unhospitable terror in them' there were sadly 'no rich pleasant valleys between them … [being] of no use or advantage either to man or beast' (cited in O'Neill and Walsh, 2000: 283). Johnson and Defoe's judgments, although out of kilter with those that are now commonplace, reflect a standpoint dominant two centuries ago that held 'wild land has value [only] as potential civilization' (Nash, 2014: 33).

Romanticism and the reconfiguration of mountains

The nineteenth century witnessed a gradual but discernible transformation in the prevailing social attitudes towards nature, rurality and mountains. At the heart of the social process that produced this reconfiguration was what became known as the Romantic Movement. It was a reorientation prefigured by the publication in 1761 of Jean-Jacques Rousseau's *Nouvelle Heloise*, a text now widely credited with having created what Macfarlane has dubbed 'secular mountain worship' (2003: 208). Rousseau in subsequent writings revisited notions of wilderness and again stressed the benefits accruing from direct encounters with nature. Rousseau's autobiography, *Confessions*, written in his mid 50s but unpublished until 1782, seven years before his death, in an oft-quoted passage tells how 'at the sight of a beautiful mountain I feel moved, though I cannot say by what' (cited in Craig, 1999: 129).

Rousseau may have provided the early momentum, but the Romantic Movement is more usually linked to the writings of a cluster of poets, literary critics and writers. Amongst the former were William Wordsworth, a native of Cumbria, and Samuel Taylor Coleridge, who singularly and together explored the Lake District and wrote extensively extolling the virtues of the mountains to be encountered there. Their excursions were not limited to wandering in the footsteps of shepherds; Coleridge made the first recorded ascent of Sca Fell in 1802, which included a descent of Broad Stand, which is now graded as a moderate rock climb. Similarly Algernon Swinburne, a late Romantic poet, made the earliest recorded ascent of a Munro (a Scottish mountain of over 3,000 ft), Bla Bheinn on the Isle of Skye (Brown and Mitchell, 1991: 85). Also prominent within the Romantic Movement were a number of writers, philosophers and social reformers, notably John Ruskin in England and Ralph Waldo Emerson, Henry David Thoreau and John Muir in North America. All were fascinated by the transient beauty of the mountains. Ruskin, possibly the most influential social and artistic commentator of his generation, who chose to make his home beside Coniston Water, and he viewed mountains as the 'cathedrals of the earth' and the 'beginning and the end of all natural scenery' (Ruskin, 1843).

Romanticism placed a new and distinctive importance on nature. But it had a special reverence for the landscapes of mountains and the aesthetic experiences one might have within them. For as Macfarlane notes, it

> *fused into the imagination of altitude a new element of attractiveness: that one was almost guaranteed enlightenment … places where you were brought to see further both physically and metaphysically … be rewarded by both far sight and with insight. (2003: 159–160)*

One legacy of the Romantic Movement has been that since the late eighteenth and early nineteenth centuries there has existed a widespread perception of the countryside as a demi-Eden, an alternative to the pressures, ugliness and friction of urban life, a place of escape and enlightenment. Affiliates of this viewpoint believed, in accordance with those ideas first articulated by Rousseau, that 'nature' and what they regarded as 'the natural' took precedence over the artificial and socially con-trived; therefore they urged that education should follow 'nature itself, in being immediate, original, free, spontaneous and simple … recognising the legitimacy of sensation and feeling' as routes to knowledge (Gutek, 1988: 74). Human experi-ence, the pre-eminence of the individual and their immersion in nature are of pri-mary importance to Rousseau, as he makes clear 'our real teachers are experience and feeling' (quoted in Boyd, 1956: 81).

Romanticism retains a significant grip on the consciousness of those who venture into the mountains. Contemporary writers share a great deal with those who shaped that tradition as the following extract taken from a popular text illustrates:

> *The view from the summit empowers you. But in a way, too, it obliterates you. Your sense of self is enhanced because of its extended capacity for sight, but it also comes under attack – is threatened with insignificance by the grand vistas of time and space which become apparent from mountain top…. This is the paradox of altitude: that it both exalts the individual mind and erases it. Those who travel to mountaintops are half in love with themselves, and half in love with oblivion. (Macfarlane, 2003: 156–157; see also McNeish, 2009)*

The Romantic reconfiguring of the experience of mountains included an emphasis on the immediacy of the encounter wherein the awareness of the world beyond the mountains fades to be 'replaced with a much more immediate hierarchy of needs: warmth, food, direction, shelter, survival' (Macfarlane, 2003: 204). Similarly the Romantic search for 'self-knowledge' or the finding of oneself via direct experi-ence has always been a strong current within climbing literature. For as Bonnington points out, climbing is an attempt:

> *to try to satisfy man's insatiable curiosity about himself and his own reactions to stress or danger, to find the boundaries of his physical capability [and] to push themselves to the limit to "find" themselves (Bonnington, 1982: 581–582).*

This in part emanates from the reality that often the individual is on his or her own in this setting and therefore reliant on their own abilities to get out of any adverse situations encountered. Or as Craig puts it, one may be obliged to galvanise oneself to 'apply these powers to ... unlock this mountain' (1999: 39). This focus on the individual means that for some the self is at times even more important than the mountains themselves. As Brown and Mitchell observed, for many climbing is 'not so much a discovery of new places as it is about the discovery of yourself and the forces that create you' (1991: 102). This heightened sense of engagement with the 'self' is not exclusive to those who climb for their own ends. Certainly many involved in delivering adventure and outdoor education programmes claim one does not really get to know the environment you are in so much as to know yourself better (see for example discussion by Hopkins and Putman, 2012).

Risk is an integral part of engaging with the outdoors, not least a mountain environment. Indeed climbers are often stimulated by the presence of risk and frequently seek out the 'dangerous'. Central also to the experience of climbing is the challenge it presents, and the pleasure, even euphoria, that comes from confronting a risky challenge and overcoming it. An integral component of this encounter is fear. But as Brown and Mitchell remind us, it is a multifaceted 'pursuit of fear', for it embodies amongst others a 'fear of the unknown, fear of failure, the fear of death ... fear of the huge voids and the darkness' (1991: 95). (see chapter 3) The examination of being afraid, the awareness of fear and the process of discovery of both one's reactions to it and attempts to control it are fundamental to the experience of climbing and central to the process of enabling others to engage in the activity. Redhead likens this to what he terms 'deep play' or 'putting yourself in a position to question who you are' (quoted in Jones, 1991: 42). Therefore it must be acknowledged that central to the climbing experience is a capacity to control those fears.

The analysis echoes Dewey's conceptualisation of experience as a 'transaction', an interplay of the individual with the world containing internal and objective conditions which combine in ways that both change the individual and the world, especially how we see the world and our place within it (Dewey, 1916: 59) (see chapter 3). The challenge also becomes a constant questioning of the 'reality' of fear, to not only control one's fears but to learn how to constantly question the 'reality' of those fears in order to be clear as to 'which are bogeys – projections of one's own phobias and not accurate images of the dangers existing in the real world' (Craig, 1999: 49) and which are well-founded and deserving of attention. This tension results in a need when climbing to manage both objective danger and internal fear. For example, when traversing a narrow ridge an individual will always be confronted with the possibility of falling. However, if they were just 20 feet off the ground they are unlikely to be concerned by the angle of the slope or the difficulty of the terrain, but if it is high they will be obliged to examine the degree to which a feeling of fear reflects 'reality'. Doing so will entail acknowledging the risks presented by traversing the ridge and facing the challenge of completing the journey.

For fear to be given its necessary 'free reign' within the climbing experience, there must be an element of the unknown or uncertainty. As Bonnington observed, 'Climbing is in its essence a plunge into the unknown' (1982: 581). Indeed many, like Joe Simpson (2003), are only really satisfied if the climb has had a serious and genuine risk of death associated with it. Given the centrality of fear within the activity, it is perhaps inevitable that a sense of conquest is not uncommonly linked to the experience of climbing. Seasoned climbers however often dismiss notions of conquering the mountains themselves, preferring to view it as relating to the individual self. Cleare helpfully explains this shift:

> Man may climb mountains but he can never 'conquer' them, the very word is out of context for how can man subdue a mountain? Mountains are merely beautiful or awesome and the only conquest by the climber is that of himself. (1980: 7)

One might question the relevance of the experience of extreme and adventurous climbers to that of the informal, outdoor and adventure educator operating in a mountain setting. However it needs to be acknowledged that those who are responsible for taking others into the mountains are almost certainly going to be climbers and mountaineers with considerable experience of the environment in which they are now operating as educators, that is, individuals 'schooled' in a tradition and who hold beliefs about the 'power of mountains' and the intrinsic value of challenging oneself and confronting one's fears in order to secure heightened self-knowledge (Hopkins and Putman, 1993). Yet it must be recognised that those participating in an informal educational programme with them may well have a different mindset and expectations so, as a result, outdoor and adventure educators should avoid superimposing their viewpoint *apropos* the mountains and the benefits of being in them unthinkingly upon such groups.

Understandably, informal educators will circumvent the taking of the kinds of extreme risks and challenges alluded to above, and sought out by Simpson and other hardened climbers. But the use of top-rope climbing and abseiling can, however risk-free the activity might theoretically be, often induce high levels of fear and anxiety for participants who have not previously encountered these challenges. Informal, adventure and outdoor educators do not turn to climbing and mountain-based activities to seek out an opportunity to terrify those they work with. However practitioners often implicitly embedded in the Romantic tradition of 'confronting oneself' and seeing 'fear [as] a true testing ground ... of ourselves' (Parker, 2001: 18) may well envisage experiencing, embracing and controlling such extreme emotions as valid educational pursuits. Where this is the case, great care must be taken to ensure although this 'testing' is embedded for them within the culture of the climbing community, it should not be unnecessarily imposed on those who undertake outdoor education programmes for alternative reasons or who are members of groups who are being inducted into what is for them an unfamiliar world of the outdoors.

Towards a post-Romantic conception of mountains

Central to the Romantic tradition is a belief in the importance of direct unmediated experiences. The natural environment, including mountains, are perceived as an entity wherein individuals can go forth and have experiences that will challenge preconceptions and foster learning. Of course experience is never as 'raw' as we routinely presume for it is invariably mediated by 'social and discursive conditions' (Roberts, 2012: 38). Nature and notions of the natural are constructed and contested, like other aspects of our lives. Therefore the belief prevalent since the late eighteenth century that the rural sphere including mountain environment is an idyll, and is a construction that needs to be dissected and interrogated. The way we perceive and experience mountains is in many ways fashioned for us and to a large extent a product of a particular culture, as Macfarlane explains:

> *In the ways we perceive and react to forms of landscape we are prompted, primed and reminded by those who have gone before ... although you might like to believe that our experience of altitude is utterly individual, each of us is in fact a complex and largely invisible dynasty of feelings we see through the eyes of innumerable anonymous predecessors. (2003: 116)*

It is essential that the informal, outdoor and adventure educator in any setting, not least a mountain environment so prefigured by Romanticism, reflects critically on the influences that shape our reading of these places and actively consider alternatives discourses.

It should be remembered that many, if not all, the mountain environments used by informal, outdoor and adventure educators are still places where others live and work. Population assessments made in 2000 reveal 10.2 per cent of the world population live above 4000 feet; 7.2 per cent between 4000 and 7000 feet; and 3 per cent above 7000 feet (Duncan, 2008). There are only nine summits above 4000 feet in the UK, all concentrated within two small areas of Scotland. Tourists, including mountaineers, came to these only recently. Long before their arrival shepherds and huntsmen would have crisscrossed their summits in order to keep themselves and their families fed. During the course of many centuries the animals owned by farmers have for good or ill altered the landscape, turning a wilderness into the 'rough pasture' we encounter today. The mountain environments of Britain so often portrayed as a 'natural' backdrop to outdoor educational experiences have, and continue to be, altered by human intervention. Deforestation in particular has fundamentally transformed the UK's upland areas. The Caledonian pine forests have long been reduced, like the oak forests of Dartmoor, to a tiny rump. The return of the original tree cover is made unlikely by the widespread grazing of sheep. Even English Nature it seems own sheep and lease out lands for grazing (Sylvan, 1995). Elsewhere this process is even more prescient. For example, any observant visitor to Nepal will encounter the chronic impact of deforestation there (Funnell and Parish, 2001). Consciousness of the flora and fauna of the environment helps encourage a sense of sharing the mountains with 'the original inhabitants' (Craig, 1999: 185) and challenges the notion that visitors, or even the humans, necessarily take precedence. Examples abound that educators can employ to show how humans have altered the mountain environment. High up in the Ogwen Valley, which is amongst the most popular destinations for mountain tourists in North Wales, can be found a small heather-clad island on Llyn Idwal. The island is tiny, perhaps six or seven feet long by three or four feet wide and close to the shore. The shoreline is easily accessible from the road by a well marked trail but the island far enough from it to deter the inquisitive. The island is unique in that the heather growing on it cannot be found on the surrounding slopes long stripped bare by the relentless grazing of sheep. Their absence has even enabled a small tree to grow on the island. This tiny isle provides a rare insight into what an alternative mountain environment might look like, yet understandably many pass by without even noticing it due to the grandeur of the surrounding landscape. Similarly Loch Maree in Wester Ross contains much larger islands than the one on Llyn Idwal, replete with a residues of the original Caledonian pine forest. Pointing out such areas of interest and opening up conversations about them can, for the educator, prompt valuable reflections about our place in the world and impact upon it.

Geology can similarly serve to reorient ourselves in a mountain environment and impart a counter discourse to Romanticism. Thomas Burnett in *The Sacred Theory of the Earth*, published in 1681 following a journey over the Simplon Pass, 'challenged the belief that the visible world had always looked the same' (Macfarlane, 2003: 31). Burnett is significant for being amongst the first writers to argue the earth is ever changing and not a fixed entity created by God. This proposition, which flew in the face of the existing religious orthodoxy, was in its way as revolutionary as that made later by Charles Darwin in his *On the Origin of the Species* (1859). By the 1830s texts of James Hutton (1785) and Charles Lyell (1830) had laid the basis for the modern science of geology, and gradually as geological knowledge grew apace, so estimates as to the age of the earth shifted from its pre-Burnett estimation of 4,000 years to many millions. By the twentieth century, with the formulation of the theory of plate tectonics, geology had become fundamental to our understanding of the formation and re-formation of mountains. Geology with its notions of 'deep time' therefore provides a challenge to notions of mountains being places of mystical permanence or Romantic idylls. Geologists might undermine naïve and Romantic notions, but we owe them a debt a gratitude for the substantive contribution they have made relating to the development of mountaineering, not least because many early expeditions, including Mallory's three Everest expeditions in the 1920s, were partly funded as a *quid pro quo* for members undertaking geological research (Davis, 2011).

Consideration of 'deep time' and the geology of mountains open up alternative experiences, for as Macfarlane points out, when 'going to the mountains … time, too, bends and alters. In the face of the geological timescales on display, your mind releases its normal grip on time' (2003: 204). For instance, the hills of Torridon are probably amongst the earth's oldest with the quartzite peaks, the rock of the original chain of mountains, around 60 million years old and the sandstone below them maybe in the region of 2,600 million years old (McNeish, 2009: 175). Such knowledge as one walks amongst these mountains invariably prompts a reconceptualisation of one's place in the world. They are, like other mountains, 'symbols of permanence' that have 'outlasted the dinosaurs and may outlast the mammals' (Craig, 1996: 8). Being in the mountains provides, therefore, unique educational opportunities to discuss and reflect upon notions of time, deep time, change and the transience of the human presence.

Mountain environments offer an almost infinite capacity for generating wonderful moments. Perhaps a valley reappearing below as a party descends through the mist, or the shifting light of the sun dancing on a hillside partly obscured by intermittent cloud. Or the wondrous delights of snow and ice, from the shifting orange and vermillion of the alpenglow, to the beauty of hoar frost or the patterns in snow drifts. Whatever the gift as Macfarlane reminds us:

> *The true blessings of mountains is not that they provide a challenge or conquest, something to be overcome and dominated. It is that they offer something gentler and infinitely more powerful: they make us ready to credit marvels. (2003: 275)*

Such aesthetic experiences can remain long in the memory, and thanks to the ever-changing interplay of weather and landscape, few visits to a mountain environment fail to offer a rewarding visual encounter for those prepared to look. For informal, adventure and outdoor educators, this interplay and the power of the mountains themselves feed both a sense of humility and a 'priceless capacity for wonder' (Macfarlane, 2003: 276), in part because no matter what one tries to achieve or undertake, be they a veteran, novice or casual visitor, within the context of the mountains individuals are obliged to accept an acknowledgement of their own limitations (Craig, 1999: 21). These hills and mountains can therefore provide a distinctive educational function; if one moves beyond the Romantic tradition and approaches from alternative perspectives, they offer an opportunity for individuals and groups to reorientate and reassess their position in the world. As Macfarlane explains:

> *Mountains seem to answer an increasing imaginative need in the West: [they] challenge our complacent conviction – so easy to lapse into – that the World has been made for humans by humans … one forgets that there are environments which do not respond to the flick of a switch or the twist of a dial and which have their own rhythms and orders of existence. Mountains correct this amnesia … they pose profound questions about our durability and the importance of our schemes. (2003: 274–275)*

Both the Romantic and the post-Romantic traditions have tended to focus on the individual. This has at times fostered an uncomfortable tendency towards individualism partially confirming the viewpoint of Bonnington that 'mountaineers are a strange bunch of individualists' (quoted in Shulman, 1992: v). This is potentially problematic for informal education with its emphasis on the importance of association, community development and dialogue (Jeffs and Smith, 2005). Before looking at some of these problems in more detail, it is important to clarify some of the benefits to be encountered within the individualised approach to the mountain experience. One benefit is that the stance on the individual need not require them to embrace an exclusive focus on the exaltation of personal accomplishments. Clearly climbing may serve as a means of achieving spiritual enlightenment, and there are many tangible benefits which can be applied directly to one's life in relation to physical and mental well-being. Brown, for one, suggests climbing encourages what he describes as 'the right amount of confidence' (1967: 17) by requiring awareness and acknowledgement of the risks involved as well as an inner belief in one's own abilities. Such belief precludes a blind leap into the dark which risks all, but embraces the calculated undertaking of actions underpinned by judgement and commitment, which enables one to both 'enjoy the risk and respect the danger' (Craig, 1999: 62).

Mountains can offer a setting where the self can best be illuminated, a venue for what Victorians termed 'character building' (Drasdo, 1998: 5). But they may equally provide experiences that create what Dewey terms 'transactions' (1916, 1938) (see Chapter 3 for a discussion of this), which can alter not merely our sense of ourselves but our sense of the world around us, and can therefore offer a valuable medium for both individual and collective development and discovery. But as we shall see mountains can provide much more besides.

Social aspects of mountains

There is another aspect to mountains which provides an alternative to Romanticism, with its emphasis on the individual self and character building, that deserves our attention. This is what Roberts (2012) refers to as the 'social' perspective, which views climbing and engaging with a mountain environment not as a quest for self-discovery, or enlightenment, but as a holistic educational experience. Brown and Mitchell help capture what this 'holistic experience' can embrace when they recall what drew them as youngsters into climbing; for them it was not a quest to unearth the meaning of life but an eclectic mix of the enjoyment to be gained from 'the hills, the pubs, the weekends, the travel, and perhaps most of all, the people' (1991: 164). At the heart of this social aspect is the value and importance of the group as opposed to the individual. By way of contrast, whilst early Romantic writers such as Thoreau and Muir spoke of walks, trips and journeys in ways that implied 'solitary endeavours', contemporary outdoor and adventure educators often talk of expeditions or treks in ways that imply a social interactive experience (Roberts, 2012: 64).

For the informal educator the 'social' aspect of taking people into the mountains is of paramount importance. The activities engaged in, whether a day's hill walk, a climb, an abseil or multiday backpacking journey will all involve to some degree or another an emphasis upon the fostering of positive relationships amongst those taking part. Indeed such activities are regularly selected by informal educators because they offer the proven potential to build genuine companionship via the need to work in collaboration one with another, a process Perrin neatly categorises as the creation of 'the comradeship of the bush, the expedition, the trek' (1983: 11). Despite the positive outcomes, this social aspect presents challenges of its own, not least because, as Brown and Mitchell point out, climbing will not of itself 'bring happiness or a release from the pressures of everyday life' (1991: 94). Indeed the mountainous environment may accentuate such 'pressures'. However, despite the inherent problems it can bestow, it nevertheless gifts the skilled informal educator exceptional opportunities to creatively work through, and with, the dynamics of group life, not least because for the group and individual alike surviving and flourishing in this landscape and completing a climb or arduous trek so often relies on the existence of trust between individuals and groups. Climbing makes what Cleare calls 'partners of the rope'; it is therefore something which has an exceptional capacity to foster 'deep trust' (1980: 9). This is because the dynamics of, for example, rock climbing, even in controlled environments, offers the experience of feeling as if you are putting your life in the hands of someone else.

One should be wary of the Romantic tradition 'trumping' the social aspects of climbing, not least when at the point of completing a climb, where it is often the personal satisfaction of surmounting the challenge rather than the reliance upon, and support of, other people that tends to dominate. For as Parker notes, 'Ego arises in many different guises, especially in the mountains' (2001: 22), a viewpoint echoed by Bonnington, who believes in climbing, at whatever level, we see the 'all-important factor, the ego, which rides in tandem with the inner urge of curiosity ... from a desire to win and also from a desire for approval' (1982: 587). A colleague once recounted how they had climbed with someone who preferred it when his second (the person following him up on the rope) struggled or even fell off, apparently because it made him feel much better given he managed to climb without difficulty. However, such excessive individualism, although not unknown, is the antithesis of the educational use of rock climbing which almost invariably helps to build trust, reliance and genuine camaraderie between participants.

The values of the informal educator will necessitate them challenging egotistic individualism and encouraging appreciation and respect for others regardless of their abilities. This is not an alien stance, for mountains and climbing can be enjoyed by all abilities and each presents unique opportunities to do so. As Stapleton explains:

> *The more I go hiking ... the more aware I become of the value of such activities....*
> *[T]here can be few activities that can bring a group of young people together in such*
> *a real and down-to-earth way ... [with] little bits of encouragement that quietly come*
> *out, sometimes from the most unlikely characters, in numerous small ways, and the*

rather wonderful atmosphere of shared hardship and sweat, where competing with one another is for once totally irrelevant. (1995: 191)

Finally the social perspective, like informal education, is linked to the promotion of democratic and associational modes of living that strengthen an awareness of the benefits of social relations based on mutuality. The mountain environment and the activities undertaken within that setting offer important and sometimes special ways of building and developing such interrelationships and interdependence. Therefore by fostering a sense of modesty and an understanding of 'deep time' it will, like the activities which take place within it, encourage fellowship, trust and shared dependency. By fostering respect for those values it can help embed democratic and humanistic principles within the lives of those who take part in outdoor and adventure education in the mountains.

Political aspects of mountains

Informal, outdoor and adventure educators operating in a mountain environment need to be aware of what Roberts refers to as the 'political current', that is, the 'sticky questions about power, equality, and justice that remained unresolved' (2012: 67). In stark contrast to a framing of the mountains as a rural idyll and an escape from the realities and tensions of modern life, Brown and Mitchell rightly argue that within the mountains there is 'no waiting rural Utopia, free from the pressures that drove us to seek it' for 'everywhere cultural entropy reproduces what we left behind' (1991: 90). The tensions, oppressions, contradictions and inequalities encountered in wider society will invariably intrude and must therefore be confronted by outdoor, adventure and informal educators. It is vital practitioners acknowledge these tensions and realities and seek ways to discuss and open up these issues to the participants. Venturing into the mountains is only partially a journey into the unfamiliar or unknown for 'our cultural baggage ... is weightless' and 'impossible to leave behind' (Macfarlane, 2003: 195). Therefore it is incumbent upon educators to ensure these inequalities and the negative 'cultural baggage' do not go unaddressed and that the experiences sought out in the mountain environment are liberating and educative, and do not even unwittingly serve to reinforce existing inequalities (Ord, 2009: 68).

As a consequence of what Brown and Mitchell (1991) refer to as a 'proletarian revolution' – signaled by the post-war emergence of a cohort of working-class climbers such as Bill Pescod, Joe Brown and Don Willans – the mountains are no longer the preserve of the upper class and public school educated. Despite this progress, class remains an issue that is still never far from the surface on the mountainside, which means there are numerous connections to wider political struggles that should be explored by educators operating in this setting, for example, the mass trespass of Kinder Scout (Hey, 2011), which played such a significant role in opening up the upland areas of the Peak District to the working class of nearby

Manchester and Sheffield. Similarly the empty sheilings of the Scottish Highlands offer stark reminders of the Highland Clearances and remain visible indicators of the presence of aristocratic and corporate landowners who retain control of large swathes of the Scottish countryside. Another example is the remote railway station at Currour deep in Rannoch Moor. This was not built as a staging post for those seeking to climb the remote Munros nearby, though this is what it has become, but as a concession to a landowner by the railway company who needed his permission to build that section of the West Highland Line. So the company constructed a station in the middle of Rannoch Moor for the seasonal use of the landowner's wealthy guests who travelled north to join his hunting party (McNeish, 2009). Informal educators operating in mountain environments should familiarise themselves with the social and political history of these localities and be equipped and ready to enter into discussions about past struggles and contemporary issues relating to their ownership, environmental well-being and responsible usage, as well as wider political struggles which still resonate.

There are other ways whereby the wider political context can be explored in this environment. Discussions regarding the role and place of women in the mountain landscape are crucial and will provide much 'grist to the mill' for the well-versed informal educator. As Brown and Mitchell point out:

> Women can never be the equal of men in climbing as long as they are subordinate in society as a whole. It is true that as the bonds which have tied women to men in the past have weakened, we have seen the emergence of good women climbers who climb independently of men. However only the socially blind would argue that the process is anything other than just the beginning. (1991: 34)

The mountains along with the rest of the outdoors were and largely remain 'gendered open spaces' (Humberstone, 2000: vii), places where women's involvement has been predominately characterised by restrictive stereotypes. Their experience may be varied and multilayered, but as Allin points out, 'physicality' in the outdoors is pre-eminently associated with masculinity; yet as her study confirms, 'women both resisted and conformed to gender stereotypes at different times' (2000: 65). This issue may be complex but it cannot be ignored. Informal, outdoor and adventure educators operating in this setting cannot be indifferent to the wider picture of political struggles which seek to achieve equality and social justice in a very unequal world (Thomson, 2007: 102). Issues relating to race, sexuality, disability, class and gender are important aspects of this context which should not be overlooked. If the educator fails to acknowledge and engage with the political aspect they become complicit with those inequalities and thereby aids and abets their continuation. The mountains may still be principally the domain of white, middle-class, heterosexual males, and although it is sometimes difficult to appreciate the complexities and subtleties of the ways in which this power operates, we must 'be prepared to engage our analytical skills and critical faculties making sense of these issues' in order address the harm they perpetuate (Thomson, 2007: 103). In doing so no small measure of 'humility' is needed. Irrespective of the difficulties, it remains important that informal, outdoor and adventure educators are prepared and equipped to engage in conversations with colleagues and the groups we work with about such issues.

Conclusion

It surely goes without saying that the outdoor and adventure educator working in the mountain environment is not solely or principally doing so for their own pleasure. Hopefully they will be enjoying their work, but in doing so are conscious that their role is that of an 'educator', not a 'consumer' exploiting participants as a means of getting paid to experience the mountains for their own selfish ends. However there is a danger outdoor and adventure educators working from the same centre or given locality for a lengthy period of time may grow jaded and overlook the capacity of that setting to inspire awe and wonder amongst those new to it. Likewise they can become blasé as to the challenge the mountains may present to those who have never encountered such an environment before. The educator must be appreciative of where those they are working with are 'coming from' and what their prior experiences, if any, of a mountain environment are, if they are to maximise their students' learning (Dewey, 1918; Jeffs and Smith, 2005).

It goes without saying that it is incumbent upon the educator to be clear about their role and purpose. As Brown and Mitchell point out, when they initially started working at an Outward Bound Centre, they had 'no clear idea regarding the use of mountains as a form of education' (1991: 94). A crucial element of both entering into this working environment and remaining fresh within it is to ceaselessly question the reasons for your presence, not merely at the outset but at all times, and also constantly ask yourself what it is you wish to teach others. With respect to both these tasks a useful point of departure for an appreciation of the role of any educator working in a mountainous setting must be, as John Redhead points out, an appreciation of the process not just the product:

> *If you climb to get to the top of a cliff or a mountain, you should very seriously question why you climb.... I think the path through is what is important, and the outcome is completely irrelevant. (quoted in Jones, 1991: 46)*

Therefore we must all be aware that climbing (as well as other related activities that take place in the mountains) should be more than 'the proving ground of character or a vehicle in the search of ultimate truths' (Brown and Mitchell, 1991: 181; reflecting the dominant Romantic tradition). They must be activities that engage with contemporary social, environmental and political currents. (Roberts, 2012)

References

Allin, L. (2000) 'Women into Outdoor Education: Negotiating a Male-gendered Space' in B. Humberstone (ed.) *Her Outdoors: risk, challenge and adventure in gendered open spaces,* London: Leisure Studies Association.

Barnes, P. and Sharp, B. (2004) *The RHP Companion to Outdoor Education,* Lyme Regis: RHP.

Beard, C. and Wilson, P. (2002) *Experiential Learning: A Handbook for Education, Training and Coaching,* London: Kogan Paul.

Bonnington, C. (1982) *Quest for Adventure,* London: Hodder and Stoughton.

Brown, J. (1967) *The Hard Years,* Harmondsworth: Penguin.

Brown, D. and Mitchell, I. (1991) *A View from the Ridge,* Glasgow: Earnest Press.

Boyd, W. (1956) *Emile for Today: The Emile of Jean Jaques Rousseau,* London: Heinemann.

Cleare, J. (1980) *Mountaineering,* Poole: Blandford Press.

Craig, D. (1999) *Native Stones: A Book about Climbing,* London: Pimlico.

Davis, W. (2011) *Into the Silence: The Great War, Mallory and the Conquest of Everest,* London: Bodley Head.

Defoe, D. (1748) *A Tour through the Whole Island of Great Britain,* London.

Dewey, J. (1916) *Democracy and Education,* Teddington: Echo Library.

Dewey, J. (1938) *Experience and Education,* New York: Touchstone, Simon and Schuster.

Drasdo, H. (1998) *Education and the Mountain Centres,* Cumbria: Association for Outdoor Learning.

Duncan, C. (2008) 'Mountain Population - 2000 Version', online. Available at: www.geo .umass.edu/faculty/duncan/iwonder/mtnpop.html (accessed 30 April 2013).

Funnell, D. and Parish, R. (2001) *Mountain Environments and Communities,* London: Routledge.

Gutek, G. L. (1988) *Philosophical and Ideological Perspectives on Education,* Boston: Allyn and Bacon.

Hey, D. (2011) 'Kinder Scout and the legend of the mass trespass', *Agricultural History Review,* Volume 59, no2 December 2011 pp. 199-216.

Hopkins, D. and Putman, D. (2012) *Personal Growth through Adventure,* Abingdon: Routledge.

Humberstone, B. (2000) (ed.) *Her Outdoors: risk, challenge and adventure in gendered open spaces,* London: Leisure Studies Association.

Hutton, J. (1785) *Theory of the Earth* 1959 ed. Weinheim: H. R. Engelmann.

Jeffs, T. and Smith, M. (2005) *Informal Education: Conversation, Learning and Democracy,* Nottingham: Heretics Press.

Johnson, S. (1785/1924) *A Journey to the Western Isles of Scotland,* London: Chapman & Dodd.

Jones, D. B. A. (1991) *The Power of Climbing,* Winster: The Vision Poster Company.

Lyell, C. (1830) *The Principles of Geology: An Attempt to Explain the Former Changes in the Earth's Surface by Reference to Causes Now in Operation,* 3 vols., London: John Murray.

Macfarlane, R. (2003) *Mountains of the Mind: A History of a Fascination,* London: Granta.

McNeish, C. (2009) *The Munros: Scotland's Highest Mountains,* Broxburn: Lomond Books.

O'Neill, J. and Walsh, M. (2000) 'Landscape conflicts: preferences, identities and rights', *Landscape Ecology* 15, pp. 281–289.

Ord, J. (2009) 'John Dewey and experiential learning: developing the theory of youth work', *Youth and Policy* 108, pp. 55–72.

Parker, G. (2001) *Aware of the Mountain: Mountaineering as Yoga,* Victoria: Trafford Publishing.

Perrin, J. (1983) *Mirrors in the Cliffs,* London: Diadem Books.

Roberts, J. W. (2012) *Beyond Learning by Doing: Theoretical Currents in Experiential Education,* London: Routledge.

Rousseau, J.J. (1761/1962) *La Nouvelle Heloise* (ed. J. H. McDowell), Philadelphia: Pennsylvania State University Press.

Ruskin, J. (1843) *Modern Painters,* vol. 1 London: Smith, Elder and Co.

Shulman, N. (1992) *Zen in the Art of Climbing Mountains,* Shaftsbury: Element.

Simpson, J. (2003) *The Beckoning Silence,* London: Vintage.

Stapleton, I. (1995) *Into the Mountains! Discovering the Victorian Alps: Stories of Timbertops and Mittagund,* National Library of Australia: E-Gee Printers.

Sylvan, R. (1995) 'Dominant British ideology: a critique of deep ecology (part one)', *Radical Philosophy* 40, pp. 2–12.

Thomson, N. (2007) *Power and Empowerment,* Lyme Regis: RHP.

Urry, J. (1998) *Contested Natures,* London: Sage.

8

WATER ENVIRONMENTS AND INFORMAL EDUCATION

Mark Leather

Veronica Strang, a cultural anthropologist, writing about the River Stour in Dorset captures in part the essence of the magical and picturesque qualities found in water:

> *The water flowing down the Stour is both natural and cultural, responsive to a changing spatial, temporal, physical and ideational landscape. Its material qualities – its composition, its transmutability, reflectivity, fluidity and transparency – are inherent, but also responsive to context. Similarly, people's biological, sensory and perceptual experiences of these qualities are universally human, and yet simultaneously a product of a particular individual and cultural moment in time and space. Their physical, emotional and imaginative interactions with water render it mesmeric, sacred, comforting, stimulating, beautiful and fearful. (2004: 245)*

Always bearing in mind the complexity conveyed in the above, the following chapter will seek to explore something of the background to water environments and their presence in outdoor education. However before proceeding it may be helpful to consider how we sense and then 'make sense' of the experiences water environments offer informal outdoor education. Over 50 per cent of the world's population live within 3 km of a body of freshwater and only 10 per cent reside further than 10 km distant (Kummu et al., 2011). The furthest point from the coastline in England and Wales is just 110 km and a third of us dwell within 10 km of the seashore (Environment Agency, 1999). Unsurprisingly Britain's cultural heritage has long been influenced by a history of living, trading and fighting on and near the sea. Although these links may have weakened, the coast remains important not merely to those living adjacent to it but to those who travel to the seashore to enjoy leisure activities. Finally the absolute necessity of water for our survival means it readily provides a fertile and stimulating environment for the informal outdoor educator.

Water environments occur in urban and rural locations alike and therefore we encounter venues for activities, formal and organised, spontaneous and informal, to be undertaken in, on, under and adjacent to the water in most parts of the UK. Some settings, swimming pools for instance, are specifically constructed for recreation and leisure activities, whilst others, such as reservoirs and canals, although built to serve other ends, are extensively used for enjoyment as well as educational purposes. The remainder comprises natural venues such as ponds, rivers, lakes, estuaries, rock pools, beaches and the open sea. Sport and recreational usage of all these is varied but amongst the most popular are fishing, boating, diving, swimming, kayaking, canoeing and sailing. Besides the more traditional water-based activities there are some recent additions to this list, such as rafting, canyoning, gorge walking, surfing, body-boarding, kitesurfing, stand-up paddleboarding, snorkelling, sub-aqua diving, coasteering, water skiing, wakeboarding and power-boating. In passing it should be noted that the educational value of some of the latter has been questioned. Cooper (2007), for one, argues there exists a distinction between outdoor activity and outdoor education centres suggesting the focus of the former, and therefore many of the pursuits they offer is upon fun, quick thrills and instant gratification. In other words they predominately operate in ways that reflect the ethos of a high energy and commercialised society. This contrasts, according to Cooper, with the stance of the latter, who in approach and tone systematically question those values by seeking to promote alternative viewpoints, notably by encouraging users to reflect on life experiences and the sustainability of existing lifestyles whilst showing respect for the natural world. However for some informal educators the distinctions raised by Cooper and others will be adjudged irrelevant. For them any shared experience, provided it generates opportunities for conversation and dialogue, will suffice as a point of contact.

Sensing the experience

Outdoor educational encounters seek to encourage those taking part to think, reflect, act and learn, often, it should be added, in complex and challenging settings. Dewey reminds us that experiences, including those offered by outdoor educators, can be both 'mis-educative' as well as educative – for 'everything depends upon the quality of experience which is had' (1938: 27). If that is the case we should perhaps ask, 'What is meant by a quality outdoor educative experience?' and 'How does this relate to informal education?" For some the starting point when seeking to assess 'quality' are the 'kite marks' and awards made by professional bodies in relation to a given activity. For example the Royal Yachting Association and the British Canoe Union respectively accredit programmes and they, like similar bodies, are in turn monitored by the Adventurous Activities Licensing Authority (AALA). These, and comparable agencies, tend to focus upon ensuring those providing the coaching are technically competent and that all accredited agencies are trustworthy and safe. Undeniably such bodies perform a valuable role, but inevitably their focus is predominately upon skill acquisition and the creation of safe learning environments rather than the fostering of opportunities for rich holistic educational encounters. Returning to Dewey we find that he divides experience into two components: (a) the immediate aspect of 'agreeableness or disagreeableness' and (b) the 'influence' that it has on future experiences independent of our aims and wishes, and whether we desire it or not. He argues that since every experience lives on into the future it is the 'effect' that matters the most. What counts is how experiences connect and achieve what Dewey terms 'continuity', which occurs 'if an experience arouses curiosity, strengthens initiative, and sets up desires and purposes that are sufficiently intense to carry a person over dead places in the future' (1938: 38). Continuity moves us towards further educative encounters that in turn promote 'growth' as part of the cumulative development of an individual. Therefore if we wish to evaluate whether our outdoor experiences are educational we might ask, as Dewey did,

> *Does this form of growth create conditions for further growth or does it set up conditions that shut off the person … from the occasions, stimuli and opportunities for continuing growth in new directions? What is the effect … upon the attitudes and habits which alone open up avenues for development in other lines? (Ibid.: 36)*

Being taken sailing for the first time by an experienced instructor, when this is done well, or 'agreeably', may be thrilling and exciting but equally it can potentially arouse a curiosity that generates a desire on the part of the novice to try steering the boat and controlling the sails. If, however, the novice is unduly alarmed, confused or feels out of control, then this excursion will probably be a 'disagreeable' one. So although sailing may essentially be a simple task, the variables and complexities can combine to make it a magical endeavour or an unpleasant encounter. There are copious skills to acquire in different settings and the continual interaction with nature, especially winds and tides, as well as with other crew members combine to provide many opportunities for growth and learning to open up what Dewey called those 'avenues for development'.

Making sense of these water-based experiences

Richard Shusterman, a pragmatist philosopher, in a number of works (2000, 2008, 2012) developed the concept of somaesthetics, which can be helpfully employed to enable us to better understand the impact of water on our informal learning experiences. In *Performing Live* (2000: 152–3) he describes how 'we cannot get away from the experienced body with its feelings and stimulations, its pleasures, pains and emotions … all affect is somatically grounded'. Shusterman, it should be noted, acknowledged the influence upon his thinking of William James, who a century earlier argued that 'a purely disembodied human emotion is a nonentity. If we try to abstract from any strong emotion all the feelings of its bodily symptoms, we find we have nothing left behind' (1983: 173–4). Certainly the emotions engendered when the body feels the splash of a breaking wave, the wobble of a kayak or the risk of capsizing serve as good examples of this. Merleau-Ponty (1962) argues that action frequently requires unthinking spontaneity, and therefore reflection can to some extent inhibit it. This contrasts with Dewey's belief that it is conscious, bodily self-awareness that is crucial to both better thought and action. Shusterman (2008) asks how we might combine critical body mindfulness with the demands for smooth spontaneity of action. Rather than some general self-awareness, he suggests body consciousness and mindfulness enrich the present experience and enhance the continuity of experience, thereby creating an appetite for further encounters and opportunities to extend the consciousness we have of our body. It was by endorsing the need for reflection whilst firmly embedding a role for mindfulness in relation to body consciousness that Shusterman was able to develop the concept of somaesthetics as a way of capturing this integrative process. There are two facets within this concept which are of particular relevance to informal outdoor education. Apart from representational or appearance issues relating to the body, Shusterman suggests self-improvement can occur as a consequence of a focus on the aesthetic quality of the body's experience, which he calls 'experiential', notably in the case of those offering the body 'a firm sense of contact and constancy from the earth so that it can afford that same sense of support to one's personality' (Shusterman, 2000: 162). The water environment is in this sense unique, especially if one is 'on' or 'in' it. The very notion of floating provides a particular aesthetic. No matter how large or small the craft, one's body invariably responds to the pulses of the moving water. This may be experienced as pleasant, as one paddles across a lake in an open canoe on a calm summer's day, or as the reverse when coping with a hefty swell aboard a 'tall ship' when the wind picks up. Being in the water is almost habitually different for it is not our 'natural' milieu given we are self-evidently land-based creatures; as such it provides a sense of being 'cut loose' or detached from what is safe and secure. When one takes to the water there is always a tacit notion of a need to return to the land, and this partially informs the uniqueness of the water environment. It also helps explain why some of those we work with, young and old, have a potent fear of being on or in water. In addition, Shusterman describes what he calls the 'performative' aspects of the body that can build strength, improve health or enhance skills. Whilst he uses weightlifting, martial arts and athletics as examples of this, one could equally, for instance, cite white-water rafting or sea kayaking as being performative. However one intellectually classifies somaesthetics, it is self-evidently about physically engaging in an activity 'by moving limbs, that is, in reflective, disciplined, demanding corporeal practice aimed at somatic self-improvement' (Shusterman, 2000: 143).

There are other ways in which somaesthetics can help us better understand the impact of water in relation to informal outdoor education, specifically in terms of (a) immediacy, (b) challenge and (c) environment. Immediacy allows us to continue in our development via a relationship with the here and now and the lived experience that offers a 'kinaesthetic sense of oneself' (Shusterman, 2000: 149).

Despite being somewhat elusive and difficult to describe, 'felt immediacy' is indispensable for the continuity of experience and for informal outdoor education if we wish to approach it in ways that turn the flow of experience into something that is not ponderous and laboured. For as Dewey explains, 'If each act has to be consciously searched for at the moment and intentionally performed, execution is painful and the product is clumsy and halting' (1998: 43), and the learning opportunities will as a consequence be impeded. Water has a unique ability to provide immediacy, for example the splash of cold water in one's face as one paddles a kayak out through the surf, or the all-embracing sensation as one jumps off the rocks into the sea whilst coasteering. Water has an inimitable facility to bring one's self into the present – the 'immediate' here and now. It also unfailingly demands our respect and attention. Even casually walking in water, paddling our feet at the beach, calls for greater care than walking on land and therefore it to a greater extent occupies the mind.

The second of the trio is challenge. If we pursue pragmatism's embracing of the experiential, whilst acknowledging the importance of felt immediacy, then this begins to undermine any assumption that our water-based activity focuses upon control of the body. Instead this idea is reversed to suggest there is a need to become bodily attentive, conscious and mindful in relation to our environmental transactions. For example, if you have been subjected to a powerful wave breaking over you and rolling you up the beach, then you will have been subjected to a lack of command over your body. The challenge posed here relates to a shift from ideas of *commanding* the body to the development of an ability to listen to it in everyday situations. This turning from the idea of command of the body in action to a heightened consciousness of it introduces the concept of bodily sensibility. Although listening to our bodies in the throes of a demanding activity may be difficult, and there must be limits to explicit consciousness during these experiences, nonetheless as the following example shows this can occur. Whilst white-water kayaking on the River Dart, the author took the wrong line approaching a rapid known as *The Washing Machine*. This resulted in me being held in the water, sucked out of my boat by the force of the river and turned around a number of times. In the moment I recall thinking, 'This is why it is called the washing machine!' Clearly I was not commanding my body, yet retained a body awareness and sense of the power of moving water.

Within the traditional view of outdoor education challenge and risk are fundamental concepts occupying a central role in relation to the design of experiences. Challenge may be considered as a complex blend of the physical, emotional and cognitive when, for example, someone is learning to stand up on a paddleboard. Outdoor education is concerned with the promotion of adventure as an alternative to normality and this is coupled with the belief that taking risks, and thus being challenged, is inherently positive. Outdoor education pedagogy can to a large extent be traced to Kurt Hahn and the 'character building' approach articulated by variations of Mortlock's (1984) model of adventure or Martin and Priest's (1986) Adventure Experience Paradigm. Typically within these there is an attempt to balance risk and the learner's level of competence with educational benefits. These assumptions have been critiqued in recent years (e.g. Brookes, 2003; Wattchow and Brown, 2011). Nonetheless, the concept of multifaceted challenge remains a useful model to help us understand the outdoor environment. Water is unique within that environment for it is an inherently unnatural place for us to be. The risk of drowning is ever present, the conduction of heat away from the body when immersed is far greater, not least in the UK, and the shock of cold water on the human body has an 'immediacy' for us to process. Yet at the same time there can be a wonderful alluring and at times mystical quality to water. There are a number of soamaesthetic stimuli: the smell of the sea, the feelings of near weightlessness that allows one to turn somersaults and enjoy the exhilaration of jumping in. Certainly when running canoeing sessions a frequently asked question is, 'Can we jump in now?'

Finally with regards to the environment the somatic self is always situated in the natural world. Therefore somatic awareness cannot really be of the self alone. Sailing in stormy waters or trudging along riverbanks in the pouring rain obliges one to 'sense' the ground or water beneath us, to be sensitive to the forces of nature acting on our bodies. An exciting aspect of this environment for informal educators is that the water milieu in which outdoor education occurs usually has a social dimension given we commonly participate as members of a group. Consequently these somatic experiences are shared ones which, as Shusterman notes, 'can help sensitise us to social relations so that we can improve them' (2012: 189). The aesthetics of experience are clear and for the acquisition of somaesthetics mindfulness they are significant. Forming these felt experiences into consciousness comes from crystallising them with reflection, something which is intrinsic to the act of expressing the essence of those experiences. Reflection can take many forms, such as writing, acting, painting, sculpting or talking, yet irrespective of the format, the worth of a skilled educator relates to their capacity to elicit learning from such shared experiences.

In summary, outdoor activity in, on or near water has great potential to urge the body into conscious awareness. For we can at different times feel wet or dry, warm or cold, challenged or discomforted, exhilarated or scared. Such activities also frequently demand we exert ourselves and therefore become tired, and therefore ever more conscious of our breathing and aching muscles. However, these activities also impart openings for individuals and groups to meditate and study the natural world, their shared experiences and the interplay of individuals within a given group setting. If being in a water environment encourages aesthetic awareness and consciousness of both the environment and body, it is the gradual development of sensibility and judgment via reflection, expression and sharing that helps to lift that experience so that it produces a lasting effect, to become in Deweyian terms something that is ultimately educationally worthwhile.

Openings for informal outdoor education

Having made the case for the creative power and sensate nature of water within an outdoor educational experience, along with an awareness of this body-consciousness

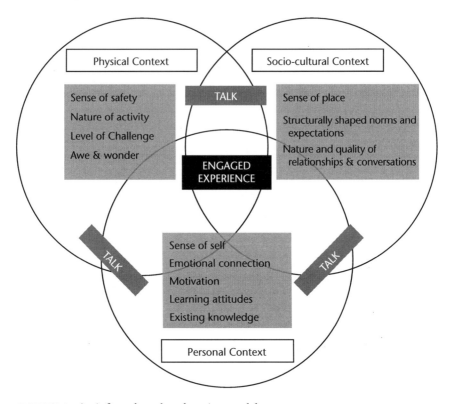

FIGURE 8.1 An informal outdoor learning model.

experience, I now proceed to offer a model of informal outdoor learning (see Figure 8.1), one that proposes that it is useful for us to conceptualise the multidimensional nature of a powerful and sensual water-based outdoor education experience and suggests how we can process this for the purposes of informal education.

The model above is partially based on similar models encountered in the work of Braund and Reiss (2004) in relation to science education beyond the classroom, Higgins et al.'s (1997) assessment of the range and scope of outdoor education and Adair's (1973) formulation of Action–Centred Leadership. In essence it is considered preferable to be able to operate in all three of the spheres described in the model and pay due attention to each in order to ensure balance and *engagement* within an informal outdoor learning experience. What connects the three contexts highlighted in this model is *talk* and the importance of learning through conversation and dialogue, both of which allow for deeper levels of engagement and the development of meanings constructed via the medium of dialogue. An example of how this can occur arose recently during the prelude to a coasteering session when the 'talk' moved towards a discussion regarding weather conditions and sea temperatures. The 'chat' and 'banter' with regards to weather forecasts, equipment and appropriate clothing for the given conditions led to a conversation that moved

forward to an analysis of the group's reactions concerning the activity, the composition of the group, individual reasons for attendance and the aspirations of both
individuals and the group in relation to the session. Translating such conversations
relating to a given activity into dialogue may, in this example and others, involve a
critical consideration of humanity's relationship with nature and engagement with
topics such as rising sea temperatures, changing weather patterns, sustainability and
ecology, just as it also demands that attention be paid to the other members of
group, to what one's companions share in common and to their discrete insights.

The significance of the spheres in the context of the model above may be critiqued from three perspectives. First a traditional outdoor activity instructor may
view the *physical context*, in this instance the water, as being more important. They
may be more concerned than the author with the sense of place (see for example
Gruenewald, 2003; Wattchow and Brown, 2011) or *the socio-cultural context*. Second
the psychologist may deem the sense of self in *the personal context* as being of greater
significance (for a fuller consideration of self-esteem and outdoor education see
Leather, 2013). Third the social theorist may consider that all learning is ultimately
social – following the work of amongst others Dewey (1938) and Vygotsky (1978)
– or indeed that all outdoor education experiences are merely social constructions (Berger and Luckman, 1967; Burr, 1995; Gergen, 1999). The author however
believes the relative size differences regarding each sphere are inevitable as those
undertaking informal education will themselves have emerged from differing backgrounds and training regimes. However the skilled facilitation of informal outdoor
education undertaken in a water environment requires an awareness of all three of
the different yet related areas. Therefore skilled *talk* connects the various aspects of
experience and allows for meaningful conversation and dialogue to develop. These
potential critiques are helpful in terms of focusing attention upon key elements, but
such shifts in emphasis will not ultimately negate the model.

Importance of *talk* for informal outdoor education

Talk incorporates many elements including chat, conversation and dialogue, all of
which may be stimulated as a consequence of the rich and powerful experiences
associated with water. So how does it relate, as a mode of intervention, to the functioning of the outdoor educator? 'Informal education' refers to learning that flows
from conversations, which can be in and around activities that are being promoted,
encouraged and facilitated by practitioners whose role it is to encourage people to
think about experiences and situations and

> *cultivate environments in which people are able to remember significant experiences,
> and to work at understanding them [as well as] create situations where people can
> experience new things. (Jeffs and Smith, 2005: 24)*

For example a group may attend their first surfing lesson. The activity and, possibly
for some, the location will be unfamiliar. Such a day will for the participants bring

to the surface a range of emotions – excitement, apprehension, frustration – as well as physical experiences – muscular tiredness, the taste of salt water, the smell of the ocean and the brightness of sun reflecting off the sea. Invariably it will be up to the leaders to give added meaning to these shared yet individually unique experiences via conversation and dialogue. The Informal Outdoor Education Model (Figure 8.1) seeks to highlight the different facets a facilitator may wish to give attention to via the medium of skilful *talk*.

Whilst it may be commonplace to view such pursuits as surfing as 'things', after all we often talk of things 'happening to us', it is essential to understand that experiences are not only 'had' but they are also 'known', or in other words they are thought about at some level. We interpret what is going on and this allows us to understand and make sense of these encounters; moreover with skilled facilitation we are less likely to avoid being controlled by or become victims of our experiences. In this way we become not just 'experiencers but also experimenters; creators as well as consumers' (Jeffs and Smith, 2005: 59). Knowing and comprehending this entails some level of personal thought involving a reflective process on the experience. Such personal reflection can be assisted through *talk* with a skilled informal educator. Dewey conceived of experience, and therefore the learning that results from it, as a 'transaction' between the individual and their environment. Therefore it is a consequence of their 'trying' and 'undergoing' that experience and, crucially, of making 'meaning' through experiential learning (Ord and Leather, 2011). In order to enlarge the experience it is important to attend to both aspects of it: the having and the knowing. Deliberative *talk*, chat, conversation and dialogue as highlighted in the model (Figure 8.1), connects the three spheres, and it is these that allow an informal outdoor educator to facilitate, frame and help articulate these experiences so that they may be better known or understood. For informal educators, part of their role is to facilitate these experiences by nurturing social settings wherein participants can look at them and attend to the feelings they invoked. Such facilitation involves interpretation of those experiences and feelings, for it is via deliberative talk that it can become possible to consider what can be learned by making connections and judgements. Part of the focus of informal educators is to enhance people's ability to appreciate and evaluate their experiences and learning. Through *talk*, formal and informal, informal educators can help others make sense of things by looking with them at their experiences. Jeffs and Smith (2005: 68) suggest:

> *We can explore what happened, examine feelings and work on making connections, forming judgements and fitting new understandings in with what they already know. More than that, we can work with people so that they can work out possible moves. In this way we may help them to engage with new situations; and to interact with others.*

The primary interest for informal outdoor educators should be the quality of the learning experience and how it may enhance, or inhibit, well-being rather than simply the thrill or somaesthetic experience of the activity. Water environments clearly provide exceptional and unique opportunities for the fostering of such learning and reflection. However the educator must be aware that some activities or modes of delivery will heighten the probability of exchanges taking place between members of the group and others will serve to dampen down that probability. For example open Canadian canoes are more likely to foster conversational interaction than kayaks. Activities requiring intense concentration and a greater degree of 'risk' are likely to restrict opportunities for the leader to engage in reflective conversations relating to the environment as opposed to more gentle and relaxed undertakings.

Centrality of relationships

The Informal Outdoor Learning Model (Figure 8.1) has at its heart relationships – both those engaged in through talk and those that connect the three related contexts (physical, socio-cultural and psychological) of an individual's experience. The model seeks to assist practitioners by providing three different lenses through which to view, focus and talk about the experiences occurring within a water environment. Jeffs and Smith describe how informal educators can build relationships through helping individuals to explore their feelings and interactions, arguing that 'by becoming part of the familiar and every day, educators can embed relationships, values and ways of being with each other that foster understanding, democracy and learning' (2005: 24–25). Similarly, the language of outdoor education embodies the concept of relationships specifically categorised into three distinct yet related areas: self, others and the environment. Helpfully the influential Dartington Conference (DES, 1975: 1–3) concluded the purpose of outdoor education was to heighten awareness and respect for:

- Self – through the meeting of challenge
- Others – through group experiences and the sharing of decisions
- The natural environment – through direct experience

Heightened awareness and respect with regards to these three areas correlates with the format of informal education. For deliberative *talk* can aid the development of each of these three 'areas'. The importance of relationships in outdoor education has long featured in much of the core literature, although this has tended to emphasise the need for learning to pay attention to relationships concerning people and natural resources. Equally this can be said with reference to adventure education and likewise environmental education, which concentrates on eco-systemic relationships.

Kalisch et al. (2011) investigated perceptions of the Outward Bound 'solo' experience. They found most of those who undertook it perceived it to have been beneficial. Participants expressed an appreciation for the opportunity it offered for them to step back from the pressures of everyday life and reflect on their personal relationships, lives and future goals. Frequently one finds that even more limited 'solo' experiences precipitate interesting and stimulating conversations. Whilst the Outward Bound solo lasts 24 hours, creating a brief gateway for quiet reflection, anything between five minutes to an hour can also nurture valuable educative encounters.

For instance a visit to a canal, river or beach will offer various activities, yet the opportunity to sit, watch and listen by the water will of itself for many prove to be a memorable and precious experience. Similarly a silent ten minutes or so with a canoeing group, instructing them to lay back in their boats, perhaps with their eyes closed, and enjoy what they notice as they drift slowly on the current invariably encourages contemplation.

The concept of utilising the outdoors to develop 'relationships with others' is discussed by Cramp (2008), who considers how best to build worthwhile relationships amongst young people 'beyond the classroom'. Whilst the value of informal education processes within a formal setting is not made explicit, it can be seen as implicit within the research Cramp discusses. In particular he looks at the importance of the child as a person and the development of pupil–teacher relationships on a residential trip by discussing the range of interactions which took place. He concludes that outdoor learning 'has actually become even more important to schools when teachers may have less time in the traditional school day to establish *effective, informal relationships* [author's emphasis] with pupils' (Cramp, 2008: 179). Relationships between people in the context of outdoor education can, it should be noted, at times be acrimonious and impede creative learning. This issue was explored by Zink and Dyson (2009), who discuss what can happen when a group 'just do not get it'. They suggest that a skilled educator can use such 'conflict' and resistance as a valuable staging post in relation to the group's development, for it can offer a useful starting point from which to investigate the relationships at work and the possibilities for living and learning in communities in the midst of the 'messiness of experience' and the 'messiness of the selves' that emerge through outdoor educational programmes.

A challenge for informal educators working experientially is to take into account how learning is recognised, a question of heightened importance with regards to settings where the learning is about relationships with others. As Zink and Dyson explain, 'It is at these sites and these moments where relationships themselves are always changing and evolving and [that] are central to the indeterminacy of living and learning' (2009: 173). For example, a canoe journey along a beautiful estuary on a windy day may see the dynamics within the group evolve and fluctuate due to many factors such as the prevailing consciousness of risk, the quality of the relationship members have with the instructor, and the content of the conversations taking place amongst participants themselves.

Martin (1999) offers a critical outdoor education perspective that provides informal outdoor educators with areas for dialogue with participants. He posits that the central issue in outdoor education is humanity's relationship with nature. Critical outdoor education accepts that there exist simultaneously local and global environmental crises, and that social and environmental injustices are both a cause and consequence of these. Working with people in the water environment offers limitless opportunities to enter into conversation and develop dialogue relating to these issues. Critical outdoor education interrogates open-air recreation beliefs and practices in terms of whether they maintain or resist the dominant view of the relationship between humans and the natural environment, namely the exploitation of the latter by the former. Examples are many and numerous. For example, interesting dialogues can often be had when canoeing the river estuaries of south Devon as a consequence of encountering the many disused kilns, mostly built during the time of the Napoleonic Wars to produce lime in order to improve wheat production, scattered along the edges of the tidal foreshore. These kilns can be used to kindle discussions relating to what is a 'natural' landscape, and wider questions linked to human exploitation of the environment. Other more profound examples of our impact on the environment are found in the many lakes and reservoirs, which to the outdoor educator may be seen merely as bases for canoeing or sailing, but which themselves exploit the natural environment and were constructed as sources of drinking water or power for hydroelectric schemes. Engaging with these settings provides ample opportunity for discussion concerning our place in the world and impact upon it. Conversations about the justifications for the original construction, as well as consideration of the destruction of natural habitats that was often required to bring them into existence, affords abundant openings for discussions about our place in the world and impact upon it. Conversations about the justifications for the original construction, as well as consideration of what alternatives might be placed on the agenda, gifts the informal educator with a myriad of conversational gambits. This is not restricted to historical perspectives, for around the world a number of hydro-electric power schemes are currently being proposed which, if implemented, would submerge some of the world's finest river valleys. Nor is such speculation limited to the impact on the natural world as such schemes very often displace native communities. How many people who kayak on the white-water course on the River Treweryn, which flows from Llyn Celyn, are aware of how contentious the flooding of the valley was in the 1950s when the Westminster government decided to drown the village of Capel Celyn in order to supply drinking water for Liverpool? Critical outdoor education must seek to foster such awareness much as it should endeavour to promote an improved relationship between humans and nature. Martin's research indicates that adventure could 'be a very powerful tool for "green" outdoor education', although he warns 'the deskilling of activities, changing the focus of a programme from skill acquisition to environmental issues, as a means of enhancing environmental outcomes may be counterproductive for some students' (2004: 20). A helpful example of how this might be achieved is to accompany a party to a remote cove following a winter storm, and then allow them to wander amongst the random flip-flops, fishing paraphernalia and assorted plastic debris mixed in with enchanting examples of weathered wood and smoothed pebbles.

Recently much outdoor education literature has provided educators with a range of stories with which to engage participants in *talk*. For example, the 'place-based' outdoor education authors Harrison (2010), Stewart (2008) and Wattchow and Brown (2011) encourage recognition of the interesting and powerful human stories that are part of the 'natural' environments in which we journey, play, recreate and educate outdoors. They discuss how the human–nature relationship has developed in ways that requires us to reconsider the conceptual basis of our relationship with 'the place', or the human story associated with these 'natural' environments. Wattchow and Brown (2011) have explored this for outdoor educators wherein identity and place-responsive education refers to a participatory and experiential phenomenon. Places change us as we change them. We need to grasp the reciprocal process of change and encourage others likewise to appreciate how our experience of a locale is always a combination of a specific physical setting, our previous embodied encounters and the cultural ideas that influence the interpretations we make when these coalesce. Dialogue here often concerns issues of social and environmental injustices. For example, when teaching sailing from a traditional and active south Devon fishing port, my students' relationship with sailing and the location can be heightened when they explore the social history of 'the place'. Reading and discussing the history of the old orphanage that subsequently became the sailing centre, visiting the local heritage museum and touring the lifeboat station all provide opportunities for critical conversations. The educational benefit of this approach is supported by Tuan (1977), who points out that eventually what was initially a strange and unknown space becomes a familiar place, where abstract space, lacking significance other than strangeness, becomes a concrete place filled with meaning. Tuan's perspective of experience is of value to us when he states that 'much is learned but not through formal instruction' (1977: 199–200).

Conclusion

This chapter has discussed the learning potential for informal outdoor education residing in physical, personal and socio-cultural contexts. These are complex opportunities not least in relation to water environments. Central to this process, as highlighted in the Informal Outdoor Learning Model (Figure 8.1), is the participants' 'engaged experience' facilitated by the talk that helps connect and make sense of the different aspects of these water-related experiences – both purposeful and accidental. The holistic and complex nature of these educational encounters may at times be difficult to link to clearly defined and prescribed outcomes, just as it can be difficult to identify exactly what has been learned. However the totality of these experiences, the richness and depth of informal outdoor education in a water environment, provides learning that is nevertheless meaningful.

Finally it is important to remind ourselves of the power and importance of the aesthetic experience, our embodied encounter with water and how informal education outdoors by, in and on the water is more than just a simplistic set of relationships between self, others and nature. Quay (2013) argues for the *balance* between aesthetic experience and reflective experience to be made more evenly balanced. He discusses how self, others and nature remain categories that outdoor educators can exploit reflectively to encompass the richness and diversity and wholeness of an outdoor experience. The same author states that 'to really understand the living experiences of the participants in our programmes we have to envision them, feel them, as aesthetic experiences' (2013: 154). This chapter has specifically considered the water environment as a special place for informal education. This may be difficult to prove or measure for informal educators given, as Tuan acknowledges, 'much of human experience is difficult to articulate … and we are far from finding devices that measure satisfactorily the quality of a feeling or aesthetic response' (1977: 200). This contribution commenced with a quotation taken from the work of Strang describing the feeling water engenders as 'mesmeric, sacred, comforting, stimulating, beautiful and fearful'. Such emotions offer informal outdoor educators' unparalleled opportunities to cultivate relationships and engage in reflective *talk*, to foster conversations and dialogue that people may recall as significant long after the event and which will help provide meaning to their lives.

References

Adair, J. (1973) *Action-Centred Leadership*, Maidenhead: McGraw Hill.

Berger, P.L. and Luckman, T. (1967) *The Social Construction of Reality: A Treatise in the Sociology of Knowledge*, New York: Doubleday.

Braund, M. and Reiss, M. (2004) *Learning to Teach Science outside the Classroom*, London: Routledge.

Brookes, A. (2003) 'A critique of neo-Hahnian outdoor education theory. Part two: "The fundamental attribution error" in contemporary outdoor education discourse', *Journal of Adventure Education and Outdoor Learning* 3(2), pp. 119–132.

Burr, V. (1995) *An Introduction to Social Constructionism*, London: Routledge.

Cooper, G. (2007) 'Activity centres or outdoor education centres?', *Horizons* 37, pp. 10–13.

Cramp, A. (2008) 'Knowing me knowing you: building valuable relationships outside the classroom', *Education 3–13: International Journal of Primary, Elementary and Early Years Education* 36(2), pp. 171–182

Department of Education and Science (1975) *Report on the Dartington Hall Conference*, Outdoor Education Study Conference N496.

Dewey, J. (1938) *Experience and Education*, New York: Touchstone.

Dewey, J. (1998) *The Essential Dewey, Volume 2: Ethics, Logic, Psychology* (L. A. Hickman and T. M. Alexander, eds.) Bloomington, IN: Indiana University Press.

Environment Agency (1999) *The State of the Environment in England and Wales: Coasts*, London: The Stationery Office.

Gergen, K. J. (1999) *An Invitation to Social Construction*, London: Sage.

Gruenewald, D.A. (2003) 'The best of both worlds: a critical pedagogy of place', *Educational Researcher* 32(4), pp. 3–12.

Harrison, S. (2010) '"Why are we here?" Taking "place" into account in UK outdoor environmental education', *Journal of Adventure Education and Outdoor Learning* 10(1), pp. 3–18.

Higgins, P., Loynes, C. and Crowther, N. (1997) *A Guide for Outdoor Educators in Scotland*, Penrith: Adventure Education.

James, W. (1983) *The Works of William James: Essays in Psychology*, Cambridge, MA: Harvard University Press.

Jeffs, T. and Smith, M.K. (2005) *Informal Education: Conversation, Democracy and Learning*, Nottingham: Educational Heretics Press.

Kalisch, K.R., Bobilya, A.J. and Daniel, B. (2011) 'The Outward Bound solo: a study of participants' perceptions', *Journal of Experiential Education* 34(1), pp. 1–18.

Kummu, M., de Moel, H., Ward, P. J. and Varis, O. (2011) *How close do we live to water? A global analysis of population distance to freshwater bodies*. PLoS ONE 6(6): e20578. doi:10.1371/journal.pone.0020578

Leather, M. (2013). '"It's good for their self-esteem": the substance beneath the label', *Journal of Adventure Education and Outdoor Learning* 13(2), pp. 158–179.

Martin, P. (1999) 'Critical outdoor education' in J. Miles and S. Priest (eds.) *Adventure Education*, State College, PA: Venture Publishing.

Martin, P. (2004) 'Outdoor adventure in promoting relationships with nature', *Australian Journal of Outdoor Education* 8(1), pp. 20–28.

Martin, P. and Priest, S. (1986) 'Understanding the adventure experience', *Journal of Adventure Education* 3, pp. 18–21.

Merleau-Ponty, M. (1962) *Phenomenology of Perception*, London: Routledge and Kegan Paul.

Mortlock, C. (1984) *The Adventure Alternative*, Cumbria: Cicerone Press.

Ord, J. and Leather, M. (2011) 'The substance beneath the labels of experiential learning: the importance of John Dewey for outdoor educators', *Australian Journal of Outdoor Education* 15(1), pp. 13–23.

Quay, J. (2013) 'More than relations between self, others and nature: outdoor education and aesthetic experience', *Journal of Adventure Education and Outdoor Learning* 13(2), pp. 142–157.

Shusterman, R. (2000) *Performing Live: Aesthetic Alternative for the Ends of Art*, Ithaca, NY: Cornell University Press.

Shusterman, R. (2008) *Body Consciousness: A Philosophy of Mindfulness and Somaesthetics*, Cambridge: Cambridge University Press.

Shusterman, R. (2012) *Thinking through the Body: Essays in Somaesthetics*, Cambridge: Cambridge University Press.

Stewart, A. (2008) 'Whose place, whose history? Outdoor environmental education pedagogy as "reading" the landscape', *Journal of Adventure Education and Outdoor Learning* 8(2), pp. 79–98.

Strang, V. (2004) *The Meaning of Water*, Oxford: Berg.

Tuan, Y. (1977) *Sense and Place: The Perspective of Experience*, Minneapolis: University of Minneapolis Press.

Vygotsky, L. (1978) *Mind in Society: The Development of Higher Mental Processes*, Cambridge, MA: Harvard University Press.

Wattchow, B. and Brown, M. (2011) *A Pedagogy of Place: Outdoor Education for a Changing World*, Monash: Monash University Publishing.

Zink, R. and Dyson, M. (2009) 'What does it mean when they don't seem to learn from experience?', *Cambridge Journal of Education* 39(2), pp. 163–174.

9

DEVELOPMENT IN THE OUTDOORS

An asset-based approach

Annette Coburn and David Wallace

The contributions to this volume illustrate how various perspectives on outdoor and experiential education resonate with informal education. Whilst the literature on all three is complex and multilayered, essentially all seek to educate people about themselves and others (Barnes and Sharp, 2004; Jeffs and Smith, 2005). Often engagement in the outdoors, even by ostensibly educational organisations, is for the purposes of fun and enjoyment, or sometimes as a reward for an 'achievement'; however if this engagement is to be designated as an educational encounter, learning must be intended and the outdoors utilised as a stimulus for development. Such development could be related as Barnes (2005: 3) suggests to self-reliance, self-discipline, judgment, responsibility and our relationships with others and the environment. Although it is multifaceted and multidimensional and operates across a variety of domains, including physical, cognitive and affective, this learning will be and is essentially 'experiential' as well as transformative (Dewey, 1938; Ord, 2009; Mezirow, 2009). Its developmental essence is in attempting to bring about change in the lives of those it seeks to educate. However it is important to think carefully about how we frame such development. As a consequence it is the authors' intention to commence by offering a critique of popular notions of development before moving on to argue that our thinking in relation to development in the context of the outdoors should be framed around 'assets'. In addition the chapter further suggests that principles of positive psychology may well provide a useful basis upon which to base such claims.

Dominance of the medical model

Traditionally concepts of development commence from a negative standpoint that seeks to identify what is wrong and then improve what is judged to be at fault. Such an approach adopts what Thomson refers to as a 'pseudo-medical model' underpinned by 'passivity and dependency – waiting for the expert to diagnose the problem and prescribe the solution' (2007: 54).This model has become increasingly prevalent in recent years, prompting Ecclestone and Hayes to suggest that what they refer to as the 'therapeutic turn' is fast becoming all-pervasive within education. This model, they argue, views young people as helpless, vulnerable victims who need to be assessed by expert practitioners, who then engage them in some form of therapeutic talk to resolve or ameliorate their condition.This therapeutic ethos they characterised as:

> . . . not merely the extension of therapeutic processes into new areas of life. Instead, it is the subtle ways in which the language, codes and symbols of therapy change our idea of what it means to be human. According to Nolan, notions of the Rogerian self, which is positive, optimistic and naturally disposed to improve, grow and learn, are giving way to a more negative, dysfunctional view of self and an acceptance of weakness caused by being only human. (2009: 135)

Plummer relates this 'therapeutic turn' directly to outdoor education, defining it as 'a purposeful intervention directed at the individual and their environment that aims to enhance health and impact functioning in many critical life domains' (2009: 291).

For almost a century advocates have highlighted outdoor education's developmental benefits, extolling its holistic virtues for mind, body and soul (Berry and Hodgson, 2011:72).This conviction, in part, was sustained by a pathologising discourse in which young people were conceived to be 'in decline'. Rather than fading over time this pathologising 'deficit' discourse has grown exponentially. For example, references to young people as 'not in education, employment or training' (NEET) or 'at-risk', 'disengaged' or 'on the margins' are not neutral but are derived from particular ideological representations of them as dysfunctional and in urgent need of expert intervention to return them to normality (Bradford, 2005). Moreover political and media constructions of young people are rarely if ever positive; as Griffin (1993) suggests they are almost invariably portrayed as 'deficient perpetrators' or as Jeffs and Smith put it as 'thugs, users or victims' (1999).

At the heart of this frequently medicalised approach to practice is the process of diagnosis which offers 'the essential foundation' and upon which subsequent interventions are based (Morrison, 2014: 238). It is this 'medicalisation of behavioural symptoms' which, as Cornwall and Walter (2006: 10) argue, consistently underpinned traditional psychodynamic therapies. Consequently outdoor education, which strives to be therapeutic or developmental, finds it difficult to avoid being consumed by the dominance of this discourse, which results in an emphasis upon the 'remedying' of those deemed 'troublesome'. Importantly, by focusing on individual problems, therapeutic education potentially overlooks the structural causes of deprivation and inequality that have created the social contexts within which such behaviours are constructed.This is unhelpful, which is why we, the authors, prefer the notion of developmental education, why we employ the terms 'development' and 'developmental education' instead of 'therapy' and 'therapeutic education'. This is because in our view the latter emphasises the need to 'fix damaged people', a stance which as you will have already gathered is not one we share. A number of writers such as Cornwall and Walter (2006) and Gesler (1992), whilst advocating a non-medicalised view of learning in the outdoors, nevertheless use the term therapeutic education. We do not do so because we view it to be unhelpful, but continue to refer to therapeutic education when discussing or citing their work.

A 'positive' approach to development

In contrast to the medicalised and therapeutic conceptualisations, we prefer to offer an alternative definition of the developmental value of outdoor education, one that moves beyond the remedial focus. Cornwall and Walter similarly argue we should be concerned with empowering participants through outdoor education, proposing we must:

> *Take into account the totality of a young person's experience, but it is more than just environmental or medical; it is holistic and encourages a young person to take responsibility for themselves, for their behaviour and their learning. Therapeutic education is the commitment to setting up an environment that enables and empowers a young person to do this. (2006: 12)*

The alternative approach taken towards development by positive psychology offers a significant challenge to both the traditional 'pathologising' perspective on development and the dominant contemporary deficit discourse. In doing so it better reflects the dynamics of the developmental changes that occur through informal and experiential education in the outdoors by both recognising and developing 'assets'.

This focus upon recognising and developing the 'assets' of participants relates closely to a central tenet and starting point of positive psychology, namely that we should concentrate on virtues rather than pathologies (Csikszentmihalyi and Csikszentmihalyi, 2006). Consequently positive psychology rejects the pathogenic paradigm which advocates of positive psychology contend focuses unnecessarily on remedial and reactive responses to health and well-being. Advocates of positive psychology have therefore constructed an alternative approach which is not rooted in negativity, an overemphasising of deficiencies and the need to identify and manage risk factors concerning the individual. Architects of positive psychology, including Antonovsky (1979, 1996), Csikszentmihalyi (1990, 2002), Fredrickson and Losada (2005) and Seligman (2003), have argued against such pathology and in favour of what has become known as an assets-based salutogenic approach. Antonovsky's principle research considered how some individuals suffer ill health whilst others, who are subjected to the same stressors, experience well-being. Health assets, he argued, serve to protect against negative health outcomes if activated and used purposefully and mindfully. A health asset is defined by Morgan and Ziglio as

> *any factor or resource which enhances the ability of individuals, communities and populations to maintain and sustain health and wellbeing and to help to reduce health inequalities. These assets can operate at the level of the individual, family or community and population as protective and promoting factors to buffer against life's stresses. (2007: 18)*

Such assets it is maintained offer significant leverage and underpin health and well-being. For example, Christian considers health from the position of 'emotional and social wellbeing rather than simply physical conditioning' suggesting that Antonovsky's work on salutogenesis helpfully highlights the importance of taking an asset-based approach with adventure education (2011: 174). Rotegard and colleagues (2010) similarly claim that assets can be utilised to overcome challenging situations. An asset-based approach eschews a focus on needs, deficits and problems and instead values the positive capacity of individuals and communities. It is in the mobilisation of both individual and collective knowledge, skills, capacities and networks that characteristics of well-being may be nurtured. Placed alongside theories of positive emotion, these facets appear to be critical to building capacities to be creative, to question and to explore (Fredrickson, 2001, 2006). Importantly this mode of working also helps foster and maintain the kind of positive frame of mind that encourages learning and human flourishing (Fredrickson, 2006; Kopela and Clarke, 2005). Positive psychology is underpinned by a belief that well-being is determined in part by the realisation of personal goals as a crucial means through which self-confidence and efficacy is improved (Ryan and Deci, 2000; Wesson et al., 2000).

Applying positive psychology

An application of positive psychology to informal, experiential and outdoor education does not merely require the providing of positive experiences. It entails the careful construction of experiences which will draw on the capabilities, knowledge and skills of participants, who will encounter those experiences within the context of meaningful action. This will enable participants to utilise and recognise existing assets, as well as develop hitherto unrealised abilities, attributes and characteristics. Within the context of outdoor and adventure education the involvement of participants in decision-making, and the devolving of responsibility for organising and undertaking activities, can in particular play a crucial role in underpinning the application of positive psychology.

This approach to development in the outdoors is consistent with the critique of outdoor educationalists' overemphasis on 'risk' and 'challenge' by Brown and Fraser (2009). Risk and challenge may play some part in the provision of appropriate experiences but they do not necessarily always provide for the development and realisation of assets and they are certainly not of themselves sufficient. What is required is a far more nuanced understanding of the interests, aspirations and capabilities of those experiencing the outdoor environment. In contrast to the overemphasis on risk and challenge, positive psychology places emphasis upon the importance of fostering feelings of 'contentment'. Izard describes this as a positive and useful emotion 'that broadens by creating the urge to savour current life circumstances and integrate these circumstances into new views of self and of the world' (quoted in Fredrickson, 2001: 220). Outdoor educators are well placed to enable participants to experience such emotions, for their working environment affords an inexhaustible array of opportunities for quiet contemplation, be it listening to the ebb and flow of the waves on the shore, watching the swaying of the grass as the wind moves gently across an open field, listening to birdsong on a forest walk or marveling at the changing hues of the trees as autumn approaches. Such experiences can help participants begin to reclaim a sense of self that is independent of their problems and proceed to reconstruct their lives by giving them awareness of what is good about a life removed from the endless focus on the apparent circumstances and actions required for a resolution.

Previous chapters within this text recount how water and mountain environments can, if competently exploited, impart abundant possibilities for educational experiences. These and other outdoor settings are also suitable for the application of the principles of positive psychology. For example, the various means of immersing oneself in or on the water provides a rich array of possibilities for constructing experiences which will enable a group or an individual to begin to realise their hidden assets – whether that is the thrill and sense of achievement acquired from standing up for the first time on a surf board, the exhilaration and sensation of freedom gained from wild swimming or canyoning or the experience of self-containment and competence supplied by exploring a region by open canoe or camping in a remote location. Similarly the mountain environment embodies the quintessential experience of climbing to the summit. The symbolic goal of simultaneously attaining both individual and collective ambition, or the individual skills and determination required to scale a rock face, can also be allied to the trust required in a partner holding the rope. Such experiences provide scope to bring out hidden strengths and unrealised potential. Gesler (1992) describes such environments as therapeutic landscapes, whilst Dunkley reminds us that these therapeutic places are nevertheless 'culturally constructed' and therefore will be 'experienced differently by different people, and not necessarily ideal or romantic landscapes' (2009: 88). Traditional journeying in outdoor education can also easily be located into this rationale, especially when this is done participatively, where those taking part decide, for example, on the terrain, location, means of travel, and the length and pace of the journey. Of course such decisions cannot be made in isolation from the expertise of the educator, but the skilled outdoor and adventure educator will 'work with' and 'alongside' a group in ways that enable them to acquire a measure of ownership and experience genuine, rather than sham involvement.

Whilst traditional outdoor education practices offer a good basis for developing an approach founded on positive psychology, in order to provide experiences which maximise the development of a participant's assets we may need to think differently about how we construct those experiences. Arguably for assets to be fully realised, they need to be part of a 'collective action' which has a genuine impact on the world such as, for example, the construction of a community garden by members of a drug rehabilitation programme (Coburn, 2008). This and similar projects have the added advantage of enabling individuals to reframe themselves as productive citizens who are giving something back to the community and equally importantly will help them be recognised in that light. By offering an opportunity for participants to work and grow together in creative ways leading to the achievement of commonly agreed goals, it can thereby simultaneously transform participants and a portion of the environment in which they reside. Participants are thereby enabled to reconceptualise their experience (Dewey, 1938), to view themselves no longer as 'wasters' but as assets, contributing towards the achievement of personal and group goals. Potentially this can offer participants a bigger boost in confidence than they previously experienced when taking drugs. Rather than taking a normalised pathological approach, based on problem diagnosis and treatment, such a developmental (some would say therapeutic) outdoor intervention offers a productive salutogenic alternative.

At the heart of outdoor education environments, as asset-based models for well-being, is the building of social connectedness (Morgan et al., 2010). In this context the role of the residential experience can be crucial. Sometimes described as a 'therapeutic camp' (Thurber and Malinowski, 1999; Kearns and Collins, 2000), they serve as 'hybrid spaces where social concerns emanating from the city are addressed in the "natural" spaces of the rural' (Paris, 2000: 90). Generally this process embodies an *escape* to the countryside and the creation of conditions wherein participants can take forward their own *journeys* and find opportunities to talk more openly about their feelings and emotions than would normally be the case.

Also central to an approach to the outdoors based on positive psychology is an emphasis on building resilience. Therefore the capacity to set goals and make choices, achieve objectives, and act within the context of challenging environments is explicitly linked with building capabilities and resilience. The role of contentment and other positive emotions such as joy and love, as well as the development of interests, are also suggested by Fredrickson (2001) as an additional means of broadening and building creativity, and establishing a repertoire of reserved coping strategies that are able to build resilience. Fredrickson also argues experiencing and sharing such positive emotions builds psychological resilience so that participants feel good about themselves at the present time, but it can also increase their chances of feeling good in the future.

Development as 'building capital'

Outdoor education has the potential to facilitate bonds between participants who are connected in both the activity and beyond, bonds that once forged can contribute towards the achievement of shared and mutually agreed outcomes (Kimball and Bacon, 1993). Such notions are redolent of Wenger's (1998) ideas regarding learning in communities of practice. In this sense, outdoor education has the potential to help the individual to move from 'legitimate peripheral participation', a term

Wenger employs to describe the participation of people 'on the edges' of a group or community of practice who stand aside in order to observe how things work whilst preparing themselves for entry, to more concerted forms of mutuality, where:

> *Mutual engagement involves not only our competence, but the competence of others. It draws on what we do and what we know, as well as on our ability to connect meaningfully to what we don't do and what we don't know – that is, to the contributions and knowledge of others. (Wenger, 1998. 76)*

Within outdoor education individual identity and collective enterprise is built from a communal experience of activity and becomes evident in a shared vocabulary, routines, rituals and symbols that begin to aid the formation of a community of practice. From this a mutual repertoire of experiences, ideas and stories may develop. This is evident in the way participants are able to identify with certain attributes of their outdoor experience and build narratives through conversation and dialogue (Jeffs and Smith, 2005), narratives that often come replete with tales of humour, trepidation, exhilaration or derring-do that draw upon experiences emanating from an activity.

Arguably, the development of mutuality and aspects of a community of practice amongst participants within outdoor and adventure education creates possibilities for the accumulation of bridging and other forms of capital (Taylor, 2011; Plummer, 2009; Putnam, 2000). Through an asset-based approach to development participant involvement in the outdoors can, individually and collectively, support a growth in social or organisational capital (Taylor, 2011: 187). Learning within this paradigm is active and participative and specifically intended to enable those engaged in it to acquire new knowledge that can be transferred to other aspects of their lives. Yet, it is also conversational and transformative (Mezirow, 2009), wherein the transformation of perspectives assists participants in using their experiences to make sense of the world and create new forms of knowledge (Sommerlad, 2003: 156). It has the potential therefore to develop capital across all three of Taylor's (2011: 187) classifications:

Human Capital	*Located in the development of individual skills and knowledge*
Social Capital	*Established through networks and norms that build relational capacity*
Organisational Capital	*Expressed through the habits of organising and the willingness to take action*

The first of the above, human capital, is perhaps the most straightforward, and many outdoor experiences focus on individual development from increasing levels of confidence to changing views of the world (Mezirow, 2009). The emphasis on mutuality and the development of communities of practice begins to explain how social capital can be built, for example in the forming of new relationships between group participants, the development of common goals and the promotion of a sense of solidarity with each other, all of which are indicative of how such experiences help young people to build social capital. Importantly, according to Bassani (2007), the acquisition of social capital mobilises other capitals, which, according to Weller (2006), can be used as compensation for a lack of financial capital.

Beames and Atencio offer a critique of social capital ideals that views their intentions as 'unabashedly idealistic', yet they do concede bridging capital is required as a tool to build richer and healthier communities and that outdoor education can 'foster social capital' (2008: 111). Their analysis strengthens the case for explicitly connecting reflection and learning in the outdoor experience to action in the locale and in the home community. In this sense not only must connections be made to the participants' lives 'back home' but action plans need to be devised to ensure concrete action results from the good intentions formulated during the time away. Arguably this also strengthens the claim made earlier that outdoor education should embrace outdoor community or social action projects as well as, or even instead of, being preoccupied with taking participants out of their community.

On reflection and transferability

It is of course incumbent upon the educator to enable participants to link experiences of the outdoor environment to their understanding of the social world 'at home'. So whilst the learning is situated in the outdoor educational setting, the educator often attempts to ensure it is transferable from the outdoors and fosters genuine development. Traditionally in outdoor education this process is ensured via the 'review of learning' (Greenaway, 2004), a process of reflection on the participant's experience. Sometimes called debriefing or processing, this is often undertaken after activities as part of the 'plan, do, review' cycle. However, we should be wary of simplistically separating experience and reflection; therefore outdoor and adventure educators need to maximise the opportunities for conversations as to what particular experiences mean to participants. There may well be advantages to pausing later in the day and reflecting with a group on their experiences, however there are also distinct benefits to be found in grasping the moment, and on a hike, at a lunch stop or at the top of a climb to find ways to encourage party members to reflect on the hidden strengths, resources and abilities required to undertake a given activity. It may well be more pertinent to encourage reflection in the moment, or as Schön (1983) describes it, 'in action', by seizing the opportunity and grasping the significance of events 'there and then' when emotions are heightened and 'realisations' possible.

The approach adopted towards facilitating reflection and the reviewing of experience is crucial if the benefits of positive psychology are to be reaped. The educator must build on the positive aspects of the experience, encouraging participants to recognise hidden strengths, abilities and characteristics. A parallel can be found in the approach described by Greenaway as 'appreciative facilitation' which 'pays attention to success and achievement ... providing positive feedback on what they did or said' (2004: 103). Building on the work of Torres (2001), Greenaway suggests that in relation to this approach it is important that the educator pays particular attention to what they are focusing on as it is that which 'gets expanded', rather than faults, that tends to result in their replication, whereas focusing on what worked is more likely to bring about positive change.

We are anxious at this point to qualify the claims being made about the outcomes emanating from the application of processes from positive psychology within the arena of outdoor education. The *feel good* factor may simply be that – and should not necessarily be portrayed as transformation in action. It must be acknowledged that at times it can be a fairly superficial or a shallow learning experience that remains isolated from deeper learning or from a process of translation into meaningful behavioural change upon return to the 'home' environment. It is a distinct challenge for informal and experiential educators in the outdoors to capture the potential in positive psychology for learning development and fostering change and to try to ensure it is transferable.

Dewey (1938) reminds us of the importance of grounding experiential education in the lives of those we are seeking to educate. Whilst in one sense outdoor education is significantly removed from the reality of everyday life, it is incumbent on the educators to make links if the experience is to be educational. It is no use merely forgetting about life back home as this is likely to provide a period of optimistic escapism and recidivism will in some extreme instances be likely to characterise the return 'home'. It is essential to try and continue the kinds of conversations that took place in the mountains, on the boat or around the campfire when back in the familiar surroundings. Research undertaken by Leberman and Martin illustrates this point. In situations where only a limited post-course review took place, a significant reduction in recall was found to have taken place compared to those settings where regular post-course reviews occurred. This led Leberman and Martin to conclude that 'post-course reflection enables participants to make meaning from their experiences with benefits of time and distance from the residential, thus enhancing transfer of learning' (2004: 173).

Person-centred approach

Developmental outdoor education must be contextualised in relation to the social lives of the participants. Those social lives with their rich and varied cultural and social components need to be acknowledged for they invariably shape the ways in which individuals and groups respond and react to the outdoor and adventure experiences they encounter. Thus, for example, what constitutes an 'informed choice' will be influenced by the ages, abilities, beliefs and backgrounds of individuals and parties. There are constraints on the kind of goals that can be set depending on the financial or other resources and the resilience of those involved. Consequently no simplistic assumptions can be made as to the capacity of participants to determine their own futures. Similarly the freedom to choose how much of an element within an outdoor or adventure education programme they will undertake may also be determined in part or whole by social class, race or gender and will be influenced by dominant ideologies that inform commonly held views. In response to such constraints Gibson (2011: 228) turned to choice philosophy and adapted this to the outdoor and adventure context, arguing the developmental use of the outdoors calls for the inclusion of three core values. These are that participants:

- Set their own goals on each element
- Must be able to choose how much of an element they will experience
- Must be able to make informed choices

This application of choice philosophy places participants at the centre of the processes through which transformative education can be developed in outdoor environments. There are strong links here with the participative practices of those informal educators and youth and community workers who advocate a form of practice that starts from where participants are, appreciates 'their' experience, and works with them to enlarge and expand that experience (Jeffs and Smith, 2005; Deer Richardson and Wolfe, 2001; Batsleer and Davies, 2010; Ord, 2016).

'Flow'

Before concluding the chapter we should perhaps consider the relevance of another important idea in positive psychology – the notion of 'flow'. Csikszentmihalyi coined the term 'flow' for what he describes as optimal experiences: 'when our body or mind is stretched to its limits in a voluntary effort to accomplish something difficult and wonderful' (2002: 3). Flow is hard to achieve and can be fleeting, but it happens when we are fully immersed in something that requires concentration, commitment and effort, and it is exhilarating and life enhancing. These optimal inner experiences have the potential to induce a sensation of harmony with one's environment as the sense of self and of the task merge in action. Carr suggests flow involves a 'total experiential absorption in an activity and temporary loss of awareness of other aspects of the self and one's life situation' (2011: 113). Fredrickson (2001) in a similar vein argues the best moments in our lives are not those when we are relaxed and passively contemplating the world but are those which approximate to 'flow' when we are wholly immersed in the completion of a task which requires effort to achieve and offers a great deal of satisfaction upon completion. There are therefore potentially significant benefits if outdoor educators are able to produce the conditions for similar feelings of 'flow' among their participants.

The outdoor environment offers many opportunities for optimal learning and for 'flow' experiences, for example the physical demands of hiking, perhaps in the mist, where the challenges of navigation are allied to the physical effort and absolute concentration is required due to the assumed presence of danger, or the sheer intensity of completing a first abseil with the need to galvanise every ounce of determination to overcome the fear associated with the chasm below and the requirement to rationalise the fear that the rope might not hold your weight. Flow experiences are of course not necessarily linked to an element of danger for equally they can arise from, for example, artistic endeavour such as when individuals during a hike become 'engrossed' in their desire to search out the perfect photograph. What unites them all is that 'flow' experiences contribute to individuals feeling a sense of harmony and discovering a new way of seeing the world and of their role in it (Coburn, 2011a, 2011b).

Ideas on optimal experience suggest that degrees of skill and challenge are relational and need to be balanced to invoke optimum psychological states (Csikszentmihalyi, 1990, 2009; Henry, 2006). To induce this optimal experience of 'flow' therefore requires a finely balanced set of conditions in which participants learn new or apply existing skills, set goals, receive feedback and take control within achievable limits (Delle Fave and Massimini, 2005). If these conditions are not just right then flow will not happen. If a learning task is set in which the learner has a low skill level and this combines with a high degree of challenge it will in all likelihood create fear and anxiety. At the other end of this continuum, when a participant has a high skill level and the task demands only a low degree of challenge it will nurture boredom and apathy. However, skills matched to an appropriate degree of challenge can be used to generate flow and bring feelings of serenity, involvement and satisfaction. At each stage, an appropriate level of challenge and skill requirement should aim to bring positive feelings of involvement and achievement.

Conclusion

Outdoor education offers opportunities for powerful learning at individual, group, social and community levels. Though deficit discourses are never totally absent in such contexts, the authors argue that a founding principle within informal and experiential education outdoors is the desire to bolster the positive capabilities of participants and the communities from which they are drawn. The starting point is about resourcing positivity, acknowledging and building assets among participants and facilitating a process through which assets are developed. Informal and experiential education therefore is not about the micromanagement of individually identified problems but should be more concerned with the holistic development of people based on the development of human capital, which in turn contributes to human flourishing (Csikszentmihalyi, 1990, 2002; Fredrickson, 2001). Such growth and development, however, takes place in a community context, and where possible, this communal and social context needs to be acknowledged in order to maximise the potential for growth. In relation to this we conclude by suggesting that outdoor educators should not overlook the benefits of fostering organisational capital through the development of community-based programmes which have the potential for genuine action, not just reflection.

References

Antonovsky, A. (1996) 'The salutogenic model as a theory to guide health promotion', *Health Promotion International* 11, pp. 11–18.

Barnes, P. (2005) *Resource Guide – Outdoor Education Higher Education Academy, Hospitality, Leisure and Tourism Network*. Available at: https://www.heacademy.ac.uk/system/files/outdoor_education.pdf

Barnes, P. and Sharp, B. (2004) *The RHP Companion Outdoor Education*, Lyme Regis: RHP.

Bassani, C. (2007) 'Five dimensions of social capital theory as they pertain to youth studies', *Journal of Youth Studies* 10, pp. 17–34.

Batsleer, J. and Davies, B. (2008) *What Is Youth Work?* Exeter: Learning Matters.

Beames, S. and Atencio, M. (2008) 'Building social capital through outdoor education', *Journal of Adventure Education and Outdoor Learning* 8(2), pp. 99–112.

Berry, M. and Hodgson, C. (2011) *Adventure Education – An Introduction*, Routledge: Abingdon.

Bonniface, M. (2000) 'Toward an understanding of flow and other positive experience phenomena within outdoor and adventurous activities', *Journal of Adventure Education and Outdoor Leadership* 1, pp. 55–68.

Bradford, S. (2005) 'Modernising youth work: from the universal to the particular and back again' in R. Harrison and C. Wise (eds.) *Working with Young People*, London: Sage Publications.

Brown, M. and Fraser, D (2009) Re-evaluating risk and exploring educational alternatives. *Journal of Adventure Education and Outdoor Learning* 9(1) 61–77.

Carr, A. (2011) *Positive Psychology: The Science of Happiness and Human Strengths* (2nd ed.), Sussex: Routledge.

Christian, E. (2011) 'Adventure education and disaffected youth' in M. Berry and C. Hodgson (eds.) *Adventure Education – An Introduction*, Abingdon: Routledge.

Coburn, A. (2008) *Measuring Holistic Well-Being: An Examination of the Characteristics and Conditions of Well-Being in Three Projects*, Hamilton: South Lanarkshire Community Planning Partnership.

Coburn, A. (2011a) *Waiting: Evaluation Report on Photo Voice at Fairbridge*, Glasgow: Fairbridge in Scotland.

Coburn, A. (2011b) 'Building social and cultural capital through learning about equality in youth work', *Journal of Youth Studies* 14(4), pp. 475–491.

Cornwall, J. and Walter, C. (2006) *Therapeutic Education: Working alongside troubled and troublesome children*, Didcot: Taylor and Francis.

Csikszentmihalyi, M. (1990) *Flow: The Psychology of Optimal Experience*, New York: Harper Perennial.

Csikzentmihalyi, M. (2002) *Flow: The Classic Work on How to Achieve Happiness*, London: Random House.

Csikszentmihalyi, M. and Csikszentmihalyi, I. (2006) *A Life Worth Living – Contributions to Positive Psychology*, New York: Oxford University Press.

Csikzentmihalyi, M. (2009) *Creativity: Flow and the psychology of discovery and invention,* London: Harper Collins.

Deer Richardson, L. and Wolfe, M. (2001) *Principles and Practice of Informal Education*, London: Routledge Falmer.

Delle Fave, A. and Massimini, A. (2005) 'The relevance of subjective well-being to social policies' in F. Huppert, N. Baylis and B. Keverne (eds.) *The Science of Well-Being*, Oxford: Oxford University Press.

Dewey, J. (1938) *Experience and Education*, New York: Macmillan.

Dunkley, C.M. (2009) 'A therapeutic taskscape: theorising place-making, discipline and care at a camp for troubled youth', *Health and Place* 15, pp. 88–96.

Ecclestone, K. and Hayes, D. (2009) *The Dangerous Rise of Therapeutic Education*, London: Routledge.

Fredrickson, B. L. (2001) 'The role of positive emotions in positive psychology: the broaden-and-build theory of positive emotions', *American Psychologist* 56(3), pp. 218–226.

Fredrickson, B. L. (2006). The broaden-and-build theory of positive emotions. In M. Csikszentmihalyi, & I. S. Csikszentmihalyi (Eds), *A life worth living: Contributions to positive psychology* (pp. 85–103). New York: Oxford University Press.

Fredrickson, B. and Losada, M. (2005) 'Positive affect and the complex dynamics of human flourishing', *American Psychologist* 60(7), pp. 678–686.

Gesler, W. (1992) 'Therapeutic landscapes: medical issues in light of the new cultural geography', *Social Science & Medicine* 34(7), pp. 735–746.

Gibson, J. (2011) 'Inclusive adventure education: better opportunities for people with disabilities' in M. Berry and C. Hodgson (eds.) *Adventure Education – An Introduction*, Abingdon: Routledge.

Greenaway, P. (2004) 'Facilitation and reviewing in outdoor education' in P. Barnes and B. Sharp (eds.) *The RHP Companion Outdoor Education*, Lyme Regis: RHP.

Griffin, C. (1993) *Representations of Youth: The Study of Youth and Adolescence in Britain and America*, Oxford: Polity Press.

Henry, J. (2006) 'Strategies for achieving well-being' in M. Csikszentmihalyi and I. Csikszentmihalyi (eds.) *A Life Worth Living – Contributions to Positive Psychology*, New York: Oxford University Press.

Jeffs, T. and Smith, M.K. (1999) 'The Problem of Youth for Youth Work', in *Youth & Policy*, Vol. 62, 45–66.

Jeffs, T. and Smith, M. K. (2005) *Informal Education, Conversation, Democracy and Learning* (3rd ed.), Ticknall: Education Now.

Kearns, R. and Collins, D. C. (2000) 'New Zealand's children's health camps: therapeutic landscapes met the contract state', *Social Science & Medicine* 51(7), pp. 1047–1059.

Kimball, R. O. and Bacon, S. B. (1993) 'The wilderness challenge model' in M. A. Glass (ed.) *Adventure Therapy: Therapeutic Applications of Adventure Programming*, Dubuque: Kendall/Hunt Publishing.

Kopela, J. and Clarke, A. (2005) *An Integrated Approach to Promoting Emotional Well-Being in the School Setting*, A Position Paper – National Programme Schools Group, Edinburgh: Health Promoting Schools Unit.

Leberman, S. and Martin, A. J. (2004) 'Enhancing transfer of learning through post-course reflection', *Journal of Adventure Education and Outdoor Learning* 4(2) pp. 173–184.

Mezirow, J. (2009) 'Transformative learning theory' in J. Mezirow and E. W. Taylor (eds.) *Transformative Learning in Practice*, San Francisco: Jossey Bass.

Morgan, A. and Ziglio, E. (2007) 'Revitalising the evidence base for public health: an assets model', *International Union for Health Promotion and Education* 14, pp. 17–22.

Morgan, A., Davies, M. and Ziglio, E. (2010) *Health Assets in a Global Context: Theory, Methods, Action*, London: Springer.

Morrison, J. (2014) *The First Interview* (4th ed.), New York: Guildford.

Ord, J. (2016) 2nd ed. Youth Work Process Product and Practice: Developing an Authentic Curriculum in Work with Young People, London: Routledge.

Ord, J. (2009) 'Experiential learning in youth work in the UK: a return to Dewey', *International Journal of Lifelong Education* 28(4), pp. 493–511.

Paris, L. (2000) 'A therapeutic taskscape: theorising place-making, discipline and care at a camp for troubled youth', *Health and Place* 15, pp. 88–96.

Plummer, R. (2009) *Outdoor Recreation – An Introduction*, Abingdon: Routledge.

Putnam, R. D. (2000) *Bowling Alone: The Collapse and Revival of American Community*, New York: Simon and Schuster.

Rotegard, A. K, Moore, S. M, Fagermoen, M. S. and Ruland C. M. (2010) 'Health assets: a concept analysis', *International Journal of Nursing Studies* 47, pp. 513–525.

Ryan, R. M. and Deci, E. (2000) 'Self-determination theory and the facilitation of intrinsic motivation, social development and well-being', *American Psychologist* 55(1), pp. 68–78.

Schön, D. (1983) *The Reflective Practitioner: How Professionals Think in Action*, London: Temple Smith.

Seligman, M. E. P. (2003) *Authentic Happiness*, London: Nicholas Brearley.

Sommerlad, E. (2003) 'Theory, research and practice – the problematic appearance of pedagogy in post-compulsory education', *Journal of Adult and Continuing Education* 8(2), pp. 147–164.

Taylor, M. (2011) *Public Policy in the Community* (2nd ed.), Hampshire: Palgrave Macmillan.

Thurber, C. and Malinowski, J. (1999) 'Environmental correlates of negative emotions in children', *Environment and Behaviour* 31(4), pp. 487–513.

Thomson, N. (2007) *Power and Empowerment*, Lyme Regis: RHP.

Torres, C. (2001) *The Appreciative Facilitator,* Maryville, TE: Mobile Team Challenge.

Weller, S. (2006) 'Skateboarding alone? Making social capital discourse relevant to teenagers' lives', *Journal of Youth Studies* 9(5), pp. 557–574.

Wenger, E. (1998) *Communities of Practice: Learning, Meaning, and Identity*, Cambridge: Cambridge University Press.

Wesson, K., Wiggins, N., Thompson, G. and Hartigan, S. (2000) *Sport and PE: A Complete Guide to Advanced Level Study*, London, Hodder and Stoughton.

10

'LIVING TOGETHER'

Making the most of the residential experience in outdoor and adventure education

Susan Cooper

Residential experiences come in many shapes and sizes. For instance they can range from an overnight stay to a month-long work camp, entail minimal travel or a long, tiring and expensive journey, and involve a single pre-existing group or individuals and parties coming together for the first time. The range of alternatives in terms of length, participants and focus is as these examples imply almost limitless. Venues on the other hand tend to be more predictable, ranging from camping under canvas to staying in hostels, hotels, halls of residence, specially adapted or purpose-built residential units, outdoor pursuit or activity centres and occasionally ships or boats. Given the variations it will therefore be helpful to ask at the outset the question 'What counts as a residential?' The definition employed within the context of this chapter will be that a residential involves a group or groups spending time away from their normal place of residence for a sufficient length of time to require them to stay overnight and live together as a transitional community. Inherent within the idea of a residential is that it includes shared experiences such as dining together and engaging in activities. Also a residential, as opposed to a holiday, a trip, a stay in a hotel or an outing, has an underlying educational purpose. Given this aim it should be organised with due attention paid to the learning needs of participants. Self-evidently the term 'residential' cannot axiomatically equate to an informal educational experience. Some, irrespective of who arranges them, will be more akin to a package holiday involving little or no meaningful educational content or intent, with the focus on leisure and fun. Others, although they have an educational purpose, are so poorly managed the opportunities for learning are lost.

Informal educators have long used the 'living together' experience to create opportunities for learning, especially in relation to fostering personal and social development. This is because concepts such as trust, respect, cooperation and communication can be 'played out for real' in a residential setting. Also given there is no easy escape from either a given activity or involvement with others such learning is both easier to manage and more likely to occur. To realise the full potential of a residential experience informal educators must possess a broad and eclectic knowledge relating to how individuals behave in groups (Douglas, 1993). They need to be able to make conscious, disciplined and systematic use of such knowledge in order to intervene wisely during the residential (Benson, 2010). Working in any residential setting, be it a care home, outdoor activity centre, adult education college or residential youth centre, can be arduous, exhausting and intellectually challenging. Certainly it requires reserves of energy, an eye for detail and acute observational skills, for many things can go wrong and opportunities for learning overlooked if the educator is not alert to what is taking place around them. Effective co-working is vital if the potential embodied in the experience is to be exploited as a learning resource. Also many avoidable difficulties arise because a staff team failed to coordinate interventions. What follows seeks to illustrate how residential experiences linked to outdoor and adventure education can promote informal education and personal growth. The focus will be on residential work with young people, although it should be noted that such work can involve adult and community groups.

Differing formats

Given the underlying purpose will influence many other aspects of the overall experience, it is essential before proceeding to consider some of the reasons workers have for organising a residential. First, let's look at the 'school residential', designed to create an opportunity for staff and students to spend time together outside of the classroom. This can focus on a particular subject or topic, for instance a visit to First World War battlefields where, although the party may have a residential base, much of the day is spent being ferried by bus from one site to another. Or an academic residential that may even be sedentary with the bulk of the time devoted to studying a subject or activity in a building or classroom. Some, such as geography or geological field trips, may, although subject orientated, entail substantial outdoor, even adventurous, activity. Alternatively a school residential may have a celebratory theme linked to the ending of an academic year or the 'passing out' of a cohort. During the 1980s outdoor and adventurous activities became part of the National Curriculum. Consequently the bulk of school students at some point in their career undertook a 'school residential' directly linked to an outdoor and adventure education programme. Following the 1993 Dearing Review, outdoor educational experiences became optional; thereafter these 'residentials', which incidentally were often more costly than the alternatives, became less and less a feature of school life. When these occur it is more usual for them to take place at 'approved commercial activity centres' licensed by the AALA (Adventure Activities Licensing Authority) which cater for large groups.

Second is the 'youth group residential'. Increasingly, as a consequence of the way in which funding is tied to 'outcomes', these tend to be issue based and involve a small 'selected' group. Youth group residentials occur in a range of settings and comprise peer groups and/or young people purposefully assembled for predetermined activities. The reasons why youth organisations, agencies and clubs organise residentials vary. For example a group might go away to be taught a specific array of skills such as how to be an effective management committee or better members of a 'youth council'. Or it might be designed to offer the youth worker the opportunity to deliver, in a controlled environment, a tailored programme relating to a specific issue or topic such as 'healthy eating' or 'sex and relationships'. Faith-based youth groups frequently employ the residential experience as a 'retreat', a period of intense reflection and attention to theological questions, or in some cases as a way of removing participants from their normal environment in order to encourage and foster conversion or the renewal of faith. It is not unusual for such residentials to include an outdoor element such as hikes and team-building exercises. With respect to these examples, although the venue might be an outdoor education centre, in some instances scant attention may be given to the activities offered. Finally the youth group or organisation may be running the residential in order to offer the young people a unique social or outdoor education experience, for example to enable urban youngsters to spend time in the countryside or vice versa.

Although far from comprehensive these examples offer some indication of what a residential experience can offer informal educators. Irrespective of the core purpose, if the group is overly large it may be difficult to generate the intimacy required for informal education to take place (Benson, 2010). Likewise if the focus is disproportionately upon a specific activity or a limited learning outcome then the paucity of free time and flexibility may result in little or no informal education occurring. Fundamentally for this type of learning to occur space has to be created for dialogue and conversation within a residential. Finally other variables need to be considered, for example: Is the group mixed or single gender? Is it a peer group or not? How long is the residential experience? All these, and other variables, will combine to shape the residential experience as well as the range of potential opportunities for learning. These aspects are explored in more detail later, although it should be noted that whilst practitioners may plan for all eventualities, it is impossible for them to anticipate all the challenges and learning opportunities a residential may present. For example a colleague was working with a group of young women with the intention of broadening and raising their aspirations. As part of this wider project a canal barge was hired for a residential. None of the young women had been afloat before and staff believed that getting them to drive the boat and operate the locks would stimulate reflection regarding preconceptions as to gender roles. The cramped living conditions on the boat, as predicted, helped erode boundaries and foster supportive relationships but what had not been anticipated was that the proximity and unfamiliar intimacy proved too great for one young woman. Eventually she stepped off the barge and 'walked away'. This obliged the staff to reflect on the impact new experiences can have on groups and individuals as well as the need to manage risk and the unforeseen outcomes that can arise from living with uncertainty. Similar occurrences are familiar to most of those who have substantial experience of managing residentials, but thankfully it is relatively unusual for someone to 'walk away'.

Why go away?

A key component of a residential is that it frequently requires participants, but not usually the organisers, to go somewhere new and unfamiliar. Understanding the significance of this 'distancing' is important in order to grasp its potential. Greenaway (2008: 348) sums this up when arguing that 'going outdoors …. *disrupts* routines, it *breaks* patterns, it *distorts* time, it *changes* roles, and it *creates* expectations' (emphasis in original). The capacity to disrupt, break, distort, change and create can be intensified when going outdoors is coupled with staying away. Roberts (2012) reminds us of the importance of taking into account the situational context, for the interactions one may have in a given place will often differ from those that take place elsewhere. Residentials can therefore be an effective way of helping people arrive at a better understanding of the intensity and complexity of group living. They often create a temporary society which can be viewed as a microcosm of a wider community. Hopkins and Putman suggest that within these 'experimental social laboratories … we can explore social relationships at a level of intensity unusual in other settings' (1993: 13). However it is essential to recognise these qua-si-transitional societies need to be connected to 'real life' if their 'learning potential' is to be realised. Two principle elements enable this to occur: first by encouraging reflection in and on action, during and, if possible, after a residential, and second by giving participants the opportunity to interrogate how that learning can be trans-ferred into their wider life. Smith argues

> *group work must be seen as an attempt to create a temporary additional group in the client's life, from which they obtain some satisfaction but whose effects are also felt in the other groups which are salient features within the client's life (1978: 47).*

Such an analysis applies equally to the residential experience. Therefore in order to maximise the learning potential of the residential experience it is necessary to enable those taking part to achieve a continuity wherein their past and present interact to help create their future (Roberts, 2012).

It may help to clarify matters if we briefly return at this juncture to the notion of 'disruption', particularly in terms of how the distancing made possible by a residen-tial experience can manufacture spaces for creative changes to take place. The act of 'going away' can promote a sense of personal freedom. Dewey (1938) suggests that increasing 'outward' freedom (freedom of movement) can further the advancement of freedom of thought and lift the horizons of the individual. However Dewey argues this is a means not an end, suggesting the educational problem is not simplis-tically solved by obtaining freedom of movement, for it leaves open what is done with this heightened autonomy. Personal freedom may be a prerequisite for indi-vidual development, however it needs to be understood as more than the absence of external constraint, for, as Button reminds us, 'the individual must also be free of internal compulsions or inadequacies' (1974: 23). Therefore in leaving our everyday context, albeit temporarily, we also, given the appropriate environment, acquire the opportunity to abandon elements of the 'self' we have created in that context. Individuals are shaped by their surrounding culture, played out in attitudes and behaviours, and unless these are confronted and transformed they may become the tacit values and norms of the group on a residential (Heron, 1989). The intimacy created by the residential experience can lead to participants confronting their normative attitudes and values, but equally it can result, for good or ill, in these being reinforced. In the light of this the duration of a given residential is something that should be carefully considered by the informal educator during the planning stages. Sufficient time is needed for participants to be enabled to depart from their customary behaviour, in order 'to take the opportunities to relate to others in a supportive atmosphere, to try new approaches and to experiment in new roles' (Button, 1974: 1); however a residential can also be 'overlong' for some, generating 'home-sickness' or possibly the emergence of unhelpful behaviourial traits within the party.

It seems appropriate at this juncture to stress that it is vital practitioners use the intimacy and intensity of a residential experience in a judicious and informed manner. It is important, for example, that workers take care to assist participants during times of vulnerability in ways that enable them to feel both supported on their journey and sufficiently safe to continue with that journey. This may be achieved through a combination of interventions focusing on individuals and the group. As Wilson points out, training plus an understanding of the theoretical underpinnings of group work are essential for

> *if enablers in groups are trained in techniques without understanding the principles and basic concepts from which they are drawn, such training raises the floodgates for streams of 'manipulation' rather than 'enabling' people to participate in decision-making processes which safeguard their rights of self-determination. (1956: 150)*

Despite certain inherent risks, the attractiveness of the residential experience for informal educators resides in the way in which the communal experience can offer a vehicle via which humanistic values can be taught and expressed (Preston-Shoot, 2007). Outdoor and adventure education residentials in particular offer opportunities for being together in a different setting, sharing challenges and successes, and reflecting on our place in the world and in relation to each other. Through skillful interventions all these opportunities, and others, can be transformed into deep learning moments for an individual and a group.

Three key elements

Three key elements are present within an outdoor adventure activity residential that more than any others make this mode of intervention a rich environment for informal educators. These are risk, relationships and power.

Risk

During a night walk through a remote forest, the party of young men became fearful, believing they would be attacked by someone lurking in the bushes. This dread, though irrational, was for them a reality. In exploring their concerns, the worker reflected on these in relation to walking in the city late at night, something they regularly did, and the greater risks of being assaulted there than in this forest. As the discussion of their current fears progressed it became apparent they were excessively concerned about statistically unlikely scenarios rather than other more potent risks to their well-being. Possibly they had acquired a range of misplaced fears (Girlguiding UK, 2009) as a consequence of the influence of over anxious adults, exaggerated media coverage and the inconsistent application of rules supposedly designed to keep young people safe. Irrespective of the cause, clearly there is a need for young people to learn to examine and make sound judgements concerning risks to their well-being. However, paradoxically, wider society seems to want to 'manage out' risk thereby denying young people the space and freedom to develop the life skills needed to manage it. Much is written about the way our risk-adverse culture is impacting on adventure education. Basically risk can be seen as operating along a continuum – moving from recreation (low risk) via adventure (optimum risk) through to misadventure (excessive risk) (Mortlock, 1984). The same continuum can be applied to the informal education process: too little and the session is recreational, too much and it can become a terrifying experience with negative, potentially long-term, harmful consequences for workers and participants. Self-evidently it is primarily the educator's responsibility to manufacture a group culture that 'allows' for 'safety and support, vulnerability and fallibility, honesty and risk-taking, liberty and autonomy' (Heron, 1989: 107), a culture that will create space for risk-taking and supports development, for example by enabling participants to voluntarily make themselves vulnerable to the reaction and control of others through self-disclosure (Benson, 2010). Practitioners must embrace 'uncertainty of outcome' in adventure and outdoor education (Allison and von Wald, 2010) as well as in informal education (Jeffs and Smith, 2005; Ord, 2016). For 'without uncertainty of outcome, without risk, we may have a very fine recreational experience, but we no longer have adventure [or education]' (Barton, 2007: 3).

Relationships

Residentials are often recalled as much for the relational aspect as for the adventurous activities (Rea, 2011). Frequently they can be the first time a young person and some adults spend time apart from their family and immediate community – an adventure in itself. Irrespective of whether that is the case, residentials open up opportunities for learning about self and others away from the constraints of 'normal life'. 'Going away' often disrupts routine and breaks patterns of behaviour (Greenaway, 1990, 2008), which means existing relationships are tested as the situation impacts on individuals' interactions with each other and the workers.

This gifts the informal educator a rich environment in which to enable participants to develop greater understanding of self and others, deepen their awareness of relationships and enhance their ability to express feelings and emotions.

With regards to relationships, a crucial distinction must be made between working with groups or using a group work approach. When working with groups, the key relationship is between members and the leader. Here the focus is on individual members and the centre of attention is not on group dynamics and process. Whereas when employing a group work methodology the informal educator will actively use group processes so that relationships between members become a focus, thereby enabling the group itself, within this relatively safe setting to become a dynamic agent of change. In this respect residentials provide an ideal mechanism for experimentation, by, for example, allowing those involved to acquire different roles and responsibilities, explore self and understand and value difference. The intensity of the residential that brings individuals together for days or even weeks can facilitate deep exploration, something that some may find disturbing or upsetting; therefore the informal educator must be prepared to manage both this intimacy and the fears that surround it if the learning potential of the occasion is to be fully realised. In these circumstances considerable expertise may be required not least because, as Benson argues, 'the first session is the moment of social and psychological birth of the group' (2010: 39) after which the group worker needs to focus on inclusion issues and the nurturing and developing of trust. As the residential progresses, staff must be alert to the possibilities for learning and readiness of the group to develop. This means they should be prepared to step aside from their central role in order to allow space for members to begin managing the maintenance functions for themselves. Facilitation of this shift in power from worker to members is something that will be explored at greater depth later.

Developing the required levels of trust and reciprocity within a group and between the group and the informal educator is crucial. Helpfully a residential can allow time for reflection during which a sense of mutuality can be fostered (Allison and von Wald, 2010). Sharing narratives of pre-residential life and stories of current events often stimulates the development of self via such exposure. Self-evidently this process demands careful and adroit management if the experience is to be beneficial for all parties. Generally a formalised process of daily reflection, which includes analysis of the spontaneous and ad-hoc moments of what has taken place during the day, works well for it helps develop a culture of openness, reciprocity and the valuing of self and others. Within such sessions the informal educator's role is critical with regards to setting the tone and leading by example.

Power

Issues of power are central to group work (Doel and Sawdon, 1999). The residential experience is especially well suited for creating conditions wherein individuals can discover and realise their potential and value, both in the context of the current group and with regards to what they can take from it to help them secure heighten control over their lives in the future (Brown, 1994). This setting has the potential to offer exceptional openings for group and individual empowerment to take place. Normally this begins slowly, with the group taking small 'action steps', realising that all opinions count, developing plans, implementing these and reviewing progress in real time. Group members may need to be facilitated to become more capable of challenging each other, the group workers and societal issues. However, as Lee makes clear,

> *the empowering potentialities of groups are only realised by the worker's skills in defining empowerment as group purpose, challenging obstacles to the work and enhancing the group process that develops the group's power as a group. (1994: 209)*

Achieving this in whole or part requires conscious commitment by the informal educator to working in a way that is explicit to the group. The 'realness' of the setting provides, for many in attendance, a rare opportunity to reflect on their own behaviour and consider what changes they might make to help achieve the future they seek. There may sometimes be a need to create a temporary additional group (Smith, 1978) in which this can take place in order to screen out the influence and impact of the cultural norms members may bring with them and that are embedded in their attitudes and behaviour (Heron, 1989). This will require the facilitators to consider from the outset which group norms they wish to promote and which they may wish to demote, for example competitive or cooperative behaviour, or authoritarian or democratic decision making. Rightly Doel asserts 'group workers have a responsibility to challenge dominant paradigms about what constitutes value in a group, and to help the group to articulate its own version of value' (2006: 145). This is not always a comfortable place for the informal educator to be but it is often unavoidable if the empowering potential of group work is to be achieved.

An informal educator's use of their power will always be a dynamic process, and the way they acknowledge, use and share their authority within a group should at all times be intentional as it is likely to be closely observed by the participants (Doel and Sawdon, 1999). As Brown notes, 'If the worker has not come to terms with her own power and authority, she is unlikely to be able to help the members discover and use theirs' (1994: 74). Here the literature on group development can be useful. Heron's (1989) guide to the basic options is particularly valuable, making clear, as it does, the correlation between group development and facilitator interventions. It is important to remember however that the style and role adopted must be appropriate to the group situation, the outcomes wanted and the members' capabilities (Douglas, 2000). Inevitably in group situations when people are interacting there will be predicaments as well as opportunities (Brown, 1994). These it should be noted will frequently be amplified by the close proximity existing within residential settings. Benson provides helpful advice, suggesting that

> *When deciding whether to intervene in a particular situation try as far as possible to understand the needs and motives of the people concerned and the position of the group so that you can focus on what is really happening. (2010: 87)*

Focusing in this way can, however, prove to be challenging for informal educators, particularly when they themselves may be tired after a long day of activities and are in need of sleep and privacy.

The key elements of risk, relationships and power persistently interact in residential settings linked to outdoor and adventure education. Therefore it is important to bear in mind that 'risk' does not merely relate to physical tasks and activities, for it exists with regards to the ways in which group dynamics and experiences impact upon the formation and development of self. After all, some participants may well be more 'frightened' of meeting strangers or sharing their thoughts within a group setting than kayaking out to sea or riding a horse. Just as the activities and residential experiences can extend the potential of group work to enable individuals to discover their worth and ability to creatively shape their future, so also the process can close down opportunities for learning due to a fear of intimacy that leads individuals to retreat into the self. Educators must also be aware that the oppressive nature of some groups can reinforce feelings of difference and support negative agency (Jeffrey, 2011). Whether the former or latter comes to pass will to a significant degree depend upon the expertise and alertness of the informal educator.

Creating climates for learning

This section explores some key ways in which employing a group work approach in residential settings can maximise the potential for informal learning. It will do so by directing the reader's attention to three key areas of intervention: (a) establishing the group, (b) meaning-making and (c) focusing on process.

Establishing the group

The objective here is to create a clear process and purpose for the group and an environment wherein risk, relationship and power can become central themes. If group members are to feel sufficiently safe to take risks, valued enough to form new relationships and sufficiently secure to allow them to experiment with power, it will be necessary for the informal educator to construct a trusting relationship between themselves and the group as well as between each group member. Brown warns that 'success' (however defined) 'is determined as much by what happens before the group comes into existence, as by what happens during the group's life' (1994: 35). This may seem fairly obvious, but when embarking on group work in residential settings it is often the case that the planning stages overwhelmingly focus on scheduling activities and preparing for the 'event' at the expense of the group work element. It is crucial that during the preparatory period all aspects are given due attention. This is required to ensure participants understand what will be expected from them including being made aware of the need on their part to commit equally to both the physical and group work elements. By talking openly about these two segments – the physical and group work – during the preliminary stages staff can begin to establish an environment in which both sources of learning are equally valued.

Developing trust and group cohesion is a key function of the pre-residential input, but it is not something that should be forced. Benson (2010) suggests it is important to be prepared to allow participants to be silent, passive or shy. Critically, he believes, informal educators should neither attempt to force or insist on trust but be prepared to seek out opportunities to lay the foundations upon which it can be built. It is the worker's responsibility to recognise and make visible the group work dimension, thereby preparing the groundwork for subsequent inputs designed to encourage the sharing of feelings and emotions. There are tasks that can help with this process, for example the formulation of a set of group norms, or the collective exploration of 'hopes and fears'. Whatever technique is adopted the purpose is to begin creating a group culture (Heron, 1989), one which may involve the onset of a process of 'unlearning' or 'unfreezing' (see Lewin, 1947) in readiness for change through a commitment to making the hidden visible. Lewin's Three Step Model for Change provides a useful reminder that before change can occur participants need to be able to accept it is necessary. Hence the process of 'unfreezing', which involves enabling participants to recognise the need and value of change for themselves, which can, for example, commence with a shared recognition and exploration within the group of habitual responses to certain situations. Once change has occurred there is a need to 'freeze' their new ways of being and establish a new place of stability.

For informal educators this stage is often a challenging one as there can be multiple tensions at play, for example the requirement to 'sell' the activity to recruit sufficient numbers to ensure a residential is viable versus the desire to place equal weight and value on the group work element; the responsibility to ensure a safe and secure environment versus the need to challenge underlying culture and values; and the wish to use power constructively and establish the worker's core role during initial stages versus the ambition to identify empowerment as a central aim. Tensions such as these (as well as numerous others) commonly arise and workers must find ways of being comfortable with them. An interesting example of how these tensions can be exploited in a positive fashion relates to menu planning for self-catering residentials. A by-product of this task lies in the fact it habitually fosters heated discussions involving all parties during the earliest stages. In the process of completing this task it usually becomes possible to introduce and cultivate the idea that the group experience will involve people doing things in different ways, eating unfamiliar foods and engaging in new tasks, all, or some, of which may be problematic. Usually there also arises at this juncture an opportunity for the informal educator to challenge, during these negotiations, dominant discourses of power, especially those relating to gender roles linked to the preparation of meals. During the process of drawing up the menu the informal educator may also find the space to introduce the topic of healthy eating. Inevitably at occasions such as this the informal educator's role in the decision-making process will be noted with respect to their use of power. These sites of tension can provide a baseline for the relationship between not only the group and informal educator but between participants. As a consequence, addressing, wherever possible, these tensions during the preliminary stages is an important part of the process of group formation and the setting of the parameters within which the residential will occur.

Meaning-making

Dewey (1938) and subsequently others, including Loynes (2000), have argued that experiential learning arises when people attach meaning and value to their experience (see also Chapter 3). Heron (1989) similarly suggests understanding is the core element to learning, a point he develops in the process of identifying three levels relating to an understanding of the (a) task, (b) group process and (c) learning process. To maximise the learning potential of a given residential experience attention must be paid to all three, in particular via review and reflection designed to encourage participants to make sense of their experience, individually and collectively. For it is these processes that provide 'the glue that creates meaning out of apparently disparate experiences' (Hopkins and Putman, 1993: 105).

While it may be straightforward to see how adventurous activities such as rock climbing or abseiling can foster stress, often a prerequisite for individual learning and development, it is perhaps less frequently considered how group processes can likewise create anxiety and fears. For instance outdoor and adventure experiences may require close proximity with strangers or talking in a group. But as Button reminds us, 'once a group has been stimulated emotionally and have begun to examine their own relationships, they will very soon be looking into themselves' (1974: 72), a process that many find stressful. So therefore it is essential that informal educators during residentials pay careful attention to what is happening in the group and the shifting dynamic of relationships between members. Meaning-making must encapsulate a holistic approach that draws on the full range of experiences, planned, spontaneous, physical, intellectual and emotional, that will transpire during a residential.

Although reflection and review can take various forms, it is important to recognise the reflective process can be a deliberate and conscious act utilising a range of associated skills relating to analysis, self-awareness, critical thinking and communication (Thompson and Thompson, 2008). Young people and many adults frequently need opportunities to acquire these skills, and informal educators should at all times consider how best to encourage their development. Freire (1972) believed the educational possibilities of activities were most effectively processed via the medium of a worker engaging in dialogue and conversation with others. However, conversation is a complex activity and therefore

> *Informal educators must be prepared to teach some of the protocols that underpin the art of conversation. This they may do through example and sensitively devising opportunities for individuals to learn how to listen and participate in dialogue and conversation. (Jeffs and Smith, 2005: 31)*

There are a number of ways this can be undertaken, but it is important that the methods adopted are developmental. For example the first evening of a residential might feature a card game similar to Bond's (1986) *Truth Game* that requires participants to pick a card and respond to the question it poses. The level of disclosure is intentionally low, and yet this type of exercise can generate a degree of stress and discomfort sufficient to initiate an exploration of the process of 'sharing stories'. Those who have used this approach tend to find groups regularly ask to repeat it on the following evening so they have an opportunity to answer different questions. The process needs to be sensitively facilitated as the valuing of appropriate behaviours and the encouragement of a climate of trust and support will serve to bond the group together. On the following evening the group might progress to a 'sentence completing' exercise that requires those present to draw on what they did earlier in the day to 'tell their story' in a way that encourages active listening and reflection. Subsequently the informal educators might use open questions, such as 'What shall we talk about this evening?' or 'Who has something they would like to say about today?'

These types of activities are designed to develop the ability and the desire of group members to engage in reflective learning conversations and dialogue. Each might last for between 60 and 90 minutes, and sit easily alongside a programme of outdoor and adventure education. There will also arise regular opportunities during a residential for the informal educator to react 'in the moment' so as to facilitate a reflective conversation. Over the course of a residential such opportunities will be identified and created by group members as well as by the informal educator. Hopefully, as a result of these engagements, reflective conversation will become a group norm. This developmental process can support a move towards individuals becoming critical co-investigators in dialogue with the worker (Freire, 1972) and thereby avoid the dominance of worker-led reflection during which the informal educator's meaning-making takes precedence. Within the context of a residential the role of the worker is in part that of facilitator tasked with enabling group members to make their own meaning, understand their own learning processes and avoid unthinkingly adopting prescribed meanings. As Mumford succinctly explains, 'If we can provide individuals with a greater capacity to learn from the widest possible variety of opportunities, we are empowering that individual to be in greater command of his or her destiny' (1991: 31).

Focus on process

If we believe learning involves an active construction of meaning then we must accept that the process of doing so will often be as important as the end product. All educators have to some extent attend to process. Informal educators however must pay special attention to the ways in which they employ their personalities and behaviour to aid the learning of others (Jeffs and Smith, 2005). For example a 'group leader' must lead by example, which in this context requires them to display enthusiasm in relation to the activities and pay due attention to any instructions given by the instructors. Similarly if they are not prepared to join in and undertake their 'share' of the less pleasant tasks, such as preparing or cleaning up after a meal or activity, then they risk forfeiting the right to ask others to do so. In the context of residential and outdoor education settings the informal educator must at all times be aware of the interplay occurring between the learning process and the dynamics of the group. Previously it has been argued that the process of 'storytelling' can support individuals to develop their understanding of self and who they want to be. However for some this is a taxing process. Therefore informal educators must be prepared to offer support to individuals in the telling of their story in ways which others can hear. They must also create escape routes for any who find the process too difficult whilst simultaneously working to ensure that the 'collective' accepts that some amongst their peers may need to move at a different pace (Doel and Sawdon, 1999). There are interesting parallels here between the personal journey towards self and outdoor activity. For instance, with the climbing of a mountain a parallel need to pay due attention to pace and escape routes is required. As practitioners we need to remember that whilst we are working with and through a group, individuals within it will have variable needs, and unavoidably each will draw selectively from the same experiences. The informal educator must consider how they can utilise the group process to support the individual by 'building a system of mutual aid' (Shulman, 1984: 163). However, as Button points out, the responsibility for constructing that 'system' will reside pre-eminently with the informal educator for 'in a supportive group situation, an individual may be able to take from his[or her] peers enlightenment that he [or she] would reject from a parent or other adult in authority' (1974: 72).

Maintaining a focus on process means informal educators must at all times, whatever the setting, maintain a conscious awareness of their role and seek to be 'in tune' with the development of the group. Observation of group and individual behaviour enables the informal educator to better respond to the needs of the group as they arise. 'Making hidden thoughts, feelings and desires visible so as to facilitate interaction and activity is', according to Benson, 'one of the most important and frequent tasks you will be called on to perform in the group' (2010: 7). This process of 'making the hidden visible' requires expertise along with competent intervention if it is to achieve a positive outcome. Within a residential setting individuals can often be observed 'playing games' with each other to produce certain responses which reinforce and confirm their beliefs about themselves and peers. They can bring habitual responses to group encounters which 'trap them in vicious circles' (Preston-Shoot, 2007: 140). Such 'games' provide participants with a way of dealing with situations they find fearful or with difficult emotions. Therefore the facilitator will need to work on opening up possibilities to address these and other underlying issues. This will require careful handling and facilitation by the informal educator. Heron (1989) offers a helpful overview citing three modes of facilitation: (a) hierarchical, (b) co-operative and (c) autonomous. These are certainly not self-contained, Heron warns: different groups with divergent purposes will usually require their own blend of the three modes.

The expertise of the informal educator therefore, in part, resides in their ability to read a group and adopt the appropriate mode when it is apposite to do so. The first mode enables the informal educator to create a climate for learning and a means whereby they can influence the formation of group norms. The cooperative mode allows the group to take shared responsibility for their learning and behaviour. Given the short life-span of most outdoor and adventure residential experiences it is important informal educators do not feel pressured into attempting to adopt an autonomous mode of facilitation before the group is ready. This can, however, be a valuable educative experience. For example in the Duke of Edinburgh Award, an autonomous hiking and camping expedition can provide a rich and rewarding experience, not least because power and responsibility are to a large extent devolved to the group. Residentials with a substantial outdoor and adventure educational content are often fatiguing for a staff team. Sleep deprivation and the usual frustrations sometimes result in personnel being tempted to operate solely or predominately according to the hierarchical mode. Awareness of the range of interventions can support a more considered response. However it is always the case that 'in order to work more intensively with group experience, the leader must learn how to focus [observe what is happening] and contextualise [make sense of why it is happening] (Benson, 2010: 188).

An excellent example of how Heron's three key features can be interwoven occurred during a stay at a residential centre on the west coast of Scotland. A large upstairs room had been given over to a 'reflective space'. It was distinct from the other functional areas used for sleeping, cooking or relaxing, being minimally furnished with no chairs or tables that would give it a pre-ordained structure. Within it, however, were some objects such as flotsam and jetsam collected from the shoreline nearby. Amongst the first tasks given a new group was to construct a sculpture from the various objects selected by each of the participants, objects chosen specifically to symbolise or represent their involvement or purpose on the residential. In making the sculpture the process of forming the group began; it became a physical embodiment of both each individual and of the group itself. Individuals were encouraged to articulate to the group why they chose their particular object, thereby beginning the process of making explicit what being there meant to them. The sculpture was unique to each group and established the unfolding process of the week together. The space around the sculpture was then used both before and after each of the day's activities, thereby providing a powerful vehicle for reflecting on the experience of the residential.

Conclusion

Residentials can provide participants of all ages and backgrounds with an enjoyable and pleasurable experience, whilst offering the outdoor and adventure educator with a unique opportunity to enable those partaking a chance to 'explore' and review, with the support of educators and peers, their own life journey – past, present and future. The use of 'journeying' as a metaphor for personal and social development is an excellent one; the similarities between physical and emotional risk are clear as too is the notion of an ongoing, unfolding process. However to make this aspiration a reality, careful, thoughtful consideration of the holistic 'residential' experience is required. Achieving a balance between confrontation and support is critical. Initially the educator needs to create the right level of support to enable participants to take the 'leap' into the unknown. This will involve both getting them ready to move and to accept the level of instability that comes with change. The emotional preparation for this personal journey mirrors the physical preparation that one engages for the physical journey of 'going on residential'. During the time away group leaders will need to step back to allow the space for participants to find their own way, to confront themselves and each other, and to support and be supported by each other. The timing of this is critical; too soon and the group may be unduly fearful, too late and the optimum time for change to happen is missed. Again this process of 'stepping back' is mirrored in the outdoor activity and will include preparing the group or individuals sufficiently in order that they are able to shift from followers to explorers, make sound assessments of risk, and support, challenge and lead one another. Finally careful attention must be paid to the process of ending the residential. Here opportunities need to be created so that individual and group achievements, both physical and emotional, can be celebrated and participants can crystallise new ways of being and commit to new challenges ahead.

The settings for residential experiences are changing; there are now numerous commercial centres offering the fully formed 'package', and whilst this takes some of the burden of organising everything away from the leaders, it can also remove some of the intimacy that can be achieved through the group, including the leaders 'fending for themselves'. To a considerable degree the move towards packaged provision has flowed from the increasing health and safety legislation linked to outdoor activity and residential living. The sense of certainty that comes from booking a week in a licensed and fully staffed centre that provides the meals and even 'entertainment' is superficially attractive to group leaders. However such facilities often separate the adventurous activity from the adventurous exploration of self, with instructors focusing on the teaching of skills and facilitation of activities, leaving the group leaders to try to focus on personal and social development. This separation unfortunately often leads to a sidelining and lack of attention to the latter undermining the holistic notion of 'living together'. Thereby valuable learning opportunities are inevitably lost. Certainly stripping away the 'luxuries' or home comforts, such as access to television or computers, prepared meals and an endless supply of hot water, will disrupt everyday patterns and routines and create the space for change. 'Doing everyday things differently' so often provides the optimum learning environment and can create a special level of 'camaraderie' within the group and between the group and the group leaders. It is this that is so often the part of the experience that is recalled most enthusiastically by participants and which makes a residential experience a lasting memory.

References

Allison, P. and Von Wald, K. (2010) 'Exploring values and personal and social development: learning through expeditions', *Pastoral Care in Education* 28(3), pp. 219–233.

Barton, B. (2007) *Safety Risk and Adventure in Outdoor Activities*, London: Sage.

Benson, J. (2010) *Working More Creatively with Groups* (3rd ed.) London: Routledge.

Bond, T. (1986) *Games for Social and Life Skills*, New York: Nichols Publishing.

Brown, A. (1994) *Group Work* (3rd ed.) Hampshire: Ashgate.

Button, L. (1974) *Developmental Group Work with Adolescents*, London: Hodder and Stoughton.

Dearing, R. (1993) *The National Curriculum and Its Assessment: Final Report*, London: SCAA.

Dewey, J. (1938/1997) *Experience and Education*, New York: Touchstone.

Doel, M. (2006) *Using Group Work*, London: Routledge.

Doel, M. and Sawdon, C. (1999) *The Essential Group Worker*, London: Jessica Kingsley.

Douglas, T. (1993) *A Theory of Group Work Practice*, Hampshire: Macmillan.

Douglas, T. (2000) *Basic Group Work*, London: Routledge.

Freire, P. (1972) *Pedagogy of the Oppressed*, Harmondsworth: Penguin.

Girlguiding UK (2009) *Redefining Risk: Girls Shout Out*, London: Girlguiding UK.

Greenaway, R. (2008) 'A view into the future: the value of other ways of learning and development' in P. Becker and J. Schirp (eds.) *Other Ways of Learning*, Maiburg: EOE, pp. 347–367.

Greenaway, R. (1990) *More than Activities*, London: The Save the Children Fund.

Heron, J. (1989) *The Facilitator's Handbook*, London: Kogan Page.

Hopkins, D. and Putman, R. (1993) *Personal Growth through Adventure*, London: David Fulton Publishers.

Jeffrey, L. (2011) *Understanding Agency*, Bristol: The Policy Press.

Jeffs, T. and Smith, M. (2005) *Informal Education, Conversation, Democracy and Learning* (3rd ed.) Nottingham: Heretics Press.

Lee, J. A. B. (1994) *The Empowerment Approach to Social Work Practice*, New York: Columbia University Press.

Lewin, K. (1947) 'Frontiers in group dynamics: concept, method and reality in social science; social equilibria and social change', *Human Relations* 1(1), pp. 5–41.

Loynes, C. (2000) 'The value of life and living: after all, life is right in any case' in P. Barnes (ed.) *Values and Outdoor Learning*, Cumbria: AOL.

Mortlock, C. (1984) The Adventure Alternative, Cumbria: Cicerone Press.

Mumford, A. (1991) 'Individual and organisational learning: the pursuit of change', *Journal of Industrial and Commercial Training*, 23(6), pp. 24–31.

Ord, J. (2016) *Youth Work Process, Product and Practice*, 2nd Ed. London: Routledge

Preston-Shoot, M. (2007) *Effective Groupwork* (2nd ed.) Hampshire: Palgrave Macmillan.

Rea, T. (2011) 'Residential centres: desirable difference?' in S. Waite, (ed.) *Children Learning outside the Classroom*, London: Sage Publications, pp. 148–161.

Roberts, J. (2012) *Beyond Learning by Doing: Theoretical Currents in Experiential Education*, Oxford: Routledge.

Shulman, L. (1984) *The Skills of Helping Individuals and Groups* (2nd ed.) Illinois: Peacock.

Smith, P. (1978) 'Group work as a process of social influence' in N. McCaughan (ed.) *Group Work: Learning and Practice*, London: George Allen and Unwin, pp. 46–57.

Thompson, S. and Thompson, N. (2008) *The Critically Reflective Practitioner*, Basingstoke: Palgrave Macmillan.

Wilson, G. (1956) *The Practice of Social Group Work*, New York: National Association of Social Workers.

11

FOSTERING SUSTAINABILITY IN OUTDOOR AND INFORMAL EDUCATION

Sue Wayman

Origins of sustainability

A helpful starting point for those unfamiliar with the concepts of sustainability and sustainable development may be to offer an explanatory outline. Below is a key section taken from working definitions of these terms prepared by Drexhage and Murphy as guidance for those attending the first meeting of the United Nations' High Level Panel on Global Sustainability held in 2010. Their paper explains these terms as follows:

> *Sustainable development is a fluid concept and various definitions have emerged over the past two decades. Despite an ongoing debate on the actual meaning, a few common principles tend to be emphasized. The first is a commitment to equity and fairness, in that priority should be given to improving the conditions of the world's poorest and decisions should account for the rights of future generations. The second is a long-term view that emphasizes the precautionary principle, i.e., "where there are threats of serious or irreversible damage, lack of full scientific certainty shall not be used as a reason for postponing cost-effective measures to prevent environmental degradation" (Rio Declaration on Environment and Development, Principle 15). Third, sustainable development embodies integration, and understanding and acting on the complex interconnections that exist between the environment, economy, and society. This is not a balancing act or a playing of one issue off against the other, but recognizing the interdependent nature of these three pillars. (2010: 6)*

The twin concepts of sustainability and sustainable development grew out of an environmental movement, which in many respects began in earnest in the 1960s. However their roots go much, much deeper (Pisani, 2006). In particular the origins can be traced to the pioneering work of a number of environmentalists, ecologists, planners, economists, architects, physicists and others, many of whom secure a mention in other chapters within this book (Mebratu, 1998). Although the concepts emerged from many traditions which frequently disagreed regarding priorities and the future direction of travel, they do, according to Caradonna, who has written the only substantive history of 'sustainability', all share a common belief that 'humans must live harmoniously with the natural world if they – or we – hope to persist, adapt and thrive indefinitely on the Earth' (2014: 8). Aldo Leopold, who played a key role regarding the development of the science of ecology, was amongst that array of pioneers (Nash, 2014). Crucially, however, Leopold promoted what he referred to as an 'ecological conscience' which emphasised our 'true place in the biotic community' (1949: 210). Overall this movement was, and remains, like Leopold and other trailblazers, profoundly critical of 'modernity', suggesting that overcoming the root 'causes' or constructions of the environmental crisis will require a fundamental questioning of the values, beliefs and assumptions that underpin modern society (Baudrillard, 1987; Hajer, 1995; Dryzec, 1997). Heilbroner not atypically holds that the problems sustainability seeks to counter are rooted in the ideological and cultural assumptions underpinning capitalism and that these rationalise 'acquisitive behaviour' and 'commodity fetishism' along with an acceptance of a belief that 'what serves the individual, serves society' (1985: 107, 143). These assumptions, Heilbroner argues, encourage a 'departure from animism', a 'depersonalisation of the natural environment' and a reduction in our affinity with nature and the natural world. According to writers from this tradition, within the heart of 'modernity' is to be found a belief in human privilege, progress and technological innovation, one that contributes to a society complacent about ecological and social exploitation:

> *Emerging within this attitude of superiority and exploitation are very powerful beliefs that govern public, industrial and frequently personal decisions. Economism, progressivism, industrialism, consumerism and individualism serve to set the direction of human actions. (Coates and Leahy, 2006: 3)*

Within this paradigm the dominant criteria by which the non-human world is evaluated is utility – that is the extent it is of use to human endeavours. As Coates and Leahy conclude, such anthropocentrism – a viewpoint which places human beings at the centre of everything – has 'contributed to a short-sighted, exploitive and unsustainable criterion for progress' (2006: 3), one that as Clark notes has produced 'an expanding economy, in which more and more material goods are produced, consumed and discarded' (1989: 30). This is an outcome which has resulted in scant attention being paid to the environmental impact this obsession with productivity and consumerism produces over time at both a macro and micro level.

The growing environmental awareness that arose post-1960 led in 1972 to the convening of the first United Nations Conference on the Human Environment (Blewitt, 2004). This gathering considered a range of environmental problems, but notably pollution and climatic change, population growth and control, and deforestation. Shortly afterwards the United Nations Environment Programme (UNEP) was established to coordinate international environmental policy-making. UNEP policies were to be guided by the concept of 'eco development', which was articulated by the chair of the 1972 conference, Maurice Strong, and subsequently elaborated upon by Jeffrey Sachs. The latter summarised it as

> *a style of development that, in each ecoregion, calls for specific solutions to the particular problems of the region in the light of cultural as well as ecological data and long term as well as immediate needs. (Sachs cited in Eckersley, 1992: 186)*

In 1980 and later in 1982, Willy Brandt, the former West German Chancellor, in his capacity as the chair of two UN Independent Commissions on International Development, oversaw the publication of two influential reports devoted to the impact of the world economic system and the causes of global poverty. Both documents made explicit the linkages between economic development, global inequality and environmental problems. Each also stressed the interdependence of developed and less developed countries in terms of labour supply, natural resources and the resultant social and environmental problems. The Commission recommended ameliorating environmental degradation by the expansion of aid programmes, the implementation of national population policies and the protection of the global 'Commons'. However like the bulk of the then existing writing on this topic, the two Brandt reports perceived market forces to be overwhelmingly beneficial with regards to the promotion of global development.

In 1983, less than a year after the appearance of the second Brandt document, the UN World Commission on Environment and Development was set up to consider global inequality and environmental problems. This produced the *Brundtland Report – Our Common Future* (WCED, 1987). Crucially this report linked social and environmental issues, citing inequality between and within countries as the primary cause of problems relating to both under-development and the environment. But it went further in suggesting that only through changes in patterns of consumption in the developed countries and population policies in the less-developed countries, co-ordinated through the UN, could 'sustainable development' be achieved. The document contained a notable 'Call for Action' which still has resonance today:

> *In the middle of the 20th century, we saw our planet from space for the first time....*
> *From space, we see a small and fragile ball dominated not by human activity and edifice but by a pattern of clouds, oceans, greenery, and soils. Humanity's inability to fit its activities into that pattern is changing planetary systems, fundamentally. Many such changes are accompanied by life-threatening hazards. This new reality, from which there is no escape, must be recognized – and managed.... Humanity has the ability to make development sustainable to ensure that it meets the needs of the present without compromising the ability of future generations to meet their own needs. (WCED, 1987: 1)*

Brundtland highlighted three fundamental components of sustainable development and made key proposals regarding each, which combined to offer a 'triple bottom line' of sustainability that involved environmental as well as economic and social considerations (Eckersley, 1992).

Despite that 'Call to Action' subsequent progress has been slow, in part, one suspects, because sustainable development was not seen as being to a significant extent a local issue, but pre-eminently perceived as a global policy discourse (Blewitt, 2004; Wals, 2012). Therefore the discourses of modernity – of economic man, and of progress, industrialisation, consumerism and individualism – remained a fundamental, largely unchallenged, part of the Western mind-set (Wals and Blewitt, 2010). Mezirow suggests this mind-set operates as a 'conspiracy of the normal', where despite our sense that we are working to make life easier for ourselves, we 'become willing prisoners who lock their own cell doors behind them' (2000: 138). Cortese similarly puts forward the case that dominant assumptions have failed to facilitate a critical questioning of our relationships with nature, as a consequence of which the following illusions are still maintained:

- Humans are the dominant species and separate from the rest of nature.
- Resources are free and inexhaustible.
- Earth's ecosystems can assimilate all human impacts.
- Technology will solve most of society's problems.
- All human needs and wants can be met through material means.
- Individual success is independent of the health and well-being of communities, cultures, and the life support system. (2003: 18)

The resultant crisis of sustainability according to Peter Dickens comprises

> both a crisis of the ways in which modern capitalist societies combine with nature, and a crisis of understanding whereby citizens of those societies fail to understand their relations with nature. (cited in Huckle, 2004: 2; see also Orr, 1994, 2009)

Beyond environmentalism - understanding of sustainability

Although it is frequently acknowledged that sustainability (and sustainable development) are conceptually broader than environmentalism (Dryzek, 2005), it still needs to be recognised that the former remains a contested term. So much so that sustainable development, and by implication sustainability, was described within one leading text as suffering from 'lexical poverty' (Harré et al., 1999: 31); and similarly by Jickling as remarkable for its 'paucity of precision' (1992: 6). This uncertainty should not, however, axiomatically be perceived as problematic. Certainly it is not viewed as such by Kagawa and Selby, who recommend we 'build a culture of learning awash with uncertainty [which] provokes transformative yet precautionary commitment rather than paralysis' (2010: 243). Nor has it prevented others claiming that sustainability is best identified as a 'motivational idea'

(Dresner, 2008; Wals, 2012) possessing the capacity to capture important issues and inspire the imagination (Hopkins et al., 1996). Sterling even goes so far as to suggest sustainability helpfully offers a 'gateway to a different view of curriculum, of pedagogy, or change of organisational policy and particularly of ethos' (2004: 55). However before proceeding it may be helpful at this juncture to examine some of the complexities within these differing perspectives on sustainability. In an attempt to clarify sustainability, Jacobs identifies six core areas but notes that a consensus does not necessarily exist with regards to each of them. The six are:

1. An integration of economic development and environmental protection
2. An explicit concern about the impact of current activity on future generations
3. A commitment to reducing pollution and environmental degradation and to the more efficient use of resources
4. A commitment to equity, attempting to meet at least the basic needs of the poor of the present generation (as well as equity between generations)
5. A recognition that human well-being is constituted by more than just income generation and economic growth
6. A commitment to participation and the recognition that sustainable development requires the political involvement of all groups or 'stakeholders' in society (1999: 26-27)

One key difference between environmentalism and sustainability is that the latter recognises the social and economic dimensions of well-being as well as the ecological elements by arguing that these are all 'deeply interdependent' (Sterling, 2001: 32). However acknowledgement of the importance of the social and economic, as well as the environmental, inevitably adds additional complexity to the notion of sustainability. Hatzius (1996) sought to clarify matters and in doing so identified three main discourses that link notions of development and sustainability within contemporary policies, each of which, he argues, have a different weight. He refers to these as the perspectives of (a) *Sustainable Growth*, (b) *Sustainable Development* and (c) *Ecological Sustainability*. The first, according to Hatzius, primarily focuses on the economic dimension and tends to take an optimistic view of social and environmental issues. The least radical of the three perspectives, it is opposed to fundamental change and predominately remains rooted in anthropocentric assumptions and a belief that the continued development of the market economy will ultimately via innovation and the 'hidden hand of the market', driven by the lure of profit, successfully resolve our environmental problems. The second, *Sustainable Development*, Hatzius suggests, accentuates the social and consequently places greater importance upon factors such as global social justice, participation and empowerment. Overall it is a reformist approach seeking to address issues of sustainability via progressive political and social change. Finally in Hatzius' trio we encounter *Ecological Sustainability*; this differs from the others in that it fundamentally challenges anthropocentrism. Emphasising environmental equity and the protection of nature it places far less stress on economic sustainability than the other two and calls for more radical change. As such it presents a more thoroughgoing challenge to the industrial and economic status quo and to anthropocentrism (Dryzec, 1997; Selby, 2005). However, this approach by giving greater prominence to the centrality of the 'ecological' can for some appear potentially dogmatic and pessimistic. To overcome this McGrail offers an alternative interpretation of 'radical' sustainability which moves towards a more positive and optimistic 'possibility-centred orientation' (2011: 124). Sometimes identified as 'Bright Green' (Steffen, 2006), this perspective endeavours to move beyond the perceived negativity of the radical approach by advocating a dual focus on 'how imperilled the planet is at present' and 'how great the future could be' in an attempt to align the radical and reformist discourses. Here the focus is on systemic change rather than individual virtue as well as upon the need to shift discourses from 'eco-tragedy and apocalyptic stories to new ones with positive framings' that can fit within the framework of new cultural movements (McGrail, 2011: 124-5).

Informal education in, and for, sustainability

Educators operating in an outdoor or adventure setting are uniquely placed to educate on issues of sustainability. For most of those taking part in their programmes the setting offers an immediate contrast to the everyday worlds they have left behind. Here they encounter fresh challenges, new experiences and an environment that has the potential to stimulate their interest in fauna and flora, the physical world and the multiple layers of rural life. All these and other environmental factors provide the perfect starting point for educative processes that focus on sustainability issues. They also gift the educators countless openings for the promotion of conversations and dialogue relating to the issues and debates concerning sustainability and development. As Zahsner, who played a significant role in the founding of the American Wilderness Society, suggests, being in nature and the outdoors is a 'pilgrimage into our species past' and offers 'sanctuaries of reorientation [which] reduce life to the essentials of food and shelter' (cited in Nash, 2014: 255). Following on from this position one can see, for example, how camping presents educators with the opportunity to provide an experience of simplicity that is far removed from the complexities of modern living. Likewise backpacking trips or longer expeditions can present to participants the experience of self-sufficiency, thereby reminding them and us what our 'basic needs' actually are. Similarly moving over the land or water under our 'own steam', whether on a day-hike, an afternoon's canoe trip or a longer expedition, demonstrates that motorised vehicles are not the sole method of getting from 'a to b' and that there are and always have been alternatives to mechanical means of transport.

Spending time in the outdoors opens up limitless opportunities to further one's appreciation of nature in all its forms and can help break down the all-pervading anthropocentric culture. Whether working alongside young people who have never left the city environment and may be bowled over by their first encounter with a cow or a sheep, or with individuals who already have had regular contact with rural life, entry into the outdoor environment alongside a well-prepared educator provides unparalleled opportunities to appreciate an interrelated ecological system and foster a deeper understanding of the importance of sustainability.

For outdoor and adventure educators the issue of **'impact'** is a potentially important transferable lesson in relation to sustainability, one more easily taught in the outdoors than elsewhere. Informal and outdoor educators can work to ensure the participant's grasp, via an outdoor or adventure education programme, of the need to minimise their own impact upon the environment. Outdoor educators can teach in the 'here and now' the importance of treating the environment with respect and integrate within their programmes material designed to change participants' behaviour in ways that foster sustainability. During activities the old adage 'take only photographs, leave only footprints' is unfailingly a sound starting point from which to commence a conversation regarding our attempts to manage impact. There are also embedded within outdoor and adventure education a multitude of opportunities to question the very notion of a 'natural' environment and thereby encourage an awareness of human influence on the ever-changing profile of the outdoors. This might flow from encouraging participants to realise that the group is climbing and abseiling in a redundant quarry or walking through a Forestry Commission plantation. Equally as we walk we may encounter places where a mono-culture has been created, or where domesticated animals have 'damaged' and reshaped a heath and downland, or deforested a hillside. Examples such as these, along with countless others, can help the educator communicate the seemingly all-pervading impact humans have had and continue to have on the 'natural' world in which outdoor and adventure education occurs. Also reflection on the topic helps the educator to build an appreciation of the need for participants to minimise their impact upon the environment and play a part in helping to sustain it into future.

Appreciation of the importance of minimising our own and others' impact can always be promoted by paying attention to the ways in which outdoor and adventure education is itself organised. If opportunities for learning about issues relating to sustainability are to be maximised, then the concept itself must be 'built into' whatever trips, outings or activities are engaged in and not merely 'bolted on'. It is a 'topic' that demands action, not merely reflection. Factors such as the environmental impact of transportation, the fuel sources used for heating and cooking, the food miles attached to the meals consumed and the degree to which efforts are made to locally source produce should all, along with similar questions, be viewed as valid topics of conversation and be utilised to furnish examples of how the informal education process can engage with the subject matter of sustainability in every outdoor and adventure education setting. Inevitably questions should and must be asked, for instance, about the environmental impact of such things as long-haul flights, and about why some groups are transported thousands of miles to partake in activities available down the road. Questions should be raised regarding for whose benefit are such jaunts organised; if it is for the staff who desire a free exotic holiday then we should not be deterred from demanding they justify such profligacy. Questions of this ilk can generate an unpleasant atmosphere in certain settings but that does not mean they should not be raised. Indeed if we are serious regarding the whole issue of sustainability these and similar questions should be constantly placed on the agenda, even if doing so makes colleagues and funders feel uncomfortable. Invariably dilemmas will emerge from such debates and discussions which will involve weighing up the educational benefits of undertaking an activity versus the impact it has upon the environment.

Being in the outdoors offers the educator an unparalleled opening to ground what can appear to be abstract concepts such as climate change or sustainability. Outdoor and adventure education offers a unique chance to correlate such issues to everyday life and connect them, and similar ideas, to the lived experiences of participants. Encountering the impact of extreme weather conditions – the aftermath of a coastal storm, damage from violent winds, or the effects of extreme drought or floods – will, for example, bestow an exceptional if unforeseen opportunity for an educator to enter into a dialogue about climate change. Even a walk on a hot summer's day, whilst not itself a consequence of global warming, presents one with an entrée to initiate a conversation on the global increase in temperatures. Similarly, a summertime walk might encourage a conversation that touches upon the disappearing summer ice of the high mountains of Europe, whilst a coast walk will present abundant openings for the educator to broach topics such as rising sea levels, receding cliffs, battered coastal defences or through observations of the flotsam and jetsam foster an appreciation of the damage caused to the ecosystem of the oceans by pollution.

Our relationships with nature

It is customary for informal educators to start from where the group they are working with is, both attitudinally and intellectually. To do so means acquiring, often rapidly, an appreciation of what is 'going on' for the participants as they enter into the world of outdoor and adventure education. It is crucial that the educator has an understanding, albeit partial, of the group's perspectives and sense of 'being' in the world. A notion of what is important for them, as well as an awareness of their value base and attitudes towards the setting they are being asked to engage with, is vital if the experience is to be appropriate and relevant. When the outdoor and adventure educator is seeking to foster learning with regards to sustainability and related topics it is essential they have 'discerned' the participants' relationship with and attitudes towards nature. That will always be a fundamental point of departure.

Helpfully Kellert (1993) suggests a number of perspectives which characterise the differing relationships humans have with nature. The first three might be termed antagonistic. These are (a) *utilitarian*, which views nature as a vast resource to be exploited; (b) *negativistic*, which associates the outdoors or nature with the individuals, previously negative experiences of it; and (c) *dominionistic*, a relationship characterised by a desire to master and control the natural world. The second three are more benign. These are (d) the *aesthetic*, wherein a preference exists for natural over human design; (e) the *ecologistic* or *scientific*, which is characterised by a motivation to systematically study the biophysical patterns, structures and functions of the natural world, and is associated with an appreciation of the complexity of natural processes, where any sense of satisfaction gained is quite detached from any utility value; and (f) the *symbolic* relationship, which is one exemplified by humans' use of natural symbols to communicate. Kellert illustrates this with reference to evidence that suggests approximately 90 per cent of the characters employed in children's fiction are animal related. Also he notes that natural symbols feature prominently in mythology, fairy tales and legends. The final three relationships Kellert portrays as positive. This trio are (g) the *naturalistic*, which believes a deep level of satisfaction is to be gained through contact with nature and that this is associated with the fascination, wonder and awe that emanates from nature's beauty as well as from the complexity and diversity of the natural world; (h) the *humanistic*, linked to the way humans can experience a deep emotional connection with the sentient aspects of nature and its individual elements; and lastly (i) the *moralistic* relationships, which are associated with a strong affinity to the natural world, and the sense of an ethical responsibility to it. It is a characteristic often associated with the belief systems of indigenous people.

Clearly those taking part in outdoor and adventure education programmes will possess differing perspectives on, and relationships with, nature. Such variable attitudes will frame the kinds of conversations an educator will have with those they are teaching. The nine perspectives identified by Kellert may not be exhaustive but they help one to delineate and trace some of the important differences in attitudes towards, and beliefs about, both the outdoors and the natural environment. His taxonomy captures some of the variations in personal attitude that may be encountered within a group which an outdoor or adventure educator is working with, attitudes that may range from a deep affinity to the natural world, through indifference, to one that is fundamentally antagonistic. Such predispositions will profoundly affect the kind of discourse and dialogue that the outdoor educator will be able to generate as well as shape the forms of intervention that might effectively be adopted. The educator must therefore seek from the outset to establish how the participants relate to the outdoors and nature. Of course, as noted earlier, the attitudes within the group are unlikely to be homogeneous; however this diversity should not axiomatically be viewed negatively but as an advantage as the variations, if skilfully exploited by the educator, will serve to generate conversations and dialogue on sustainability and similar topics.

For these to be fully productive the outdoor or informal educator must be aware of their own relationship to nature. Given their background and presence it is unlikely their stance will be hostile, but they may well have subtle or slight differences of appreciation and opinion from that of their colleagues. These may impact on how they engage not only with the outdoors but also with the groups and colleagues they work with. For example, they may have a geographical or geological background and therefore approach their encounters with the environment in which they operate from a radically different perspective to that of a co-worker who grew up in the region and enjoys a deep spiritual connection with the same locale.

In reality we all have a discrete lens through which we view the outdoors and we must therefore be prepared to do what Crosby refers to as the 'internal work of the informal educator' (2001: 55). That is, we must reflect upon and be aware of how our deportment and phraseology impact upon our modes of engagement both with others and the environment in which we operate.

There is however an additional stumbling block that can potentially undermine our attempts to educate in, and for, sustainability. It is what Nikel and Reid (2006) and Zeyer and Roth (2011: 36) refer to as the 'dangers of Post-Ecologism', an attitude of mind characterised by a recognition of the problem but which rationalises the situation in a way that allows the individual or group to avoid the necessity of making any fundamental changes apropos either their lifestyle or political commitment. Orr in this respect reminds us that the destruction of the planet 'is not the work of ignorant people' (1991: 99). Post-ecologists tend to call for political leadership, but their environmental concerns are frequently delegated to 'experts' and 'professionals' and they are likely to reformulate ecological problems as scientific or technological ones. Engaging with the post-ecologists in debate and beginning the perhaps slow but necessary process of re-engagement with them is an essential task if substantive progress is to be secured on a number of fronts. For Stibbe, doing so will entail discovering 'discourses which encode worldviews that inspire people into action for sustainability', although he acknowledges 'different discourses motivate different audiences' (2009: 4).

Sustainability for Grove-White (1997) is crucial for the role it can perform in providing new space for political explorations that offer an alternative to trying to promulgate vague calls for action. As we have seen both outdoor and informal education are well placed to play a part in undertaking this task. Blewitt (2004: 6) argues that practitioners such as outdoor and adventure educators should be prepared to act as exemplars, and in essence have, a moral duty to penetrate via dialogue and conversation the masks and veils of media spin, political rhetoric and instrumental rationality that envelope environmental issues. The challenge is perhaps even greater when attempting to educate those with a post-ecologist perspective than it is with those who are simply unaware of the impending environmental catastrophe and the debates pertaining to it. As Orr notes, 'The crisis we face is first and foremost one of mind, perceptions, and values; it is an educational challenge' (1994: 27).

Pedagogies of informal and sustainable education

Dominant ideologies are reflected in current formal education curricula, indeed they may be so dominant that critical debate in many settings is closed down or at best curtailed. (Cortese, 2003; Karol and Gale, 2004; Tregidga et al., 2011). Consequently, according to Orr, the risk arises that 'more of the same kind of education can only make things worse' (1994: 27). Education for sustainability as it has emerged in the wake of the 1992 Rio Earth Summit has, as a result of this widespread malaise, sought to promote, with varying degrees of success, an alternative curriculum, one that involves a synthesis of environmental and development education and which sets out to challenge the traditional pedagogies and ambitions of education (Wals, 2012; Sterling, 2010). UNESCO has, with this in mind, linked education for sustainability to notions of citizenship education and political literacy; by doing so it has drawn upon its own ongoing emphasis on rights, responsibilities and participatory development. Specifically arguing for:

> *A curriculum reoriented towards sustainability would place the notion of citizen-ship among its primary objectives. This would require a revision of many existing curricula ... [to] emphasize moral virtues, ethical motivation and ability to work with others to help build a sustainable future. Viewing education for sustainability as a contribution to a politically literate society is central to the reformulation of edu-cation and calls for a 'new generation' of theorizing and practice in education and a rethinking of many familiar approaches, including within environmental education. (UNESCO, 1997: paragraphs 67 and 68)*

This 're-visioning' of education in a way that places sustainability at its heart is con-sistent with many of the central features of both informal and outdoor education. So, for example, when Sterling (2001) calls for education for sustainability to con-tain interactive enquiry-based and student-centred pedagogies that are dialogical, critical and involve active (deep) learning, founded on more equitable learning relationships, this is not something new to informal educators. Indeed it is largely a restatement of the methodologies that already comprise the core element of its essential pedagogy (Jeffs and Smith, 2005; Ord, 2016). Nor would this method-ological format sit uncomfortably alongside that adopted by experiential educators, not least those operating in outdoor settings. There is also a shared emphasis on process within informal and outdoor education and education for sustainability. Blewitt's suggestion that we need to move to a process curriculum which tran-scends traditional subject and content-based curriculum likewise echoes a sub-stantive element of the approaches adopted by informal and outdoor education alike. The International Expert Review of Education for Sustainable Development undertaken by Tilbury for UNESCO reflected this shared heritage when it placed a particular stress on 'processes of collaboration and dialogue ... processes which engage the "whole system" [and] processes of active and participatory learning' (Tilbury, 2011: 7).

Education for sustainability and informal education also both stress the centrality of values. A focus that is in tune with that which is advocated by the authors of the International Implementation Scheme supported by UNESCO, which advocates:

> *Understanding your own values, the values of the society you live in and the values of others around the world is a central part of educating for a sustainable future. Each nation, cultural group and individual must learn the skills of recognising their own values and assessing these values in the context of sustainability. (2005: 3)*

Educators operating in the outdoors are much less inhibited by the organisational and bureaucratic constraints that often make life difficult for those working in formal educational institutions. Consequently they are arguably better 'placed to change society, by changing the habits and instilling the ideas of future citizens' (Tripp, 1992: 22). However informal educators are not immune with regards to the topic of sustainability from accusations of hypocrisy – of failing to practice what they preach. Clearly it would be far more effective to engage participants in education for sustainability if the agency and practitioners themselves were seen to be taking meaningful steps to minimise their own environmental impact and carbon footprint. For instance, many participants will doubtless be aware as to whether the electricity is generated from renewable sources, or whether the food and other produce is locally sourced. Informal and outdoor educators who seek to teach others the importance of sustainability must be ready to adopt a measure of humility and, as Scott suggests, at every opportunity seek to

> exercise their social responsibility exploring with learners what sustainable development might be; doing this in ways … without prescription or proselytization. And then, they need to share their work so that they – and we – might all learn what has been done, how effective it was, and why. (2002: 13)

Seizing the moment

Politicians, with, of course, some conspicuously high-profile exceptions, appear to be ever more mindful of the importance of sustainability. The Stern Review (2006) placed an increasing importance on it for the UK government and John Beddington (2009), who was chief scientific advisor to the UK government from 2008 to 2013, suggested an imminent 'perfect storm' of food shortages, water scarcity, insufficient energy resources and social conflict was to be expected by 2030 unless the current direction of policy altered. Such a prospect, articulated by senior scientific figures, is one that no responsible government can readily dismiss in a cavalier fashion. Subsequently the intergovernmental Panel on Climate Change (IPCC) unambiguously stated that 'climate change will amplify existing risks and create new risks for natural and human systems' (2014: 1). Similarly, alongside the UK and most developed economies, the US for the first time signed a major commitment to reducing carbon emissions in the Paris Agreement on climate change (UNFCCC, 2016).[1] Of course we cannot assume that because this has occurred opposition to policies designed to foster sustainability will go unchallenged in the future. Prominent politicians in Europe, North America and elsewhere can be found who deny the very existence of climate change and set aside the need for policies designed to encourage sustainability. The case therefore still needs to be argued and re-argued and the facts relentlessly marshalled to sustain that case. It has perhaps never been more pressing or pertinent to engage in education both in and for sustainability. We know that doing nothing is not a socially responsible option – if we do not at least try to be part of the solution we will inevitably remain part of the problem. Informal and outdoor educators have an obligation to educate in, and for, sustainability. And there is no better backdrop or setting for them to do so than the outdoors.

References

Baudrillard, J. (1987) 'Modernity', *Canadian Journal of Political and Social Theory* 11(3), pp. 63–73.

Beddington, J. (2009) Food, Energy, Water and the Climate: A Perfect Storm of Global Events? Available at: http://webarchive.nationalarchives.gov.uk/20121212135622/www .bis.gov.uk/assets/goscience/docs/p/perfect-storm-paper.pdf (accessed 24 Mar 2014).

Blewitt, J. (2004) 'Sustainability and lifelong learning' in J. Blewitt, and C. Cullingford (eds.) *The Sustainability Curriculum: The Challenge for Higher Education*, London: Earthscan.

Caradonna, J. L. (2014) *Sustainability: A History*, Oxford: Oxford University Press.

Clark, M. (1989) *Ariadne's Thread: The Search for New Modes of Thinking*, New York: St. Martin's Press.

Coates, J. and Leahy, T. (2006) 'Ideology and politics: essential factors in the path towards sustainability', *Electronic Green Journal* 1(23), pp. 1–22.

Cortese, A. D. (2003) 'The critical role of higher education in creating a sustainable future', *Planning for Higher Education*, March–May, pp. 15–22.

Crosby, M. (2001) 'Working with people as an informal educator', in L. Deer Richardson and M. Wolfe. (eds.) *Principles and Practice of Informal Education*, London: Routledge Falmer, pp. 54–61

Dickens, P. (1996) *Reconstructing Nature, Alienation, Emancipation and the Division of Labour*, London: Routledge

Dresner, S. (2008) *The Principles of Sustainability* (2nd ed.) London: Earthscan.

Drexhage, J. and Murphy, D. (2010) 'Sustainable development: from Brundtland to Rio 2012', paper presented to 1st Meeting of the High Level Panel on Global Sustainability, New York: United Nations.

Dryzec, J. S. (2005) *The Politics of the Earth: Environmental Discourses*, New York: Oxford University Press.

Eckersley, R. (1992) *Environmentalism and Political Theory: Towards an Ecocentric Approach*, Albany: University of New York Press.

Grove-White, R. (1997) 'Environment, risk and democracy', *The Political Quarterly* 68(B), pp. 109–122.

Hajer, M. (1995) *The Politics of Environmental Discourse: Ecological Modernization and the Policy Process*, Oxford: Clarendon Press.

Harré, R., Brockmeier, H. and Mühlhäusler, P. (1999) *Greenspeak: A Study of Environmental Discourse*, London: Sage.

Hatzius, T. (1996) *Sustainability and Institutions: Catchwords or New Agenda for Ecologically Sound Development?* [IDS Working Paper 48], Falmer: University of Sussex.

Heilbroner, R. L. (1985) *The Nature and Logic of Capitalism*, New York: W. W. Norton.

Hopkins, C., Damlamian, J. and Lopez Opsina, G. (1996) 'Evolving towards education for sustainable development: an international perspective', *Nature and Resources* 32(3), pp. 2–11.

Huckle, J. (2004) 'Critical realism: a philosophical framework for higher education for sustainability' in P.B. Corcoran and A. E. J. Wals (eds.) *Higher Education and the Challenge of Sustainability*, Dordrecht: Kluwer, pp. 33–46.

Intergovernmental Panel on Climate Change (2014) *Climate Change 2014: Impacts, Adaptation, and Vulnerability*. Available at: www.ipcc.ch/report/ar5/wg2/ (accessed 22 March 2015).

Jacob, M. (1999) 'Sustainable development as a contested concept' in A. Dobson (ed.) *Fairness and Futurity: Essays on environmental sustainability and social justice*, Oxford: OUP.

Jeffs, T. and Smith, M. K. (2005) *Informal Education, Conversation, Democracy and Learning* (3rd ed.), Derby: Education Now.

Jickling, B. (1992) 'Why I don't want my children educated for sustainable development', *Journal of Environmental Education* 26(4), pp. 20–45.

Kagawa, F. and Selby, D. (2010) *Education and Climate Change: Living and Learning in Interesting Times*, London: Routledge.

Karol, J. and Gale, T. (2004) *Bourdieu's Social Theory and Sustainability: What Is 'Environmental Capital'?* Available at: www.aare.edu.au/publications-database.php/4291/Bourdieu's-social-theory-and-sustainability:-What-is-'environmental-capital (accessed 23 April 2014).

Kellert, S.R. (1993) 'The biological basis for human values of nature' in S. R. Kellert and E.O. Wilson (eds.) *The Biophilia Hypothesis*, Washington, Island Press.

Leopold, A. (1949) *A Sand County Almanac: And Sketches Here and There*, New York: Oxford University Press.

McGrail, S. (2011) 'Environmentalism in transition? Emerging perspectives, issues and futures practices in contemporary environmentalism', *Journal of Futures Studies* 15(3), pp. 117–144.

Mebratu, D. (1998) 'Sustainability and sustainable development: a historical and conceptual review', *Environmental Impact Assessment Review* 18(6), pp. 493–520.

Mezirow, J. (2000) *Learning as Transformation: Critical Perspectives on a Theory in Progress*, San Francisco: Jossey-Bass Publishers.

Nash, R. (2014) *Wilderness and the American Mind*, New Haven, Yale University Press.

Nikel, J. and Reid, A. (2006) 'Environmental education in three German speaking countries: tensions and challenges for research and development', *Environmental Education Research* 12(1), pp. 129–148.

Ord, J. (2016) *Youth Work Process, Product and Practice: Creating an Authentic Curriculum in Work with Young People* (2nd ed.), London: Routledge.

Orr, D. W. (1991) *Ecological Literacy: Education and the Transition to a Postmodern World*, New York: SUNY Press.

Orr, D. W. (1994) *Earth in Mind*, Washington: Island Press.

Orr, D. W. (2009) *Down to the Wire: Confronting Climate Collapse*, Oxford: Oxford University Press.

Pisani, J.A. Du (2006) 'Sustainable development: historical roots of the concept', *Environmental Sciences* 2(3), pp. 83–96.

Scott, W. (2002) *Sustainability and Learning: What Role for the Curriculum?* University of Bath: CREE.

Selby, D. (2005) 'Responding to Globalisation and the Global Condition. Technocratic Skills or Normative Ideals? A Critique of Douglas Bourne's Conception of Global Education', Zeitschrift fur Bildungsforschung und Entwicklungspadagogik, *Journal for International Education Research and Development Education*, 28(1): 35-39.

Steffen, A. (2006) *World Changing: A User's Guide for the 21st Century*. New York: Abrams.

Sterling, S. (2001) *Sustainable Education: Re-visioning Learning and Change*, Dartington: Green Books.

Sterling, S. (2004) 'An analysis of the development of sustainability education internationally: evolution, interpretation and transformative potential' in J. Blewitt and C. Cullingford (eds.) *The Sustainability Curriculum: The Challenge for Higher Education*, London: Earthscan, pp. 43–62.

Sterling, S. (2010) 'Learning for resilience, or the resilient learner? Towards a necessary reconciliation in a paradigm of sustainable education', *Environmental Education Research* 16(5–6), pp. 511–528.

Stern, N. (2006) *Stern Review Report on the Economics of Climate Change*, HM Treasury. Available at: www.hmtreasury.gov.uk/d/CLOSED_SHORT_executive_summary.pdf (accessed 3 June 2007).

Stibbe, A. (ed.) (2009) *The Handbook of Sustainability Literacy: Skills for a Changing World*, Totnes: Green Books.

Tilbury, D. (2011) *Education and Sustainable Development: An Expert Review of Processes and Learning*, Paris: UNESCO.

Tregidga, H. M., Milne, M. J. and Kearins, K. N. (2011) 'Sustainable development as a floating signifier: recognising space for resistance', Launceston, Australia: *The 10th Australasian Conference on Social and Environmental Accounting Research*, 5–7 December 2011. Full conference papers available at: www.utas.edu.au/__data/assets/pdf_file/.../Tregidga_Milne_Kearins.pdf (Accessed 13 February 2014).

Tripp, D. (1992) 'Critical theory and educational research', *Issues in Educational Research* 2(1), pp. 98–112.

UNESCO (1997) *Education for a Sustainable Future: A Transdisciplinary Vision for Concerted Action*. Available at: www.unesco.org/education/tlsf/mods/theme_a/popups/mod01t05s01 .html (accessed 27 January 2013).

UNESCO (2005) *Values of Sustainable Development*. Available at: www.unesco.org/new/ en/education/themes/leading-the-international-agenda/education-for-sustainable-development/sustainable-development/values-sd/ (accessed 21 February 2012).

UNFCCC (2016) *United Nations Framework Convention on Climate Change*. Available at: http://unfccc.int/paris_agreement/items/9485.php (accessed 19 January 2017).

Wals, A. E. J. (2012) *Shaping the Education of Tomorrow: 2012 Full-Length Report on the UN Decade of Education for Sustainable Development*, Paris: UNESCO.

Wals, A. E. J. and Blewitt, J. (2010) 'Third-wave sustainability in higher education: some (inter) national trends and developments' in P. Jones, D. Selby and S. Sterling (eds) *Sustainability Education: Perspectives and Practice across Higher Education*, London: Earthscan, pp. 55–73.

WCED (World Commission on Environment and Development) (1987) *Our Common Future*, Oxford: OUP.

Zeyer, A. and Roth, W. M. (2011) 'Post-ecological discourse in the making', *Public Understanding of Science* 22 pp. 33–48.

Note

1   As this goes to print President Trump has begun to pull the US out of the Paris Agreement, despite wide spread condemnation from across the globe.

SUBJECT INDEX

AUTHOR INDEX

Printed in Great Britain
by Amazon

55765028R00120